Ian Stafford is a prolific journalist, bro_____
sports reporter for the *Mail on Sund*_____
Reporter of the Year in 1990 and Mag_____ ...
1995. He now contributes to the *Mail on Sunday* as well as writing sports
and general interest features for a wide range of national and international
publications, including *Esquire*. He also broadcasts on television and
radio. Ian Stafford has written five books, including *Playgrounds of the
Gods* – his first participatory book – which was shortlisted for the William
Hill Sports Book of the Year prize. He lives in Kent with his wife and two
children.

Also by Ian Stafford

Playgrounds of the Gods

in your
DREAMS

How one man fared when he played the best

at their own game

IAN STAFFORD

headline

First published in 2001
by HEADLINE BOOK PUBLISHING

First published in paperback in 2002
by HEADLINE BOOK PUBLISHING

10 9 8 7 6 5 4 3 2 1

ISBN 0 7472 3689 5

Picture credits
Football Dave Pinegar (except team photograph)
Wrestling Richard Dean
Rugby Union Jackie Sloan
Rugby League Richard Dean
Athletics Dan Smith
Cricket Anthony Robinson
Motor Racing LAT, Richard Dean

Typeset by Palimpsest Book Production Limited,
Polmont, Stirlingshire
Designed by Jane Coney
Printed and bound in Great Britain by
Mackays of Chatham plc, Chatham, Kent

HEADLINE BOOK PUBLISHING
A division of Hodder Headline
338 Euston Road
London NW1 3BH

www.headline.co.uk
www.hodderheadline.com

To Karen, Charlotte and Harry – still the best team in the world.
And to my mother and father. Sleep well.

contents

foreword

Having seen Ian Stafford in action, when he joined me and my Great Britain coxless fours colleagues for a week of intense training and racing at the Leander Club in Henley a couple of years ago, I know that he gives everything he possibly can to his cause. Matthew Pinsent, Tim Foster, James Cracknell and I didn't believe he would be able to last the pace of a week's training with us, such are the mental and physical requirements of rowing. However, what he lacked in natural rowing talent, he made up for in determination and doggedness, willingly putting up with everything we threw at him – even when we pushed him into the Thames to baptise him! At least our training must have done him some good – he might not have made the Olympic team, but two years on he could still beat Eddie Irvine on the rowing machine.

Now Ian has gone on to sample top-level sport in a whole host of new challenges and adventures, each posing their own demands: who else is deranged enough to keep on getting up for more after being repeatedly hurled to the ground by the Wigan Warriors, for example?

Only by participating in such sports is it possible to get a proper idea of what it is like to train and play at the highest levels: many writers, for obvious reasons, can never truly know. Ian's inside view of sportsmen on their own turf reveals what they are really like, and gives a fascinating insight into what it is that makes a team like the Leicester Tigers the champions they are.

Because royalties from this book will be going to the NSPCC, there is an added incentive, too, to enjoy Ian's account of the bruising effort involved in following his dream. And, you never know, if I ever decide to come out of retirement, I might give Ian a call to team up again as partners, just as we were in Henley.

Sir Steve Redgrave, June 2001

introduction

It had something to do with reaching my late thirties, with an unwillingness to accept the obvious, and with a desperate yearning to transform myself into something that lay not just on the periphery of my dreams, but at their very kernel.

I had a grand plan, three years ago, to see out my youth with an unlikely series of sporting challenges that would permit me to travel to distant lands and share a life of sporting prowess with the best in the world. This I duly achieved, and the result was my previous participatory book. And then? Well, then I was supposed to slip quietly into my late thirties and beyond, warmed by the glow of such memories.

But this failed to materialise. My Indian summer became my Indian spring. My earlier attempt to satisfy my wannabe urges, to meet, head-on, the first signs of a rather premature mid-life crisis, only served to whet what seems to have become an insatiable appetite.

In my mind, as I speed through first my mid- and now my late thirties at an alarming rate of knots, I am still that young twenty-year-old with the world at his feet. People said to me then that before I knew it I would be well into my thirties. I scoffed back then, but they were so right. In a blink of an eye, seventeen years have passed by. My children are no longer the babies I once held in my arms, but fast-growing, independent youngsters who form their own opinions and answer back. And, worst of all, a few unwanted and uninvited white hairs have started to appear on my chin whenever a couple of days' stubble is allowed to prosper. As this book testifies, growing old is something I am clearly unwilling to accept.

There must be a mistake somewhere on my birth certificate, or in my passport. I'm convinced I haven't even reached thirty yet.

I still shout abuse at the television set when an England football player misses what I consider an open goal, an England rugby player fails to make a vital tackle, or an England cricketer drops a dolly of a catch. I should know better. I really should. Yet I have retained the naive assumption that I, placed in an identical position, would have done the business and completed the job. Just, I suspect, like most readers of this book.

Something else, and something rather odd, has developed, too. Even though my earlier experiences revealed to me in no uncertain terms that the world has not, after all, missed out on a great sporting talent, the passing of even a brief passage of time has stoked up the fires of delusion once more. Like a wound that has healed, time has allowed the conviction that I really can prove myself at a very high sporting level to return, bigger, bolder and uglier than ever before. It seems that the last occasion failed to prove that I did not belong in such superlative sporting company. On the contrary, indeed, it merely added fuel to my self-delusory fires. I had proved myself before – well, almost – and I would prove myself again, more so than ever.

This time I was not only going to train and hang out with some of the best sportsmen around, but I was going to play in a real-life, pressure-filled situation, the sharp end of every sport's business. This, after all, is what happens in my dreams. The sight of me ambling on to the Wembley pitch, jogging around the Lord's boundary, or preparing for a line-out on the Twickenham turf was already a common occurrence in my imagination. Now I wanted to make it a reality.

The rules would be simple. I would spend what would amount to at least a week with the best teams or individuals in Britain. There would be absolutely no dispensations. I would have to go through everything the country's top sportsmen underwent on a daily basis, culminating with an appearance in a big game or event. Only then could I say, to myself as much as to the reader, that I had truly sampled life, with all its ups and downs, as a leading sportsman in a wide range of contrasting sports.

Three years ago I plunged into a similar set of challenges unaware of the pain, both mental and physical, that lay awaiting me. Three years on, and three years older, I knew exactly what had to be done. I had kept myself in reasonable shape during this time, but for me even to be able to walk in the same arena as the sporting stars with whom I was planning to play would require a massive improvement at an age when the barriers become significantly higher. It wasn't easy. Only three years may have passed, but they were crucial years in terms of waning physical capability, and my body found the preparations a great deal more demanding second time around. And it certainly wasn't easy, either, when I was required to match the professionals I attempted to lock horns with.

Persuading some of the best teams and individuals in British sport to allow someone of my questionable skills to join their ranks took some doing, and the individuals' stories are explained in the book. Suffice here to say that my participation was wholly dependent on leading sports figures being willing, or mad enough, to take the gamble. I think most enjoyed the experience in the end, as much for its novelty as for the fact that their hapless guest suffered acutely in the process of discovering what they are all about.

Last time I travelled the world. This book is a story much closer to home. It is a story about a number of well-known sportsmen, superb exponents of their special craft, but also emotional human beings who thrive on the joy and the despair of life in sport.

It is the story of what makes sporting stars the successes they are, both as individuals and as members of teams whose only currency is winning. Along the way it sheds some light on their methods and practices, and shares in their moments of glory and grief.

Above all else, *In Your Dreams* is a story of a man clinging to his fast-fading youth like a climber to a rock. Sometimes it is painful, sometimes amusing, and sometimes just plain embarrassing, but although my seven sporting moments in the spotlight may not have left much of a mark around the playing arenas of Britain's best sportsmen, they have left me with some indelible and highly personal memories that will keep me content for a long time – at least as long as it takes before the next rebellious attempt to beat time rears its ridiculous head inside my child-like mind, and my dreams make a desperate bid for reality once more.

chapter one

 **THE BOY DONE GOODISON**

It was a pretty preposterous notion when you think about it. A top English Premiership football team regroups for the start of a new campaign. A great deal of money – and therefore pressure – rides on a successful season. People's hopes, their dreams, the very focal point of their lives, pivot upon the ability of their team to win many more matches than they lose. Thousands upon thousands of hard-working supporters will pour through the turnstiles expecting to be entertained, and expecting to return home with a victory to celebrate. Often the whole mood of the remainder of the weekend can be gauged by what takes place in the space of ninety minutes. Emotions, inevitably, run deep.

For these reasons astronomical amounts of money are invested in the right managerial and playing personnel. Nothing is left to chance. Those who have reached such elevated heights have succeeded against all the odds: they are the crème de la crème of a nation of wannabe footballers. This is the world of seniors professional football, the big league.

Amidst all this enters a punter off the street, someone whose recent football-playing experiences amount to kick-arounds with his six-year-old son and a host of dubious recollections of sensational goals scored in the distant past – or was it in his imagination? He means well, of course, and he will try his damnedest to keep up with his illustrious colleagues during pre-season training, the crucial time of the year when the players' engines are stoked up for what always proves to be an incredibly gruelling ten months of Premiership football, but the reality is that he will probably be about as much at home as a painting-by-numbers picture in the Tate Gallery, as welcome as a streaker at the Trooping of the Colour.

It was with all this in mind that I tried to compose a letter to some of the top football teams in England. I knew that if I stood the remotest chance of being invited to join a Premiership outfit, with a view to featuring in a game at some point, it would have to be during the pre-season period, which always includes a number of 'friendlies' against fellow teams looking for some match practice and pointers before the serious business begins in August.

Nick Mallett, the South African rugby national coach, and Steve Bernard, the Australian Test and one-day cricket team manager, had both written kind references on my behalf following my experiences with their teams during the course of 1998 (chronicled in my book *Playground of the Gods*). I hoped that endorsements from such achievers would help my cause. In April 1999 I sent desperate pleas in the post to a number of Premiership teams, working on the basis that if I waited for each team to turn me down, even the opportunity of playing pre-season would be long gone. It was then just a question of waiting for the inevitable rejections.

It took a few weeks, but then they began to arrive: a steady stream of often polite, sometimes impolite, refusals to accommodate me. Some were understanding, others almost incredulous that I should so much as contemplate playing with them. Manchester United, for example, sent a short and terse response, Liverpool likewise. Arsène Wenger explained how he likes all his training at Arsenal to be behind 'closed doors', while George Graham at Tottenham wrote: 'I do not like any distractions whatsoever.' Others never replied.

David O'Leary made the effort to telephone me, though. I was driving west along the M4 motorway at the time and had to pull over at a junction for what transpired to be the nicest rejection of the lot. The Leeds manager took the best part of half an hour to explain how much he appreciated my interest and liked the concept, but how when he put the notion to his predominantly young team they reacted as if O'Leary had lost his sanity. It was good of him to make the call, but as I continued my journey to the West Country that day, I was still without a willing club.

All this changed during the following week, when a flurry of positive responses suddenly came my way. Danny Wilson at Sheffield Wednesday wrote: 'You can spend as much time as you like with us.' Jim Smith at Derby left a message asking me to call him to discuss arrangements. Coventry's Gordon Strachan contacted me at home. I began to blather down the line to him about my understanding why he should not want me when he interrupted me with: 'Who said I don't want you? You can come and join us, and I'll even try and get you a game against West Bromwich Albion in our pre-season derby. I know I must be mad, but we'll give it a go.'

I was minutes away from becoming a Coventry City player – albeit for a week – when the telephone rang again. It was Walter Smith on the line, and if there was one Premiership manager I had half-expected to hear from, it was him. I had got to know Smith a couple of years earlier, when he was nearing the end of his tenure at Rangers, and had always enjoyed my trips up to Glasgow to interview him, often over soup in his wood-panelled office at Ibrox. A decent and honest man, Smith always talked openly about any subject I broached, from his key personnel to his success and failures and, ultimately, his reasons for quitting Rangers: he had, quite simply, lost the buzz for the job. A change of scenery was required, and when the post at Everton came up, at the beginning of the 1998–99 season, the Scot saw a challenge he could not ignore.

Everton was at the time a club in turmoil, with four managers in the previous five years and a seemingly annual flirtation with relegation. Smith was to discover that the problems at the old (and once successful) club were even deeper than he had suspected, or had been told. By instigating a spate of signings he merely added to the club's already severe debts, a situation that led to the sale of Everton's top striker, Duncan Ferguson. Devoid of finances, and in the grip of internecine war within its own board, Everton lurched from one crisis to another. Somehow Smith kept the club from relegation, and was now looking forward to a better second season in charge, although still facing hurdles that would prevent Everton from mounting any serious challenge for honours. I certainly hadn't assumed that Smith would run with my idea, but I had been hopeful. My hope stemmed from his interest in my other sporting experiences around the world, especially the time boxer Roy Jones Jr beat me up in Florida, in 1998. A couple of weeks after that incident I had gone to Everton's Bellefield training ground to interview the manager. After the interview I showed him some gruesome photographs of Jones and me slugging it out in the ring. Smith had summoned into his office Archie Knox, his assistant manager, and Dave Watson, Everton's long-serving central defender and then player-coach, and the three of them had pored over the pictures with obvious glee. Knox had appreciated the shot of my bloody face, Watson had gone for the photo of my body slumped against the ropes, while Smith had favoured the post-fight pose, with a smiling, unruffled Jones and a clearly concussed Stafford blinking at the camera. I knew, when I wrote to him later, that at least he would not question my commitment or serious intent.

My hunch was correct. Smith did not even bother to discuss the proposal. Instead, it was straight down to business. 'We're all going off to Tuscany for a week or so in a training camp,' he told me down the line. 'You can come with us and become part of the squad. Then I'll play you in one of our matches at the end of July.' This was terrific news. Everton may not have been the powerful force they once were, but they were still a major club and a global football name, with a magnificent old ground bursting with tradition and ardent, near-fanatical support. 'I'll try my hardest to impress,' I started to say, failing to hide my child-like excitement. 'You never know, I might even surprise you and not be as useless as you'd imagine.'

'Ian,' responded the deadpan voice with the soft, Scottish lilt. 'I'll decide if you're useless, not you. Now, we're supposed to be playing against Fiorentina [the Italian Serie A team from Florence] but, with all due respect to your talent, you might find Gabriel Batistuta a bit of a handful.' It's probably fair to say that a clash with Fiorentina's Argentinian star striker might have been testing. I waited for his laughter to die down. 'So how do you fancy coming on as a sub against Manchester City?'

Man City? Really? 'Well, we've got them at home in one of our last friendlies before the start of the Premiership. It'll be a big game, and I'd expect a good crowd. I'm prepared to put you on for the last fifteen minutes if you want, providing you come through the training camp okay.'

This was more, much more, than I could have possibly hoped for. A week in Tuscany, living, eating and playing with Everton, and then a match, in front of the Goodison Park faithful, against a City side that had just been promoted into the First Division. This was still some way short of their assumed role as one of the most prestigious English clubs, but it nevertheless represented a big game between two, somewhat sleeping, north-west giants.

Smith promised that he would get back in touch to arrange the details. The flights and the accommodation would all be paid for by the club. All I had to do, according to the manager, when we next made contact, was to 'bring my boots'. In the week before departing for Italy I stepped up my fitness campaign. I had a notion that pre-season training would be tough and as my previous sporting adventures had taught me, the ability to be accepted by my new team-mates would hinge, to a large degree, on whether I could last the pace in training. Each afternoon I would don a pair of football boots and run around the local park kicking a leather ball along the route, side-stepping any terrier that advanced towards me and dodging the dog turds as if they were defenders.

With three days to go, Smith and I spoke again. 'Don't panic,' the Everton boss insisted. 'I've told the boys not to mess with you. Cause him any grief, I've said, and Ian will flatten you. He's been in the ring with Roy Jones, you know.' It was a sure sign of things to come. Somehow I knew there would be a great deal of humour in the forthcoming week, and most of it would be directed at me. I had seventy-two hours to develop a few extra layers of skin.

At 6 a.m. that Friday I arrived at Stansted Airport with my suit and luggage. I could see an impatient Archie Knox standing by the departure gate. 'You're late,' he said, by way of introduction. 'That's a good start, isn't it?' I fumbled with the luggage labels, prompting the assistant manager to help. 'I can see you're going to be trouble straight away,' he added. My only hope of salvation lay in the fact that there seemed to be a small glint in his eye. Later the players would confirm that his bark was always worse than his bite.

Walter Smith invited me to sit with him on the plane as we headed for Pisa. Archie was alongside. Behind sat an array of international talent. Richard Gough, the former Scotland captain, remembered me from an interview we conducted when he was at Rangers. Chris Woods, the former England 'keeper, was now the club's goalkeeping coach. Scotland's John Collins, an expensive signing from Monaco the season before, said hello. Dave Watson, still playing, and the darling of the Goodison faithful, recalled the boxing photos he'd seen the year before in the manager's office. Slowly I introduced myself to as many of the players as I could. I discovered that they all seemed to know why I was there. Walter had told them of the idea a few days' earlier after training, and had reassured them of my methods and approach. All appeared friendly, welcoming, and interested to hear of my sporting adventures around the world.

Much of the two-hour flight was spent working out answers to sporting quiz questions. After much agonised debate over the finer points of sporting trivia we were taken by bus from Pisa airport to our destination in the Tuscan hills. 'Il Ciocco' is a hotel and conference centre not far from the city of Lucca and in the heart of Garfagnana, one of Tuscany's most beautiful regions. The hotel's idyllic setting could hardly have been further removed from the torture that lay ahead. On entering my room – most of the team shared with another player, but I, alongside Smith, Knox and Dave Watson, was lucky enough to have one to myself – I discovered a pile of sportswear from Umbro, the team's kit providers. Shorts, t-shirts, polo shirts, tracksuit tops and bottoms, sweatshirts, even trunks were laid neatly on my bed – just one of the perks of being a 'professional' football player. All sported the club motto, 'Nil Satis Nisi Optimum', which translated means 'nothing but the best'. I was told to wear a blue polo shirt and blue shorts for lunch and discovered, on entering the dining area, that every member of the team was kitted out the same.

I collected my salad and went to sit at what appeared to be the management staff's table but Walter Smith, who everyone referred to as 'the gaffer', stopped me from pulling up a chair. 'You're supposed to be one of the team, remember,' he whispered, nodding his head towards the players. He was right. I sat down at the end of one of the two long tables provided for the players and, over lunch, discovered that on the basis of my long-distance running experience in Kenya the previous year, I had been built up to be some kind of supremely fit athlete. Don Hutchison, the team's captain and a Scottish international who had won the FA Cup with Liverpool back in 1992, and Terry Phelan ('Phelo'), likewise a Cup winner with Wimbledon in 1988, both seemed interested in this particular adventure. 'I'm a bit like the Kenyans,' Phelan announced. 'Coming from the part of Salford that I do, it was either football or nothing.' Gough and Watson, meanwhile, reminded me that, at a couple of months before my thirty-sixth birthday, I could not use my age as an excuse for a poor showing in training. Gough was thirty-seven years old, and Watson had been at Everton for so long it would not have surprised me if he had had Dixie Dean for a room-mate.

All members of the team were told to retire to their rooms after lunch, and sleep. Such 'suggestions' would never be optional. Now I was grateful for a couple of hours after such an early start to the day. Later in the week I would discover that an afternoon nap was a necessity. At 4 p.m. Jimmy Comer, the team masseur, banged on everyone's door. He handed me a white t-shirt, yet another pair of blue shorts and, a little strangely to a grown man and father of two, a pair of white underpants, all of which I was instructed to wear that evening for dinner.

First, though, came training. The team wore their training gear for the week: yellow t-shirts, black shorts and black socks. I was kitted out in white and blue, my garments all sporting my initials, 'IS'. I noticed that the management wore the same gear, with Walter's brandishing 'WS' in large capitals, Archie's 'AK', and so forth. A bus dragged us up the mountain above the hotel to a football pitch perched on a plateau close to the peak. After a few sums we worked out that we would be training at over 2,000 feet. Dave Watson took charge of the early proceedings, a daily routine that saw us all jog around the field before enacting a series of stretches, sprints, and backwards and sideways sprints. The stretches, in particular, took some time; they are a relatively new element to training in British football and one that has probably lengthened the career of the professional player.

A game of handball followed, using miniature footballs. The aim was to score a goal in the small nets by either heading or volleying the ball from someone's pass. This would be another part of the daily routine, designed to encourage quickness of foot and mind in creating space, but also providing enjoyable competition for the players who appeared, to a man, determined to win. This would become my favourite part of training, too, if only because my lack of talent did not reveal itself so much in these games. We ended the warm-up period with a series of pitch-length sprints.

It was during the practice match at the end of the first training session that I was reminded of the reason why I embark on fantasy trips such as this. The game was just five minutes old when – ludicrously, and laughably – I scored the pre-season training camp's first goal of the week. Don Hutchison started the move, sending his pass out wide to Mitch Ward, his former Sheffield United team-mate. Ward sprinted down the right wing before crossing the ball to the far post. Terry Phelan directed his header back across the face of the goal, eluding defenders Dave Watson and David Weir in the process and there, from the edge of the six-yard box, the new signing half-volleyed the ball half-way up into the net.

Walter Smith would lament later that with millions of pounds' worth of footballing talent on the pitch that afternoon he was hardly expecting to see some newcomer off the street score the first goal. It was as good a way as any, though, to break the ice with my new-found playing colleagues. I thought about embarking on an orgy of joyous celebration, but decided a quiet punch of the air with my fist would suffice. Quite a scramble for credit followed. 'Don't forget it was my pass,' Don Hutchison ('Hutch') insisted. 'Never mind that, it was my cross that made it,' Mitch Ward followed up. Terry Phelan couldn't believe his ears. 'What about my header?' he asked. 'Split the defence completely and sent him clear. Don't forget to write that, Ian.'

As we trooped off the pitch Dave 'Waggy' Watson put his hand on my shoulder. 'I can see we're going to have to watch those sneaky runs of yours on the far post,' he said, with a friendly smile. Richard 'Goughie' Gough followed up. 'I bet you'll say it was a 25-yard screamer, won't you,' he added. Walter Smith and Archie Knox had overcome their initial shock and were now chuckling away. 'Not bad,' Smith said. 'Just a bit rusty, but it's been a year since you played with Romario, hasn't it?' he said. I felt as happy as any frustrated football fan could. So far it had all gone better than I could have possibly hoped.

After a dinner of salad, pasta, soup, meat and fruit we retired to the hotel lounge. Hutchison, Ward and Paul 'Gezza' Gerrard, the likeable and maverick goalkeeper, settled down to a series of lengthy games of chess. Dave 'Unsy' Unsworth, Nick 'Barms' Barmby, Davey 'Peas and Gravy' Weir and myself took on the challenge of Richard Gough, John Collins, Dave Watson and Craig 'Shorty' Short over a Trivial Pursuit board. In Barmby and Unsworth my side possessed two players who seemed to know the answers to all the TV soap questions, but it was not enough. The opposition won 6–4, after a high degree of questionable tactics that might have produced yellow cards on a football pitch for time-wasting and gamesmanship, and spent the next twenty-four hours reminding us of this historic victory. Hardly rock and roll, I'll admit, but the players were under some scrutiny from the management, were keen not to cause any upsets just prior to the start of the season, and were painfully aware of the physical hardship that would befall us all the following morning.

Each of us found a timetable lying on our bed when we retired for the night. A bang on the door at 7.45 started the first full day's proceedings, which began with a freezing dip in the outdoor swimming pool, designed to loosen up our muscles and joints. The players looked far from eager, wrapping their arms around their shivering bodies to keep warm, and forced to don multi-coloured swimming caps that made it appear like a Duncan Goodhew lookalike convention. By 9.30, after a quick team breakfast, we found ourselves back up the mountainside training pitch. Dave Watson, and then Archie Knox, took charge of the preliminary jogs, sprints and stretches. Walter Smith watched the handball session, shaking his head dramatically when my chance to volley into an empty net ended with the ball soaring into orbit. 'Bearing in mind you did all those technical skills with Romario and Flamengo, what's happened?' he asked.

The 'killer', as Dave Unsworth had been warning me all morning, came at the end of the session. All the players had noticed during their other exercises how Archie Knox, Chris Woods and Jimmy Martin, the team's kit-man, had been placing plastic cones on all points of the pitch. The aim was this: pairs of players would start from the corner of the pitch and run to a cone at the edge of the centre circle, then on to the touchline on the half-way line, and back to the centre circle. From there they would continue a series of return sprints, to each corner of the pitch, and the other touchline at the half-way point. In all this would incorporate twelve consecutive sprints and turns, taking around two minutes to complete. Gasping for breath and clutching their stomachs, the pair had to recover in the time it took another two to complete the same route. Then they would be off again. Dave Unsworth was my partner and, for a while, allowed me to keep up with him, before recognising the need to push on, leaving my desperate figure lunging behind. Archie Knox had promised that we would perform this exercise three times. As it wore on so my legs grew heavier, and my speed, never exactly impressive, began to falter. The players yelled shouts of encouragement as I drew every remaining ounce of energy from my fatigued body. When we had completed three sprints, and I had sunk to my knees in exhaustion, Archie decided to throw in one more leg of the exercise for fun. The collective groans from the Everton squad must have echoed around the whole valley, but we had little choice but to drag our bodies around for a fourth time.

It was a quieter bus journey back down the hill to the hotel that lunchtime, with most of the exhausted players staring vacantly out of the window unable to muster much of a conversation. Feeling ready to drop myself, I found their state of tiredness encouraging. Walter Smith, however, had other ideas. 'The lads are going too easy on you,' he said. 'They're being far too nice. I've got to get them to give you more stick. That's what it's like in football, you know. It's a team game, and you've got to act under pressure in a match situation.' Great.

Just before lunch a small piece of drama was played out. Seven of the team, including Don Hutchison, Danny Cadamarteri and Paul Gerrard, found themselves stuck in the hotel lift. Predictably, too many had piled in, and the elevator, having shut its doors, then refused to open them again, or move. The rest of the team soon gathered around, helpless with laughter as they heard the increasingly frantic pleas from inside the lift. Eventually, after what seemed like an eternity, a technician came to free the 'Everton Seven'. Gerrard announced to anyone who cared to listen: 'That was one of the most frightening experiences of my life.' His statement, and his sincere expression, was greeted with yet more howls of laughter.

That afternoon's nap was gratefully received after the early start and the rigours of the morning's training. It felt like the beginning of a new day when the now-familiar banging on the bedroom door woke everyone up in time for the late afternoon session. A small crowd of mainly young locals had gathered to watch us go through our paces – which included a practice match where I failed to add to my scoring tally – chanting 'Ev–er–ton' and receiving waves from Archie Knox in return. Later, before dinner (and a game of Trivial Pursuit in which our side avenged the previous night's defeat), I made the first of my numerous trips to the physiotherapy room. Steve Hardwick, who had just joined the club as team physio from Bournemouth, went to work on my blisters, while Jimmy Comer gave my aching calves a rub.

Comer used to be an apprentice footballer with Liverpool, alongside Paul Jewell, the man who took Bradford City up into the Premiership. 'You were blowing out of your arse towards the end today, weren't you Ian?' he said, with a big grin on his face. 'But the lads would have appreciated it.' 'Blowing out of your arse' was a favourite expression of Jimmy's, and it was one he would be using repeatedly in my presence for much of the week.

Day three, a chilly, misty Sunday morning, began in difficult circumstances. My legs felt like blocks of concrete. It seemed as though I had been already at Il Ciocco for a week, such was the intensity of the training. To make matters worse, a large frog was found floating in the cold swimming pool as the unwilling squad of Duncan Goodhews leapt in. Even Walter Smith started to complain about wearing the swimming caps.

Like most of the team, he was not at his best early morning. Archie Knox took charge of all pre-training that morning, which was initially greeted with enthusiasm by the players, if only because he jogged around the pitch at a slower pace than Dave Watson. He also added a few extra dimensions before a practice match, including touch wrestling (my partner was the young and promising striker Phil 'Jevo' Jevons), and then touch British Bulldogs. Guess who was the first player to be caught? Scot Gemmill took one look at me and decided there and then whom his prey would be. It was during the bending and stretching exercises that some of the players saw fit to release some wind, causing initial comments from the assistant manager, followed by threats of fines to anyone found guilty. The problem was, nobody would own up, and when Archie Knox asked for supergrasses within the camp, all remained quiet, save for some stifled giggles and false accusations. But Knox had the last laugh. The morning's training ended with a fifteen-minute spell of sprinting, incorporating full-length, two half-length and four quarter-length sprints, repeated over and over again. As we collapsed to the ground and gulped down mouthfuls of iced water, Knox made an announcement. 'If you work well this afternoon you can all have a very big spangle,' he said. 'We'll have the day off tomorrow, go to the beach, and have dinner out.' He received a round of applause from the team, leaving me to whisper to John Collins: 'What's a spangle?'

'You remember Spangles, don't you?' he said. 'You know, the sweet. Well, sweet rhymes with treat. So in Archie's language a spangle means treat. Got it?'

Right. Obvious, really. The afternoon, again, was not as demanding as the morning, with more ball skills training and practice matches to enjoy, although my early scoring touch seemed to have eluded me as the tackles began to fly in at a greater rate of knots than previously. Afterwards Jimmy Martin, the kit-man, gave me his typically forthright opinion. 'You looked like a bag of shite,' he told me, with a big grin over his angular face. This was Jimmy's way, which made him popular with the management and players, especially when he became the brunt of Archie's sometimes sadistic sense of humour. He, Archie, Woods and often Walter Smith would often play 'foot tennis' before the start, and sometimes after training, heading and volleying the ball over a bench that served as a net, as if their lives depended on a win. The victors would then hurl abuse at the vanquished, with Jimmy Martin being the chief provider and recipient.

I chatted to Walter Smith over a cappuccino the following morning. He seemed more relaxed than I had seen him for some time. 'Despite all our problems at the club, I'm beginning to see a ray of light here,' he said. 'It was a gamble to come in the first place, but I thought they just had to stop going through managers. They had to recognise that they needed some stability.' He began to reflect on the team's progress: 'I arrived too late last summer to get to know what the players could and couldn't do. This time I know a great deal more, and I can see a good spirit developing here in camp. No matter how many talented individuals a club may possess, having a united team who will fight for each other is always the number one priority. Managing this club is a tremendous challenge to me, and I needed it at the stage I had reached in my career.' It was a brave decision to turn his back on Rangers and almost certain success in Scotland, but Smith appeared genuinely contented with his current lot.

Soon we were all in the bus and on our way to the coast at Viareggio. There, after a couple of hours sunbathing on the beach, I took a walk with John Collins through the town. It turned out to be an interesting discussion, centring on how the younger players of today's game have it relatively easy.

'Do you remember "Jim'll Fix It"?' John asked. 'You know, that TV show with Jimmy Savile. Well, I wrote to it as a kid asking if I could train with Celtic for a morning. The club refused.' He looked quite upset as he recounted this story. 'You can imagine how good I felt when I later joined Celtic. I used to get stick from my peers because I never drank or got caught up in the kind of things that have wrecked careers. I was so desperate to succeed, and so hungry, that I wasn't prepared to let anything jeopardise my goals in life.'

We stopped at a shop window to gaze at some leather bags. 'You know what I'd do if I was a manager right now?' he asked. 'I'd send my young players down a coal mine, or into a steelworks. When they returned for training they'd be so grateful for what they have, and so desperate not to go back to the pit, that you'd never hear them utter a moan again. I just happen to think that many of today's young players are not hungry enough because it's all been too easy for them. It won't do them any favours, though. When the going gets tough for them, as it surely will, they'll find it harder to recover.'

It was a sobering thought as we joined some of the others for a quick drink – non-alcoholic in Collins's case – before clambering back on to the bus for a journey home that would include a stop at a restaurant. Archie Knox bought me a beer and watched with an amused expression over his tanned face as I drank. 'Make the most of it lad,' he said. 'Cos tomorrow I'll work you so hard your legs will be up your arse.'

The bus journey home was eventful. The Italian driver possessed such a shocking black perm, that it took no time for the team to re-christen him Kevin (as in Keegan). The good-natured driver was either happy with or oblivious to his new name. Not so Jimmy Martin, whose angular face and nose provoked parrot imitations from at first a couple of the players, and then almost the whole team. Terry Phelan proved to be the most adept parrot impersonator, and in an almost surreal ten minutes or so, I sat on a bus hurtling through the mountains and valleys of Tuscany listening to some of British football's finest screeching.

Finally, and to the great horror of most of the squad, Dave Watson decided to treat us to a few songs on the microphone. Clearly a dangerous man when in close proximity to a karaoke machine, the stalwart of the Everton side bashed out a series of rather painful Beatles numbers, his favourite being 'Just Seventeen'. Collins and Gough at the back of the coach were beginning to take umbrage over Watson's terrible din when

Gough joined Walter Smith, Archie Knox and former Rangers player Alex Cleland in a series of favourite songs from the Ibrox terraces (not sectarian, I hasten to add) – directed, of course, at a defenceless John Collins.

As we made our way back to our rooms, after a merry evening that seemed to serve its purpose in terms of team bonding, Dave Watson explained his life's predicament to me: 'I had a tough career choice to make when I was younger,' he admitted with a wry smile. 'Seeing as I come from Liverpool, I was obviously a born singer. In the end football just got the nod, but it was a close call.' Thank goodness for that, I thought, as I bade him goodnight.

On the fifth morning injury struck. I had felt a twinge on the inside of my left thigh early on and may well have over-compensated as a result, but for whatever reason I suffered a small tear on the outside of my left thigh during the course of a series of sprint exercises. I withdrew and had the damaged area iced up by Steve the physio. This all provoked more stick from the players, led by Dave Watson. 'When the going gets tough,' he started to sing, looking at me and shaking his head. 'Twenty-two pre-seasons,' he added. 'Never injured.' Hutch joined in. He had already decided to refer to me as 'Wobbly', on the basis that my legs were all over the place after a couple of days' training. 'It's all about working through the pain barrier,' he said. 'We have to do it all the time. But if you can't . . .' He left his sentence dangling in the air, finishing his remarks with a tut-tutting and a look of mock disappointment.

Jokes apart, I felt surprisingly low that afternoon as I sat out training. I knew I could not match the players in talent, technique or skill, but at least I had felt I was making a fist of keeping up with them in the physical department. Now I had been hit by injury, and as Steve explained to me, if I had pushed the damaged area too much it could have resulted in a serious tear, and a six-week lay-off. It turned out to be an interesting cameo of life as a professional footballer.

'It's just the worst experience for a player,' Richard Gough said that evening, as I sat with John Collins's special ice-pack strapped to my thigh. 'You're just desperate to play, but you're out of sight, out of mind. People think that players enjoy taking the money when they're injured, sitting on the bench not exerting themselves. Nothing could be further from the truth. It's a depressing and worrying period of your career, and we all have to go through it at some point.'

That night Don Hutchison and Mitch Ward appointed themselves the team's 'casino' bankers, producing a mini roulette wheel and happily taking bets. Hutchison was the collector, and Ward, wearing what he thought was his lucky baseball cap, the spinner of the wheel. Through the course of the evening they each managed to lose £200, mostly to the young Danish midfielder, Peter Degn – and both looked rather dazed at the end of it all.

The injury felt a little better in the morning. While the rest of the squad gathered around, I was forced to stretch and jog in front of them. It was when I tried a sprint that the damaged thigh muscle pulled again. Steve Hardwick shook his head, and a groan, followed by chicken noises, arose from the assembled players. 'Five training sessions, then they've always had enough,' Goughie uttered, just loud enough for me to hear.

Terry Phelan took pity on me. He had had his fair share of injuries, particularly during the previous eighteen months, and decided to cheer me up by showing his battle scars. 'Don't worry, big man,' he said. (Phelan tended to call me 'big man', although most men are 'big' compared to the former Wimbledon and Manchester City defender.) He sported a huge lump on each of his thighs, the result of thigh strain injuries turning to ruptures.

Walter Smith suggested that I should attend a management meeting after lunch, in order for me to experience all aspects of life within a football club. Present that afternoon were Walter, Archie, Chris Woods, physio Steve Hardwick, team masseur Jimmy Comer and Jimmy Martin. It proved to be a short meeting. Schedules and injuries to the team were discussed, then the arrival of striker Kevin Campbell later that day, and the return home of Michael Branch, who was considering a transfer to

Portsmouth. Nick Barmby came to say his goodbyes, too; he had to fly home that afternoon to be with his expectant wife in time for their baby to be induced. (Little George Barmby was born the following day.)

After the management meeting Jimmy Comer announced he wanted a quiet word with the manager. He was clearly nervous about my presence. 'It's rather personal, gaff,' he said. 'It's all right,' Walter told him. 'Ian's one of us. I want him here.' Jimmy then proceeded to talk of how uncomfortable he felt in the company of one of the players. 'He seems to want to be rubbed down more than the rest,' he said. 'It's getting to the stage where I want someone else in the room with me, just in case. I'm telling you, much more of it, and I'm leaving.' The manager said he would sort something out, and then, once Jimmy had left, asked me for my views. I had sat there in an astonished state listening to all this. Eventually, once I gathered my composure, I told him it could prove to be a problem in the dressing room, even more so if it were ever to emerge in the press. Later that afternoon, as I joined the squad for stretches, Walter pulled me aside. 'I've got to tell you something,' he said. 'Jimmy and the boys are trying to wind you up. It's supposed to be a set-up.'

I thanked him for his tip-off, and then felt foolish having offered him my considered 'advice' earlier on.

'Wobbly' was becoming a popular nickname for me by now, although Alex Cleland had also come up with 'Choccy', as in chocolate thighs. John Collins could see that I was far from enjoying the experience of being injured.

'I injured my toe in January and missed the rest of the season,' he recalled. 'There I was, joining a big club with a bit of a reputation to live up to as a player, and all I could do was sit there for the rest of the season as the club sank into the relegation zone. I felt completely helpless. It was the worst spell of my career. That's why I'm so happy now.' As if to prove his point, he pumped the air with his clenched hand. 'It's just great to be playing again.'

You could tell this in the way he approached his training. He and

Gough, and sometimes Watson, would spend an extra half an hour or so each day in the gym, working on the weights. It showed in their physiques, especially in the case of Collins, who would invariably shine in training. 'That's the way to do it,' Archie Knox would often shout out when John produced a perfect sprint or a textbook exercise. Good-natured but sarcastic comments of 'Well done John' would then be heard from some of the others, a response meted out to any player singled out by Archie in training. Gough was another player whose eagerness belied his age. 'Not bad for a thirty-seven-year-old,' he'd say to me as he raced past during the jogs that began every training session. 'I reckon there's another season left in me yet.'

Before dinner, Don Hutchison and I had a game of table tennis. Earlier, on the team bus, I had declared (buoyed by my ping-pong success against the Springboks in South Africa) that no Everton player could beat me. I knew that on a bus overflowing with so much competitiveness, someone was bound to respond. Hutchison took the bait, but my boast was to backfire badly. I was clearly beaten three sets to nil, as Hutchison delighted in telling any passing figure. Not only that but he was richer for his exertions, having placed a £10 bet per set.

Hutchison and Ward returned to the casino wheel later that night, determined to recoup their own – rather more substantial – losses from the previous evening. It was obvious it was going to be their night after an extraordinary coincidence – some might say too extraordinary a coincidence – took place. Gough and Collins had been ragged all day about their unwillingness to part with their money at the roulette wheel the previous night. Eventually, more for some peace than any other reason, the two Scots formulated a plan. Gough would place £10 on the red, and John a further tenner on the black. That way, one would definitely win, the spoils would be split between them, and the self-styled casino bankers would get off their backs. It was a no-lose situation. Or so they assumed.

Mitch spun the wheel. A hushed silence followed: all eyes followed the route of the ball as it whizzed its way around the roulette wheel. As soon as it lodged itself in a slot there was uproar. The ball had landed on the figure nought, the one place on the whole wheel where neither Gough nor Collins could win. Hutchison and Ward celebrated as if they'd just scored the winner at Wembley, while the rest of the players roared with laughter. Gough and Collins just blinked. Collins, in particular, would spend the next few days convinced that Hutchison had managed somehow to control the ball. 'They did us,' he'd say to the rest of us. 'I know they did us.'

They were still talking about the roulette incident on day seven. The players were awarded a small spangle, the morning off, although for me, this meant a rigorous session in the swimming pool and in the gym, working on my thighs. Some of them were by the pool sunbathing as I worked out. 'It would be funny if you scored against Man City,' Dave Watson said. 'I've seen most things in football, but you scoring for us at Goodison would be a real first.' Walter Smith declared that there was more chance of me being stretchered off. Craig Short took up the theme. 'They've got this big, central defender called Andy Morrison,' he said. 'You won't want to mess with him. Just think, one pass a little too short for you. It's either you or Morrison. You stretch out your leg, he dives in two-footed . . .' Shorty then shook his head demonstrably and let out exaggerated sighs.

There, too, was Scot Gemmill, the Scottish international midfield player who had joined Everton that summer from Nottingham Forest. He recalled life growing up as the son of Archie Gemmill, the famous Scottish midfielder, during the 1970s. 'Brian Clough signed my dad for Derby County the day before I was born,' he said. 'Our families have remained close ever since. I remember having a fight at school once. My dad had missed a penalty on the previous Saturday afternoon. I scored a penalty with a tennis ball in the playground on the Monday morning and started to celebrate, as small kids do. Then someone said: "Shame your dad couldn't do that on Saturday", and all hell broke out.' Gemmill Snr obviously had his son's footballing interests at heart: 'Later, when I was sixteen, he'd force me to stay in on a Saturday night if I had a game on the Sunday morning. I thought it was ridiculous at the time, but now I understand that he wanted to see if I had the right application. You just don't get signed up as a professional football player because your dad was a bit useful.'

Kevin Campbell ambled over to say hello. Having arrived on loan from the Turkish club Trabzonspor, at the back end of the previous season, his goals had proved crucial to Everton's Premiership survival. Now Everton had signed him, although some inflammatory comments from the Turkish chairman meant that the former Arsenal player had to make a last visit back to Turkey to clear the air before being allowed to leave for good. It was a ridiculous case of football politics and Campbell, the person abused in all of this, was the one who was forced to smooth things over. Needless to say, he was delighted to be in Tuscany, although judging by the enormity of his suitcase he must have thought we would be there for the whole month. 'He must be carrying all the money Everton's paying him in that suitcase,' Hutchison remarked.

Shortly before the afternoon training session began, the week's 'wind-up' came to its fruition. The previous day Jimmy Comer had asked Chris Woods, in my presence, to remain in the room with him while he rubbed down Craig Short. That night I happened to come across Short and Comer having a glass of wine on a bedroom balcony. Unhappily for them, I had failed to make any connections. At 4.15 Steve the physio asked me to wake up Jimmy Comer next door. I banged on his door a few times and then opened it to find Jimmy lying on his bed with a pair of Everton socks acting as a gag, and Craig Short bending over him making rather staged movements. I had been preparing for some kind of surprise, but not exactly this. Comer and Short fell about laughing when they saw my terrified face, at least until I told them that Walter Smith had tipped me off about the whole thing. This prompted Jimmy to ring up Walter. 'You've done me,' he complained down the line. 'You've bloody done me.' Short took no time in assuring me of his sexual preferences. 'I'm happily married with two children,' he stressed. 'You do realise it was only a joke, don't you.'

I underwent a second fitness test in front of the team back on Il Ciocco's pitch to see whether my thigh would allow me to train. It still pulled considerably but, mindful of the watching players, and after forty-eight hours of derogatory comments, I announced I would rejoin the main squad and play through the pain barrier. This was met – much to my delight – with a round of applause. 'He's back,' Dave Watson added, with a smile. 'I've got to look out for those sneaky back-post runs again now.'

As training finished I was summoned to the head-tennis court. Walter Smith told me I would be his partner against Woods and Jimmy Martin. He added, with a menacing glare, that he had never lost a game of head tennis in his life. Half an hour later, and with the rest of the team enjoying showers back in their rooms, Walter had lost his first game. He decided to lay all the blame on me. Later he heard from some of the players that I had been apportioning some of the blame his way. I'd just turned out my light and was fast descending into a deep sleep when the telephone rang. 'Right,' pronounced Smith's now familiar voice. 'Let's play head tennis right now. If you're going to criticise me then we'll have it out on the head-tennis court.' It was past midnight, it was pitch black outside, and the head-tennis court was up the mountain. I told him I'd see him in the morning, assuming he was joking. To this day I can never be sure he was.

On our penultimate day in Tuscany, we endured our last double training session. Once again Dave Watson began the proceedings – the friendly sergeant major in charge of the infantry men – and then Archie Knox would take over. Walter Smith would observe everything with great interest, leaving his trusty lieutenant to bark out most of the orders. For some reason I always seemed to perform better in front of Knox than in front of Smith. I'm not suggesting I was exactly impressive in the assistant manager's presence, but at least I scored a few goals in the handball and five-a-side matches, something the 'gaffer' missed out on on a consistent basis. The intensity of training had also increased noticeably. A combination of physical tiredness and stress as the start of the season drew nearer meant that tackles were flying in. At one stage Danny Cadamarteri objected to a physical challenge from Dave Unsworth. Words were exchanged between them. Five minutes later, however, they were all smiles. 'It's never personal,' Unsworth explained later. 'But it happens a lot in training at most clubs. It's just our natural competitiveness and the fact that we all need to impress. All the players understand this, and they rarely fall out with a team-mate.'

At the end of the afternoon session the management staged an England versus Scotland five-a-side game. Despite England boasting Chris Woods, the former national goalkeeper, I found myself between the posts after an hour spent in the company of Paul Gerrard and reserve goalkeeper Steve Simonsen. Chris Woods, our captain, played up front. Alex Cleland officiated, which proved to be a big mistake. The Scot was without doubt the most biased referee I have ever known, and by the end of the 2–2 draw, accusations and counter-accusations were being levelled at each and every one of us. A penalty competition resulted. The Scots missed their first four shots – with Smith and Knox both blasting their efforts over – before Jimmy Martin beat me with a low shot that bent back three of my fingers. Woods saved the day for England with an equaliser, and Jimmy Comer won the game by virtue of a successful chip from the half-way line, in a new competition following the drawn penalties.

Our last night was the occasion for the squad's big trip out. The lads were let loose and were allowed, within reason, to do what they liked. 'Kevin', the jovial bus driver, took us to a local nightclub called 'The Skylab'. Gough and I soon found ourselves hogging a table football game, the former Scottish captain revealing yet again his competitive nature. The first game went to me, 8–2. Towards the end of the game Gough started to chide himself and, somewhat bizarrely, his defenders – who, implanted in a row of four on to a steel rod, were in no position to answer back. 'That's crap, Goughie,' he would say to himself after I'd scored a goal. 'Your defence can do a lot better than that!' Sure enough, in the second game he hit back to win 6–4, his glee obvious to all. I argued that I still won when the two legs were added together, but he would have none of it. 'It's 1–1,' he insisted. 'I bounced back.'

Some of the younger players were helping themselves to huge litre-glasses of beer. 'I'll give you a grand if you drink one of those on the head, Ian,' Michael Ball said from across a crowded table. The others encouraged me and, like a fool, I accepted the challenge. Hutchison gave my shoulders a last-minute rub, like a boxing trainer, and wished me luck. After what seemed like an eternity, and only after a number of very slow gulps, I downed the lager in one final, concentrated effort. Everyone cheered and clapped, even more so when Bally produced his 'grand' – a one thousand lire note, worth around 32 pence.

Oh well. I suppose it produced a laugh and a talking-point. But worse was to come. Don Hutchison, Mitch Ward and Craig Short seemed eager to show me a trick. Hutchison planted a small silver coin on to Ward's forehead. Ward then slapped the back of his head three times. On the fourth occasion the coin dropped into his hand. 'Now you try,' Hutch suggested. Short planted what I thought was a coin on to my head. I began to slap away, but with no success. After ten slaps I suggested Hutch should try. The offer was gratefully accepted. Eventually, the penny dropped, or rather it didn't. Short had never placed the coin on me in the first place. I had just spent the last few minutes slapping the back of my head for no good reason at all.

The players began to slope off back to the hotel. I managed to persuade a local to give Hutchison and Ward a lift home, leaving behind me, Short, Phelan and Alex Cleland – all of us wondering just how we would find our way back to Il Ciocco. Cleland, normally one of the quieter members of the squad, was by now muttering about flying the flag for Scotland, and when Short tried to relieve himself in a bush, only to tumble through it and down a hill, we knew it was time to leave.

Phelan could not stop himself laughing at the sight of an embarrassed Craig Short re-emerging from the bush, but his attitude changed when I found a friendly Italian football fan who agreed to drive us home. 'I've got a new baby at home,' Phelan would wail in the back of the car as we veered from one side of the road to the other. The collective relief was immense when we were dropped off outside the hotel main gate, although some of my fellow passengers that night would rue their excesses in the morning.

The phone rang in my bedroom six hours later. It was Walter Smith, who had remembered a coffee we had arranged the day before. 'We'll have to sit down and discuss your fees,' he said, his wry smile betraying his mock seriousness. 'When can you sign for us?' He did, however, confirm that I had done enough to warrant a fleeting appearance against Manchester City, adding that I had mixed well with the team and worked hard. He was dead right about that last statement. Pre-season training with Everton proved to be as physically demanding as any sporting challenge I had ever encountered. By that morning I could hardly walk.

This was our last day, and a half-day because of our flight back to Stansted. Archie Knox led the squad jog, waving like royalty to the group of young fans that he seemed to have adopted during the past week. After some head tennis and a five-a-side, we left for a stopover in Lucca, en route to Pisa airport. Phelan – who turned out to be a bit of an antiques buff – and I toured the market stalls. 'I love all this,' he enthused as we strolled through the cobbled streets. 'There's a lot more to us footballers than you might think,' he added.

Indeed there is. I was quite sorry to leave them at Stansted late on that Saturday night. I was to return home by taxi, and the rest of the team would drive up to Liverpool. Walter was threatening to show *Braveheart* on the coach video yet again, but the players voted for *Dumb and Dumber* instead. I would be back with my new-found team-mates the following week. Indeed, as I climbed into the taxi and headed for home I realised that I was nine days away from making my debut at Goodison

Park. It seemed an unlikely dream – even after nine days of training in Tuscany – and the very thought of wearing the blue of Everton for real began to set my pulses racing.

During my time back home I continued training, following Archie Knox's stretching regime in my back garden, running around the local recreation ground, eating pasta, drinking water, even wearing flip-flops, like all proper footballers, at home. Walter Smith fixed me up for two nights the following week in Liverpool's Swallow Hotel, which was Richard Gough's base while he searched for a more permanent home in the city. 'Don't panic,' Walter would say to me once again when we spoke at the weekend. 'Everything's arranged. Just get yourself up here.'

I drove north on the Monday night. In forty-eight hours I would be playing for the Everton first team against Manchester City in what was a testimonial game for John Ebbrell, the former Blues midfielder, whose career had been cut short by injury. Strangely enough, I recalled interviewing a young Ebbrell when he made the news by becoming the first graduate from the FA Soccer School at Lilleshall to break into the top division of football. How odd it seemed that his whole career had flown past since then, and that it was me, at the age of nearly thirty-six, who would now be playing at Goodison. Duncan McKenzie and Ian St John were on a radio phone-in that night reminding the listeners about the testimonial. 'It's a big game,' the former Merseyside football stars insisted. The butterflies in my stomach bore testament to that.

Early on the Tuesday morning, I arrived at Bellefield, the Everton training ground in West Derby, only to discover that I'd left my football boots at home. That, for obvious reasons, was not a good start. Luckily Jimmy Martin alleviated my rising panic by finding a spare pair of Kevin Campbell's boots. I checked with Kevin to see if he minded, and rather hoped that his natural scoring touch might remain in the boots. Ronnie Ekelund, the former Barcelona and Odense midfielder, had joined the club for a week's trial. If all went well, the Danish international hoped to sign for Everton. Francis Jeffers, the talented young striker who had enjoyed an instantly fruitful partnership with Campbell, had recovered from the injury that had forced him to miss the trip to Tuscany.

We began training with the usual series of stretches and five-a-sides. I managed to score twice in a 2–1 victory in one of the games, but my form failed to last the distance. I came somewhat unstuck when required to dribble quickly in and out of a series of slalom poles. Walter Smith surveyed the scene of wreckage after one such foray. Two poles were bent, and another flattened to the ground. 'Do that again,' he said, as he picked up the poles and hammered them back into the turf, 'and tomorrow night will be the last time you play for Everton.'

A short afternoon session followed where moves for the next day's game were worked out, and a series of short-passing exercises were enacted. At the end of the session we all took turns to fire free kicks over a metal wall of defenders, with the player deemed to have taken the worst kick having then to become the goalkeeper. Hutchison decided to lend me a hand by distracting Gerrard in goal long enough for me to hit the back of the net. 'I saw that,' Walter Smith shouted across the field, shaking his head in the process.

Walter left for a typical evening's spying mission at Bradford City versus Nottingham Forest, the unseen work of a manager. I took a drive around nearby Stanley Park until I came to Goodison Park. I had only ever been to the famous old ground once, and that was many years earlier when I was starting out in sports journalism. I parked the car and circumnavigated the stadium, walking along the small roads with terraced housing – it seemed that little had changed around here for decades. The stands sent huge shadows across the surrounding streets. Quite a few people were wearing Everton shirts – and this was not even a match day.

Training the next morning was brief. There was no point over-exerting the team on the day of a match. The players still had enough time for a few last-minute digs, however. 'I can't remember the last time we substituted a sub,' Watson announced, as I jumped into the large communal bath. Jeffers got wind of the fact that I would be replacing a striker at some late stage of the second half. 'If it's me, I'm slapping in a transfer request,' he said. Unsworth was already talking up my chances. 'If you score,' he said, as the steam rose from the bath water, 'I'll wet myself laughing.'

While the rest of the players returned to their homes for a restful afternoon, I stayed at Bellefield with Walter Smith and Archie Knox, killing time. A youth match was played out on the training pitch, but my mind was elsewhere. Walter could sense this. 'You're beginning to make me feel nervous,' he said. 'Don't panic.' This had now become his favourite phrase, at least while I was around. As he pondered his dubious decision to allow me to play for Everton, however, his 'don't panics' were beginning to resemble those of Corporal Jones in 'Dad's Army'.

After an interminably long afternoon, in which I showered twice to calm my nerves, I followed Walter by car to Goodison. People were already beginning to mingle outside the ground, the familiar smell of burgers and hot dogs permeating the air. The water sprinklers had been switched on and were spraying the magnificent turf, hardened by a day's sunshine that still bathed the pitch. Some of the players began to arrive, walking along the touchline carrying their holdalls. The ever-enthusiastic John Collins saw me and pumped the air with his fist. 'This is it,' he shouted. 'This is what it's all about.' Unsworth and Hutchison followed suit, great beaming smiles plastered over their faces. It was clear that this was always the highlight of their week.

The blue shirts of Everton were hanging on individual pegs in the dressing room. I was number 22. I slipped the shirt over my head and changed into my white shorts, blue socks, shin-pads and Kevin Campbell's boots. Walter Smith feigned a double-take when he saw me kitted out, for the first time, in the full Everton strip. 'Eighteen years in coaching and management,' he said, 'and I reckon I've just made my biggest mistake.' With less than forty minutes left before the big kick-off, my churning stomach prevented me from fully sharing the joke.

We ran on to the pitch to stretch and warm up. A sizeable crowd was beginning to file into the rows of seats, a steady chatter rising from the stands, and the latest chart hits blasting out from the stadium tannoy system. Dave Watson took charge once again as we jogged and then sprinted across the width of the pitch, occasionally glancing across to the other half where City were performing similar exercises. They were sporting some familiar names themselves, with the likes of goalkeeper Nicky Weaver, Ian Bishop, Mark Kennedy and a young man called Shaun Wright-Phillips – Ian Wright's son, no less – all playing. So too was Andy Morrison, a big tough man, about whom Craig Short had earlier waxed so lyrically when describing my potential meeting with the City defender on the pitch.

Someone in the crowd was intrigued. 'Who's the new player, then?' he shouted out to Scot Gemmill, who just happened to be jogging alongside an advertising hoarding. Scot's response was immediate. 'I can't believe you don't know him,' he replied. 'After all, he's cost us £3 million.'

The humour disappeared, however, once we had returned to the dressing room. It may have been just a pre-season testimonial match, but its importance was not being belittled. Smith had already made it perfectly clear that Manchester City, just promoted into the First Division after their play-off heroics a couple of months earlier, would be up for the game. And so they were. Their manager Joe Royle, Smith's predecessor in the Goodison hot seat, was so focused on proceedings that when he emerged from the players' tunnel, he instinctively turned to sit in the Everton dugout rather than the away team's.

Dave Watson, standing up and bouncing a ball on the dressing room floor, told us to knuckle down and make sure we were the first to the ball. He then took time to shake every player, including me, by the hand and wish us all luck, a process repeated by many of the squad. I felt rather honoured, almost touched, that they should involve me in this small and rather poignant ceremony. More than ever before, I felt as though I were really a part of the team. There was a host of high achievers, medal winners and international players that night – men like Collins and Gough, Watson and Phelan, England's Barmby, Scotland's Gemmill, Hutchison and Cleland – yet a look of nervous tension and serious intent was etched on each player's face. If this is the pre-match intensity of a friendly, I thought to myself, heaven knows what it will be like in the Goodison dressing rooms prior to a Liverpool derby game.

It was time. Both teams seemed to emerge from their respective dressing rooms simultaneously. A few of the players nodded in recognition to each other. We remained lined up on either side of the players' tunnel, waiting to receive the official sign to make our entrance. Someone broke wind, causing great consternation, and turning a tense scenario into a farcical one. There I was, about to run out for one of the truly memorable moments of my life, only to be surrounded by a bunch of football players holding their shirts up to their noses.

We jogged out on to the pitch. The crowd had increased noticeably in the last half hour before kick-off. I later discovered that it numbered around 13,000 – not a massive crowd by Goodison standards, but a good turnout for a pre-season testimonial. We formed two columns as John Ebbrell emerged, holding his daughter's hand, to general applause. The formalities over, the Everton reserves returned to the dugout while the two starting teams ran into their positions.

Walter Smith was sitting high above in the stands, alongside various board members. Archie Knox was in charge of the more immediate proceedings. I sat next to Alex Cleland, with the potent smell of Deep Heat all around us. Copious amounts of gum were chewed as we settled down to watch the first half. Everton took charge of the game from early on, peppering in a series of attacks that were thwarted by City's determined defence. Francis Jeffers broke the deadlock, rifling in a shot from the edge of the penalty area that flew through a couple of defenders and past Nicky Weaver thanks, in part, to a slight deflection. One–nil, which was good for Everton, and good for me. Despite all the team's promises, I was wondering whether they would still play me if City were losing.

At half time the reserves warmed up on the pitch, passing the ball to each other and enacting a series of stretches and jogs. I would have liked to have seen what was going on in the dressing room, but when I tried to make my entrance, Walter Smith sent me packing back out on to the pitch. 'You're a sub,' he said. 'Go and practise.' And so I joined Ward, Scott, Phelan, Cleland, Ekelund, Cadamarteri and the big young central defender, Richard Dunne, for a quick kickaround before the teams returned for the second half.

An hour into the game, wholesale changes took place. On came Gough, Phelan and Ward to replace Michael Ball, David Weir and Dave Unsworth. Within a couple more minutes Scot Gemmill and Peter Degn took over from Nicky Barmby and Don Hutchison. I was just beginning to wonder whether Archie, in all the excitement, had forgotten my presence. Hutchison and Unsworth told me to perform a couple of stretches and sprints under the nose of the assistant manager to serve as a blunt reminder. The large clock on the far stand was ticking away, and as the time drew close to the seventy-five-minute mark, so my nerves reached a state of near-frenzy. Archie ordered Ekelund, Cadamarteri and me to leap off the bench. We stripped off our sweatshirts and lined up on the touchline. The assistant manager beckoned me over for a final tip. 'If you get the ball, Ian,' he said, as I bent down to listen earnestly to his advice, 'just get rid of it.'

I cannot recall ever having felt so fit in all my life. Some of the players later put it down to the effects of the adrenalin that was flowing through my body like a river that had burst its banks. I felt strong, even fast, and when I entered the fray I bounded like a spring lamb on to the pitch – well, at least that's how it seemed to me.

The press report after the match said that I replaced Dave Watson, while Kevin Campbell and Francis Jeffers were removed for Ekelund and Cadamarteri, but in fact I ran straight up the field to my favoured position of outside right. Cadamarteri joined me in a new-look Everton strike force, and Ekelund settled into a midfield berth. As I ran on to the pitch, trying my hardest to look the part and to appear unperturbed by the extraordinary circumstances in which I found myself, I heard a singular tannoy announcement. 'Wearing number 22, making his first and most definitely last appearance for Everton, Ian Stafford.'

There then followed what seemed to be the fastest quarter of an hour of my life. Within a couple of minutes Cadamarteri had received the ball to my right. I was standing on the corner of the penalty area, with my back to the City goal, convinced that the dreaded Andy Morrison was breathing down my neck. In that split second the obvious move was to return the pass to Danny, enabling him to cross the ball into the area. The first part of the plan worked quite well. I sent the ball back down the flank with a first-time touch, and then looked with horror as Cadamarteri stood still. The ball trickled harmlessly out for a City goal-kick, amid a loud roar of disapproval from the Everton section of the supporters.

The *Liverpool Echo* was quick to pick up on this in the following morning's edition. 'Stafford may wish to forget his first touch, which saw him lay off a pass on Everton's right flank for an overlap that wasn't there,' it reported. I saw a replay of the action later, courtesy of a cable television channel that had broadcast the game live that night. The pass indeed looked appalling, and was made worse by my effort to give Ekelund – who had turned his back on me – a public rollicking. Moreover, Morrison was a good five feet away from me at the time. Had I known this, I would have turned round and attempted a shot. Who knows, my effort might even have found the back of the net. Or perhaps not. Hindsight is a wonderful tactic.

For the next eight minutes or so, play was mainly in Everton's own half. Gerrard produced an athletic save, but in general the threat to our lead was minimal. There was little I could do except loiter with intent close to the half-way line. I made a few sprints in vain, finding space but no team-mates willing to risk passing the ball to me. I found solace in the fact that the City defence, unaware of my purpose that night, considered me a sufficient enough threat to keep a constant eye on my darting runs. Eventually I helped the ball along to Peter Degn out on the wing, before becoming involved in a tussle with Morrison for the ball. He won the encounter, after I twice attempted to hack away the ball, prompting the City fans to chant his name. 'Morrison, la, la, la', resounded around Goodison Park, while I rubbed a finger that had somehow been bent back in the clash.

The referee blew for time. Everton, despite my presence, had won the game. We all shook hands with each other, returned the home support's applause, and jogged off the pitch. My initial disappointment at my negligible contribution was soon swept away by the Everton players, who made a point of congratulating me and asking whether I had enjoyed myself.

My answer, of course, was yes. Very much so. In fact, I felt so good it was as though Everton had just won the Cup. The rest of the team had seen it all before, many times. They showered, changed, and said their goodbyes. For them it was just another game. In four days' time they would face yet more opposition in their last pre-season friendly. In ten days' time Manchester United would be paying Goodison Park a Premiership visit. To them, thrilling as it is to play football, it was their job. To me, a frustrated sportsman, it was a dream that had rather abruptly come to an end.

'Old Ian's as high as a kite,' Archie Knox observed, chuckling away and asking Walter Smith if they should sign me up. 'Ring me tomorrow,' the manager said. 'I'll give you my answer.' It proved to be a late night drive back to London, but the buzz of having appeared for the Everton first team kept me wide awake as I ventured further south along the empty motorway. Seven hours after slipping into a dreamy sleep back home, I telephoned Walter for a final verdict.

'Give it to me straight,' I said. 'Maybe you can grade my performance.'

He cleared his throat, as if he were about to make a major speech. 'Your one redeeming feature is your attitude and application,' he began. 'For that I'll give you an A. No, make that an A plus. I could name a few talented football players who could become huge stars if they possessed your determination.'

Well, that wasn't so bad, was it? The problem was that I had a feeling that Walter's report would take a sudden nosedive.

'What about ability, then?' I asked, failing to hide my hesitancy. 'A to E.'

'Can we go down to Z?' he asked.

'Sure,' I replied. 'So what's my grade, then?'

'Z,' Walter said without any pause. 'At least it's Z when compared to a professional footballer. I can see that you are a decent park player, though.'

He waited for a response, but there wasn't much I could say. 'We're talking about the very highest level here, Ian,' Walter added, softening the blow a little. 'There's quite a lot of work to do on technique, but your attitude was first class. You've got to remember that the vast majority of hopeful football players hear exactly the same kind of shattering news you've just received – at least it would have been shattering if your attempts to become a full-time player were serious. It's a hard game.'

Of that there is no doubt. And at that level it is a highly professional game, too. English footballers have had their share of bad press – and in some cases they deserve it – and created images that send out all the wrong kind of signals to the public. Yet I found with Everton a group of highly committed sportsmen who took what they did seriously, and although they shared plenty of lighter moments along the way, the game, and the result, seemed to matter more than anything and anyone else. It was a fascinating, if short, insight into a Premiership club.

Or at least I assume it was a short insight. A comeback cannot be ruled out completely, of course. For a start, how many players can safely say that Everton never lose when they play for the first team? That, if nothing else, is my claim to fame at Goodison Park. Walter Smith's departing words left me with a small degree of hope, and I felt a rush of adrenalin when, a few days after the match, I found him at the other end of the phone. 'I've just thought of another, truly important, advantage you have over all my other players,' he said.

'What's that, Walter?' I asked, as the words 'cool', 'calm', 'calculating' and 'mature' flashed through my mind.

'You're cheap,' he said, with a chuckle to himself. 'You could come in useful yet, my boy.'

chapter two

 THE RED SHADOW

When I was training with Everton Walter Smith used to warn his players that if they messed with me I would punch their lights out, just as I had done to Roy Jones Jr the previous year. Hardly likely. But my next challenge was to provide me with another weapon in my arsenal: I was going to become a professional wrestler. Had he known this, it would have simply confirmed his conviction that he had just allowed a certified lunatic to play for his first team.

You have to be in your mid-thirties or older to appreciate what wrestling used to represent in Britain. Saturday afternoons for a vast number of people meant wrestling on ITV's 'World of Sport', and for the best part of an hour all generations crowded around the television set to cheer their heroes, and jeer the baddies. Bizarre as this may seem, it became cult viewing.

In time Jackie Pallance and Mick McManus gave way to the likes of Big Daddy, Giant Haystacks and Kendo Nagasaki, all household names in their day and larger-than-life, comic-strip figures, who filled such illustrious venues as Rochdale Town Hall and Morecambe Pier. 'Grapple' fans knew that some choreographed theatre came into play, but they neither noticed nor cared. So long as Big Daddy saw off Haystacks with his trademark belly flop, they went out on a Saturday night content with the world.

When ITV decided to halt the transmission of wrestling in the 1980s it all but destroyed the sport. For ten years the heroes of yesteryear continued to ply their trade, but for pennies rather than pounds. This would have continued but for one important new development. The creation in the US of the World Wrestling Federation served to reinvent the sport and introduce it to a fresh and young audience.

Today British wrestling is clawing its way back, thanks to the influence of American WWF stars such as the Rock, the Undertaker, Mankind and others among the unlikely bunch of meathead characters. At the same time, however, it has also maintained a link with its traditional past. The notion of the WWF coming to Bognor Regis to play out its over-rehearsed acts in front of the blue-rinse brigade does not somehow sound like a recipe for success. The British public still likes its wrestling raw, with imperfect wrestlers, imperfect bodies, and plenty of audience interaction.

It was this that I wanted to explore. Is wrestling, at least British wrestling, genuine, or is it just a game? Is there an element of skill required, or do you just need to be a big lump with a third rate diploma from a third rate drama school? And what are these wrestlers really like? Even though I had vowed never to return to the ring after my severe beating by Roy Jones Jr the previous year, I decided that what I really meant was that I would not return to a boxing ring. A wrestling ring? Well now, that was different.

Having made this somewhat rash decision, and then researched the subject using old books and the Internet, I came to the conclusion there was only one man to turn to in this situation, one man who might just be maverick enough to teach me how to wrestle, and perhaps even partner me in a tag bout, where teams of two take on each other in a physical spectacle that rarely respects the rules.

Pat Roach is recognised these days to be 'The Guvnor' of British wrestling, partly because he has been doing it for so long – he was often the 'whipping boy' for the likes of Haystacks and Nagasaki in their heyday before graduating to become the star turn himself – and partly because his film and television fame means he is the one practising professional wrestler in Britain that most people have heard of.

His biggest claim to fame is most probably his role as 'Bomber' in the hugely successful British television series 'Auf Wiedersehen Pet', but Roach has also appeared in a number of high profile films, including the Bond movie *Never Say Never Again*, all three Indiana Jones movies (viewers may recall him as the bald man who got chopped into tiny pieces by the aeroplane's propellers while chasing Harrison Ford in *Indiana 2*), *A Clockwork Orange* and *Clash of the Titans*. On each occasion Roach played a gigantic and often sinister figure.

When I telephoned him, however, he was at a more down-to-earth location: his Birmingham scrapyard. The conversation did not begin well. When I mentioned the fact that I earn part of my living through journalism Roach all but hung up in disgust, before launching into a lengthy rant about how despicable journalists are. Having first endured his vocal disgust and then managed to keep him from hanging up, I told him of my serious intentions. A stunned silence followed before the Bomber threw a host of questions at me. 'Are you serious?' was the obvious first one. 'Have you any idea how hard this will be?' came next. 'Do you like pain?' followed shortly afterwards.

Slowly, as we talked, Roach began to warm to the idea, especially when I agreed to take, to use his words, 'everything that was coming to me'. We ended the conversation with this verdict from the Bomber: 'I've never heard anything as crazy in my life. You're a madman, but I like the challenge of turning a madman into a wrestler. And I like the idea of beating up a writer.'

Within a couple of days Pat had found a willing wrestling promoter. John Freemantle is the most successful promoter in the south of England. After receiving a call from my new-found partner, and a man the promoter is always delighted to feature, Freemantle agreed to present a tag match between the Bomber and myself against two, yet to be decided, opponents.

He was staging a promotion at the Pavilion Theatre, Worthing, the following night, and suggested I should come down to watch Pat in action and meet both of them.

It was a cold and foggy night down on the seafront, and the five hundred or so people who had come to the theatre to watch the Bomber and friends were no doubt relieved when the auditorium doors were flung open and they could reach the warm comfort of their seats. In recent weeks such luminaries as The Joe Loss Orchestra, Sooty, 'The Ken Dodd Happiness Show' and John Mann, the BBC Radio organist, had appeared at the Pavilion; now, the neon light outside the theatre informed us, it was the turn of 'All-Star Wrestling'.

Pat had arranged to meet me before the start of the show. It was as I was queuing for my seat that I felt a large, bear-like claw clasp my shoulder. The man, quite simply, is enormous: 6 ft 5 in tall and weighing in at 19½ stone. His age is more difficult to gauge: an enquiry in that regard is met with an ugly glare and a puffing out of his vast bulk, but he will quite happily admit to fighting all the big names during the 1970s, when British wrestling enjoyed its halcyon days.

'It's the oldest sport in the world,' he explained as we sat down with a cup of tea in the theatre's cafeteria, now awash with cigarette smoke and pale ales as the mainly middle-aged audience got stuck into their pre-show refreshments. 'For the sake of decency we wear trunks, but that's about it. There are no props and you're out on your own, on active duty for sixty seconds a minute. You're either dishing it out or getting it.' He gave me a slightly disdainful look at this point, and added: 'In your case, you'll be mainly getting it.'

The conversation would be punctuated by autograph seekers, some referring to Pat's acting days, but most seeing him as the most respected man in British wrestling. 'Show him who's boss,' one demanded.

'Don't worry,' Roach would reply, his Brummie accent seemingly more prevalent that night. 'We all know who's the boss.'

As we made our way to his dressing room I asked Pat if my wrestling debut was really likely to hurt. His answer came in the form of a sudden headlock, taking me completely by surprise, that ended just as a click sounded from my neck. 'I could have ripped your head off if I'd wanted to,' he explained, as he shut the dressing room door and prepared for his bout. 'Does that answer your question?' As I rubbed my neck and found my seat in the theatre I was left with little illusion that he was telling the truth.

John Freemantle ambled over to say hello. Looking resplendent in his wrestling promoter's attire – white dress shirt, black suit, bow tie, microphone in hand – he explained how he had been brought up on wrestling from an early age, and loved the traditions of British boxing. 'The WWF does nothing for me,' he said. 'I'm convinced it wouldn't work in Britain because we like our sport to be for real, and our performers to be more like us. Wrestling used to be a massively popular sport in this country, and I'm convinced it will be again.' He added that he would feature me in a tag team contest at a show he was promoting at the Brighton Centre. 'It should be really interesting,' he said, with a glint in his eye that seemed to spell trouble.

What then followed was a rather surreal night of part-staged, part-violent entertainment, involving the likes of Doug 'The Anarchist' Williams versus 'Wildcat' Robbie Brookside, and the baddie, Lee Darren, against 'local favourite', Barry Cooper, fighting for the 'prestigious' Sussex Championship and trophy. 'You've got a big mouth,' Darren would shout at old ladies who would step up to the ringside to deliver one-fingered salutes, but it was Cooper who won in the end.

Top of the bill, however, was the Premier Wrestling Federation's heavyweight champion, 'Bomber' Pat Roach, who would be facing John 'The Bear Man' Elijah, a big, balding man who entered the arena wearing a bearskin. Bomber arrived to the theme tune of 'Auf Wiedersehen Pet', and as the audience clapped along to 'That's Living All Right' Pat clapped, waved and smiled. With his rather weather-beaten face he was at one time a class baddy, but the growl has since turned to smiles, and experience and time has transformed him into the best of the good guys.

I noticed a large scar on Roach's left shoulder and wondered how he had managed to acquire such an indelible mark. It didn't seem to affect him, however. Although The Bear Man managed to engineer a fall on Roach, our hero came back with two of his own – the second following a body slam in which our man hoisted the heavy Elijah up above his head and then threw him down to the canvas – to win the bout and accept the cheers from the audience. Not content with that he grasped the microphone and praised his beaten opponent for playing a part in what he determined to be a good, old-fashioned wrestling match. 'It's how it should be,' he informed his followers.

As he left the auditorium to yet another blast from 'Auf Wiedersehen Pet', he caught sight of me and nodded his head. 'I'd look forward to two plastic hips, if I were you,' he quipped, and went back to the dressing room to change and collect his pay for the night. Later I saw him as he stepped into his car, before driving back up to Birmingham. 'I'll see you on Monday, then,' he said. 'Make the most of the next few days, because people take for granted life without pain.' Monday would be my first ever lesson as a wrestler, and I had absolutely no idea what was going to happen. But on the evidence of this night I had grown to understand one very important aspect. Whatever else might occur, it was clearly going to hurt.

Pat Roach has a fitness centre in the Erdington district of Birmingham, beneath the shadow of Spaghetti Junction. He seemed keen to take me on a tour of his facilities to start with, stopping at various framed photos on the wall, such as in character alongside Laurence Olivier or Harrison Ford, or old wrestling posters featuring bouts between himself and Giant Haystacks.

In the centre's back garden he had erected a large green army tent that housed a rickety old wrestling ring. This would be my school for the half dozen lessons Roach was prepared to teach me. 'It won't nearly be enough, you know,' he would tell me. 'But you might pick up enough not to get killed. Maybe maimed, but not killed.' Reverse psychology, as I would discover throughout my time with him, was one of Pat's strong points.

We began with some gripping exercises, clasping each other's arms with our hands and pushing. As we did this Roach recalled wrestlers he had witnessed over the years who had lost their composure in the ring and ended up causing serious damage to their opponent. 'I've seen some terrible injuries in my time,' he'd say, as he would lock my head in his arms and squeeze. 'Absolutely terrible.'

There then followed what he later termed my test of heart. Roach started to pick me up and throw me over his considerable frame, doing this repeatedly. Each time I would land flat on my back on the floor, making a loud smacking sound in the process, and lie there numbed by the experience. It would all happen in a flash. One second I would be tangling with this big brute, the next he would be grasping my thigh, slinging my body up over his shoulder, and then slamming me down again. I had no say, nor influence, in the outcome.

Previous experiences in similar company had taught me not to complain about such treatment, but after the tenth time, with absolutely no sign of abatement, I was just beginning to wonder when a seemingly happy Pat would be putting a stop to this. 'Well,' he said eventually, as I lay prostrate, winded, and somewhat frightened on the floor. 'I can see you don't particularly like that, but I can also see that you have a heart. That's a positive sign, you know. If you'd failed that test, there wouldn't have been much point in going on.'

That sounded like potentially good news, but it merely heralded a number of other painful moves. 'I'm going to show you how a good wrestler can kick and punch you enough for you to feel it, but without it really hurting,' my teacher explained. For starters, he began to kick me on the forehead. The trick is to brush the sole of your boot across your opponent's forehead with enough force to send him over but without causing too much damage. 'Let me show you,' Pat said, before adding: 'This won't hurt – much.'

I had to stand on all fours like a dog in the middle of the ring as the man who beat up Sean Connery lunged forward and planted his huge right foot on to my forehead with a rather menacing dart of his leg. As I picked myself up from the canvas, having been sent crashing into the corner by the blow, Pat said: 'See, I told you. It didn't hurt, did it?' Actually it bloody well did. And it continued to hurt each time he did it, with me, a willing compliant, on all fours in the middle of a ring in an army tent. Each time I prepared myself for the next blow I asked myself why on earth I found it necessary to do this.

When it was all over, and I walked gingerly to my car, Pat told me what was to come. 'That was just preliminary work, you understand,' he said. 'The hard stuff's coming next week. But for now I suggest you go home and rest, because you're going to feel it tomorrow.'

Never mind tomorrow. By the time I reached home my back felt broken in three places, and my head, previously the recipient of Roach's size 13 boot, was throbbing. Raiding my wife's homeopathic box I took vast quantities of arnica to ease the bruising, before throwing some geranium, lavender and camomile oils into a hot bath. 'How's your day been, then?' my wife asked as I sank into the water. 'It could have been better,' I replied, as I visualised myself being kicked in the head by a 19-stone bearded brute. 'A lot better.'

By the morning I was finding movement, any movement, very difficult. I telephoned Pat, who seemed to enjoy my discomfort. 'I'm not at all surprised,' he said. 'I feel like that all the time. You've never been slammed before, have you? Your body's not supposed to take that. It's not really built for it, is it? It's a very unnatural thing to do. Anyway, I wouldn't worry about today.'

'Why's that, then?' I asked.

'Cos you'll feel worse tomorrow.'

On the morning of my next lesson I called in at Lonsdale Sports in Beak Street in London to see my old friend, Ruben Shohet. Ruben had provided me with my boxing gear when I went out to Florida to fight Roy Jones Jr. Now he had some wrestling shorts and boots for me. The shorts were more like cycling tights, clinging firmly to my thighs and rather revealing in certain places. The boots, specially ordered by Ruben, were long, black and patent. I tried both on and looked rather kinky – all the more so since I was standing in the middle of Soho early in the morning looking as though I'd just finished a night's work. 'I didn't want to say anything at the time, but I thought you were mad when you fought Jones,' Ruben said, showing me to the door as I clasped my booties. 'But now I know you are. It's actually making me feel quite nervous having you in my shop.'

Pat was momentarily impressed with my new fancy gear – that was, until he forced me into the first headlock of the afternoon's lesson. 'Your fancy boots aren't going to help you now,' he announced as I slapped my hand against his vast torso in a vain attempt to release myself. After the usual introductory body slams – all of which were as frightening and as unwanted as the previous time – we went to work on a few moves. As he flipped me over from a head lock that he referred to as a 'head mare' I found myself learning to somersault; this was partly for effect and partly to regain my balance as quickly as possible. The better you can somersault, apparently, the better it looks and the less painful the consequences. If I landed messily Pat would deliver a stock comment: 'You look like a sack of shit.' I heard this on an annoyingly regular basis over the coming weeks.

We then progressed to what wrestlers refer to as the 'clothes line', a stiff arm across the top of your opponent's chest that sends him crashing to the floor. Of course, in order for Pat to teach me how to deliver such a move he needed first to demonstrate on me, which meant another ten minutes of reacquainting myself with the canvas. Each time I would bounce off the ropes, run at him, and be met by a straight arm that pounded into me so hard that I was almost sent backwards, my legs flipping up in front and my body falling down like a bag of potatoes.

'You've got to learn to use the full area of an eighteen foot wide wrestling ring,' Pat explained after the last clothes line had been delivered. 'And you have to respond to what your opponent does to you if you want to avoid the pain,' he added as he picked me up from the floor by my hair. I was still winded and in recovery from the last clothes line, and the last thing I was expecting was to be hauled by my hair to my feet. 'That hurts, doesn't it?' he said, as I winced and tried vainly to release his hold. 'Well, you'd better get used to it, because they'll be doing it to you all the time. They won't care one jot if they rip half your hair out. That's your problem, not theirs.'

I was just digesting all this when Pat suddenly went berserk. Pushing me into the corner, he began kicking and kneeing me in the stomach before punching me with his forearm across the chest. It looked far worse than it really was, but I was still scared witless by this attack. Although the pain was minor, the thought of what he might do must have made me look like a cat caught in the headlights of a car. To make matters worse Pat adopted a look of sheer rage on his face, and delivered each blow with a huge roar.

'Well done,' Pat said brightly, stopping as abruptly as he had begun and acting as if nothing had happened. I slid down the length of the corner post and on to my backside, breathing heavily now and sweating profusely. 'You're still alive then, I see,' he added, now with a friendly smile. I remained on guard. You just never knew what might come next. He was beginning to remind me of Cato, Inspector Clouseau's oriental assistant, who would attack the Peter Sellers character at the most unfortunate times and in the most unexpected places. When I walked out of the fitness centre's front door I ran to the car as soon as Pat's huge frame had disappeared, started my engine and was away before he could return to administer any further punishment.

A couple of days and hot baths later John Freemantle made contact. He seemed excited about what he deemed to be 'good news'. He knew who my opposition would be in a fortnight's time at the Brighton Centre in what had now become his top-of-the-bill tag match, and he wanted to christen me with a name that would stand the passage of time.

'You're up against Dick the Bruiser and Pretty Boy Stuart,' he announced, with triumphant aplomb. 'You won't find anyone tougher or nastier than those two. They won't be doing you any favours at all.'

'Thanks John,' I muttered. 'Any other good news?'

There was a pause as Freemantle geared himself up for a name which he, at least, was clearly proud of. 'Go on, have a guess,' he said.

I didn't have a clue, but offered 'The Orange Squash' and 'The Orange Crush' on account of my hair, as well as the irresistible suggestion, 'The British Hunk'.

'No, no, I'm calling you Ian "The Red Shadow" Stafford,' John replied. 'It's on account of your red hair. In fact, it's already being printed on all the posters. Are you wearing red shorts, or maybe red boots?'

I told him that I would be in grey and black. 'Okay, then, can you get hold of a red cloak or something for the night?' John was entirely serious.

And so The Red Shadow was born, a man of mystery and intrigue, who was coming to Brighton and, with the help of The Bomber, would see off the evil challenge of Dick the Bruiser and Pretty Boy Stuart. It just didn't bear thinking about.

On the morning of my next date with pain in Birmingham John Freemantle faxed me a press release he had just issued. 'Action man Ian Stafford makes his debut in the grappling ring when big-time wrestling returns to the Brighton Centre,' it stated. 'He teams up with "Bomber" Pat Roach, the reigning PWF heavyweight champion, to take on two of wrestling's tough guys, Dick the Bruiser and Pretty Boy Stuart, in a special tag team bout at the Brighton Centre. The show also features appearances by former world champion Steve Grey, The Anarchist Doug Williams,

"Mr Vain" Peter Collins and local favourite and Sussex champion, Barry Cooper.'

When I appeared in the tent I told Pat that we would be on the same bill as Mr Vain and The Anarchist. 'What's your name, then?' he asked.

'The Red Shadow,' I told him, a little self-consciously. Pat stood in the ring, shaking his head and muttering: 'Dear, oh dear, oh dear.'

'And who are we wrestling against?' he asked after a moment's contemplation.

'Dick the Bruiser and Pretty Boy Stuart.'

Again, Pat stood there, with his hands on his hips, staring down at the floor and shaking his head. 'Well, they won't be doing you any favours,' he announced, finally. 'One look at you, in your black boots and red cloak, and they'll probably want to murder you. As wrestling debuts go, you could have picked easier opposition than those two. Catch them in the wrong mood and they won't give a shit if you're new to the game. They'll just enjoy beating you up. Come on then, Red Shadow, we'd better do some work.'

And so we did. After the usual preliminaries – gripping exercises, followed by a few slams that I was beginning to grow wearily used to but still did not enjoy – Pat announced that this day, with our big date looming fast, we would be 'robust'. He never got round to answering my query about how he would describe our previous lessons. I noticed that his grip was firmer, his head lock tighter, and his whole approach more physical. It was during this lesson that I learnt a sequence of moves that, if executed properly, and with the delays created by interaction with the crowd, could last five valuable minutes.

First, after sending me into a headlock, Pat would throw me over but as I landed I would perform a roly-poly and leap right back on to my feet. 'The crowd will like that, and it will annoy your opponent,' he informed me. 'It will show that you are not hurt nor fazed by the situation.'

Then Pat would throw me over again, but this time I was to land, as Pat would so poetically put it, 'like a sack of shit'. He would pick me up and throw me over again, this time following me down to perform what he termed 'skulduggery'. This took the shape of little pinches and digs in the side and the ribs, a foot on the head and a twisting of the arm. Like most of my previous experiences in the training ring, it looked worse than it was, but it was still a series of uncomfortable experiences.

I was then supposed to clamber to my feet, twisting his arm round so that he was in a lock of my making. Pat's response would be a kick to the stomach and a headlock, but I would throw him against the ropes and prepare to deliver a clothes line on the rebound. Unfortunately for me, he would react quicker and send me crashing to the canvas with his own clothes line.

It sounds a lot to remember and even more to carry out successfully, but that was only half of the sequence. Having felled me with a clothes line Pat was to pick me up by the hair, lock his huge, tree trunk arms once more around my head, and send me flying to the floor. This time I was to hold on to his arm and twist my body round so that an unbalanced Roach would be forced to hurl himself to the canvas.

Although I would have him in a hold, he would climb back on to his feet, twist my helpless body around, and end up holding me once more in a head mare. Dragging me over to his partner in the corner, both would then proceed to perform Roach's 'skulduggery'. The referee is supposed to stop such goings on, but he is too busy telling my complaining partner to get out of the ring and back to his own corner on the other side of the ropes.

To make the sequence as realistic as possible, Roach has to pound my body with a series of kicks and stiff arms to my chest, stomach and thighs. Eventually, the referee gets to my opponent and tells him to drag me back into the centre of the ring, and away from his nasty partner. Pat would then grab me by the hair and send me into yet another head mare. I would throw him against the ropes once more but this time, on the rebound, I would duck under his outstretched stiff arm and hit him with a clothes line on the return journey, with both of us bouncing off the ropes like an elastic band.

This is a moment of triumph, and to celebrate I am to run across the canvas to deliver a forearm smash to the chest of the other opponent standing in the corner, before performing a theatrical roly-poly and releasing Roach, my partner, into the ring with a victorious high five.

Still the move was incomplete. Pat now proceeds to beat up whichever opponent is in the ring, suffers a little retaliation, and then softens him up once more for me to deliver the *coup de grâce*. I vault over the ropes, hit the baddy with two consecutive, upper cut forearms to his chest and then, having bounced off a rope, hurl my body horizontally towards him to produce a flying fall. The force of my body hitting his, close to his neck, results in him toppling over backwards with me falling on top of him, from where I pin down his tired arms for the crucial count of three. There! Simple really. God knows how many times it took for Pat and me to perform the whole sequence without any memory lapses or errors, but eventually we did. The series of moves took nearer ten minutes in the end, and when it was all over I slumped to the floor in a sweaty exhaustion. 'I don't believe it,' Roach said, in mock disbelief. 'You're just beginning to look like a wrestler.'

That night I viewed a videotape that the BBC's 'Arena' programme had sent me about the cult and myth of Kendo Nagasaki. It took me back to those Saturday afternoons in the 1970s, with the distinctive music of ITV's 'World of Sport' and the commentary from Kent Walton. In particular it showed the night that Nagasaki had his mask removed in the ring by Giant Haystacks, the only time it was to happen in his professional career. In the corner, heaping abuse at Haystacks, and attempting to put a stop to the bad man's efforts, was one Pat Roach, looking small in comparison to the hairy monster ripping off Nagasaki's mask. Underneath the mask was a shaven-headed man with a pigtail who quickly covered up his face again and replaced the mask over his face.

'I'll never forget that night,' Roach commented when I told him that I had watched the documentary with fascination. 'It was quite sad to see in a way.' Masked wrestlers have been an integral part of wrestling tradition since the sport's fairground beginnings, but Nagasaki had other reasons why he should remain anonymous. 'Naggers was a highly successful businessman,' Pat explained. 'As far as I know he was a millionaire. He didn't need to do the wrestling, at least not for the money. But he loved the game, the buzz, and the action. That's why he wore a mask. By day he would be sitting in a boardroom, but at night he'd be in the ring.'

I asked Pat why he still insisted on wrestling, after all these years, and after everything else he had achieved in his life. I expected an instant answer, but Pat had to give it some thought. 'Do you know, it's not something I've ever really analysed,' he replied. 'It's definitely not for the money. I've made a few bob in my time, and you don't make a good enough living out of wrestling, at least not these days.' He stood in contemplation for a moment. 'I suppose part of the reason is that it keeps me fit and in shape. But the main explanation is that I still love the buzz I get each time I enter the auditorium, and the challenge of the ring. It can be a little scary sometimes, because you never quite know what's going to happen, and how you're going to emerge from it all, but the adrenalin makes it all worthwhile. I guess I'd miss it, even after all these years. The game's not how it used to be, and I don't know whether it will ever return to the great days, when we packed out the venues and there were some magnificent, colourful characters, but I've been wrestling longer than anything else I've done in my life, even acting, so it's hard to give it up.'

Pat snapped suddenly out of this rare moment of self-examination and motioned for us to get down to work. Lesson number five began in the Roach ring with a reenactment of the sequence of moves I had learnt the previous time. When I made a mistake Pat would storm across the ring and slap me in the face. 'What the bloody hell was that for?' I asked the first time, part in anger and part in shock. 'You've got to be in the zone,' he replied. 'It's nothing personal, but you can't afford to make mistakes.

It looks bad on you, and therefore on me, and it could be dangerous. So I'm going to slap you every time, until you stop making errors.'

I wasn't exactly happy with this promise, but when faced with the prospect of wrestling a giant with twenty-five years' experience under his belt, there was not much I could do about it. Besides, his methods, crude as they were, seemed to work. The thought of a Roach slapping did wonders for my powers of concentration.

After we had successfully run through the sequence, Pat announced that we would now learn a completely new and different set of moves. These proved to be as long and complicated as the first.

We began with what he referred to as 'arse bumps'. These followed a move in which I performed a head mare on Roach before sending him crashing to the ground. I would follow him up by sitting behind him and entwining my legs within his. I would then tip backwards, forcing his body to be hoisted upwards before flinging it back down again on to the canvas. Performing this on a man weighing almost 20 stone was not easy, especially as I was called upon to produce three successive arse bumps.

Eventually he would roll over, grab my leg and get to work with what he endearingly referred to as his 'bits and pieces'. This constituted a kick in the stomach, a twist of the leg in a move known as the 'leg snatch', a further kick in the head, a pull up by the hair, and a final thrust that sent me crashing, once again, to the canvas. 'If I tell you that you landed like a sack, I'm sure you can tell me its contents,' Pat would say, leaning over me and looking down.

Next came the bear hug, where Pat would wrap his far-from-welcoming arms around me and squeeze the life out of me. I was supposed to plant the palm of my hand across his face, his reddish whiskers scratching me in the process, but a further constriction from the Bomber would leave me limp and lifeless.

The only way out would be for me to perform a sudden spin of my body so that my back ended up against his chest. Then my hand would wrap around his head and send him flying to the floor. This was a more enjoyable aspect of the move, but it was always going to be short-lived. Roach would then launch himself at me, twist me round into a half nelson – where my arms were forced behind and above my head – and send me somersaulting back down to the floor. Although I would butt his stomach with my head as I rose from the ground, he would drag me into a corner and perform another assault, this time hitting and kicking me noticeably harder.

The sequence would end with what Pat termed the 'Irish whip', a move in which I would have his outstretched arm in a lock, before whipping it round in a circular movement that resulted in my opponent spinning to the floor. Put all together, the combination of arse bumps and bear hugs, half nelsons and Irish whips, punctuated by Roach's skulduggery, would last ten minutes. With Roach also spending time in the ring this, together with our first sequence of moves, would be ample.

There was one more lesson remaining before the big night, but at last I was beginning to believe – in my naive way – that I might just be able to survive my 'top of the bill' date with Dick the Bruiser and Pretty Boy Stuart. John Freemantle invited me down to the Winter Garden in Eastbourne a week before my bout in Brighton. This particular promotion boasted a tag team challenge between four pairs, and I thought it would be interesting to see how tag partners worked together. The Winter Garden's clientele appeared strikingly similar to the crowd that I had seen in Worthing, a collection of elderly and middle-aged men and women, plus a bunch of rowdy kids who would heap abuse on the wrestlers before scurrying back to the safety of their seats. The evening's solo bout featured 'The Rock and Roll Express', Blondie Barratt, against a young newcomer called Paul Phoenix. 'It's hold on to your seats time,' promised John Freemantle's programme, even if Blondie Barratt looked more like Rick Wakeman when he finally snarled into the ring.

There were a couple of throwaway passages in the programme that made disconcerting reading, too, at least to an utter novice such as me.

'Sid Cooper is currently sidelined by an injury which may end his ring career,' it stated. 'Good, though, to see Gerry Finch back in action after a long injury lay-off.' It reminded me to double-check my insurance the next day.

Yet it was the tag matches that I had really come to witness in Eastbourne: Flash Barker and Steve Grey versus Barry Cooper and Kris Kay in the first bout; father and son combination of Ricky and Roy Knight, otherwise known as 'The Superflys', against Steve Minelli and, once again, The Anarchist Doug Williams, in the second.

The only rule there seems to be in such bouts is that there are no rules. All sorts of mayhem went on, with the referee seemingly – or probably purposefully – powerless to halt the proceedings. I sat at ringside open-mouthed at the speed of the fighting, the high degree of technical skill and the amount of skulduggery that went on. Most of the contestants may have looked overweight or out of shape, but years of wrestling experience had given them the know-how to use every spare inch of the ring, and to adopt every move I had learnt, plus a whole host more. I drove home in the small hours convinced that my getting seriously hurt would be a foregone conclusion. I asked John Freemantle for his thoughts, hoping he might have some words of encouragement for me. 'No, 'fraid not,' he said, with a shrug of his shoulders. 'I can't see you not getting hurt at some stage. It's just a question of how badly.'

In what was my last lesson in Birmingham, Pat hardly improved my nerves. 'I've got to tell you, the Bruiser and Pretty Boy won't be impressed that you, a writer, have taken the place of a good, honest professional wrestler, robbing him of the chance of a decent pay day,' he said. 'They'll be looking to exact some kind of revenge.'

Now, I know what many people will think: Roach was just enjoying making me as nervous as possible; the bottom line is that wrestling is fixed, it doesn't hurt, and it's hugely choreographed. After all, that's what I had always been led to believe, too.

Well, the painful truth is that although the outcome of some bouts is arranged in draft form, few bouts are completed without someone being hurt to a degree, and often the best-laid plans fall alarmingly apart. As for the choreography, there is a good reason for the exaggerated somersaults and twists. When a wrestler the size of a whale begins to throw you over his shoulder, and there's nothing you can do about it, you perform as high a loop as you possibly can in order to land as safely as possible on the right part of your back. Believe me, there is no real 'right' part of your back to land on, and it still feels like a slab of concrete being slammed into your body, but it creates a better outcome than if you were to fall, in Roach's words, like a sack of shit. And why don't you merely refuse to be sent spinning into the opposite corner? That's an easy one. The fall untwists an arm that could otherwise be broken.

Roach and I got down to business. We went through the first sequence of events, with my flying dive on the Bomber and a subsequent fall ending the proceedings. It was during the second session that I caught him in the very place where you do not want to catch any man, especially Pat Roach. Midway through the next move he paid me what wrestlers euphemistically refer to as a 'receipt'. In other words, if I made a mistake on an opponent that led to some pain on his behalf, as opposed to a recognised move – even if it was a complete accident – I should prepare myself for some painful retribution. This usually took the shape of a pinch of thigh or arm but this time, just to spice up the afternoon, he gave me a hefty tug of my armpit hair.

'Sorry, did I catch you?' he asked, all innocently, as I ran around the ring clasping my armpit. 'That'll teach you to be a bit more careful, hey!'

The session ended as it began, with more of Pat's own brand of psychology. 'Make sure you bring fifty quid with you on Thursday night, won't you?' he ordered.

'Why?' I asked, awaiting one of Pat's characteristic witty retorts at my expense.

'Because there's no way you'll be able to drive after Dick the Bruiser and Pretty Boy have finished with you. You're going to need a cab to take you home, my lad.'

On a more serious note Pat admitted that he and John Freemantle had lined up a replacement partner for him if I had failed to come through the training. 'I had to decide if you were up to it, and you also needed to avoid getting injured over these past few weeks,' he explained. 'It looks like you've come through.' He continued: 'But you've got to understand something. If you remember half the moves you've learnt from me on the night you'll have done well. It'll happen so quickly, and you'll be so nervous, so frightened and so exhausted after just a couple of minutes, that you won't be able to think straight.'

That was all I wanted to hear. We then worked out how we would start the bout, with Pat and me alternately entering the ring from the ropes to confuse the opposition as to which of us would lead off. After all, given the choice between a man that not even 007 could beat up and me – 7 inches smaller and 7 stone lighter – who would you rather wrestle with?

Eventually I would stay in the ring. If things went to plan – and Pat assured me that they would not – I would allow my opponent to fling me on to my back so that I could enact my roly-poly more and land smoothly on my feet. This would no doubt anger bad guy number one, who would then perform Roach's 'bits and pieces' on me.

Then came the part I liked the sound of. I would perform the latter section of that first sequence learnt in Roach's tent. I would throw my rival on to the ropes, duck under his swinging arm and hit with an elbow on the rebound. That would be the sign to run across the ring and straight arm baddy number two, somersault back towards my own corner and tag Roach. Pat would then rough up the opposition sufficiently for me to enact the final flourish, a couple of further punches followed by a flying leap which would, or at least should, result in a fall to us.

A slightly grey area, assuming any of this worked, followed. 'What happens after that, Pat?' I asked, with understandable inquisitiveness.

'Oh well,' he replied. 'Then the Bruiser and Pretty Boy grow really angry and spend the next ten minutes beating the crap out of you, making sure it's sufficiently away from our corner to prevent us from tagging and allowing me to enter the fray.' I was glad I had asked.

We said our farewells and I drove back to London for two nervous days and restless nights. I played down the potential consequences of my date with two of wrestling's baddest of baddies with my family – who found it hard to believe that they were suddenly living with a professional wrestler – and tried to flatten my stomach as much as I could with a series of sit-ups and a fasting campaign.

On my day of reckoning the hours passed by excruciatingly slowly, and so my state of frenzied anxiety developed. Eventually, in the mid-afternoon, I packed my boots and shorts – making sure a cylinder of arnica and a small bottle of whisky were included in my bag – and set out for 'The Green Room', a fancy dress shop in West Wickham.

In the store they had prepared a row of red capes and cloaks for me, but at first I had to wait ten minutes before being served on account of Scarlett O'Hara being unable to squeeze into her dress and Wonder Woman taking an eternity to look at herself in the mirror. I was thwarted in my original favourite cape when I discovered that a long devil's tail protruded from the bottom. Most of the others made me resemble Little Red Riding Hood or Superman, but eventually I settled for a large heavy cape with white lining which, if matters became too awful, could always be reversed and waved as a white flag.

It was a dull, grey early evening when I arrived in Brighton. Unbeknown to me, Pat had already spent a couple of hours at the Grand Hotel taking tea, as cool as the cucumber in his sandwiches. 'I always like to prepare myself for a bout in Brighton with high tea in the Grand,' he informed me later, sounding not unlike Bertie Wooster. I discovered that the local newspaper had run a feature that day, after John Freemantle had alerted them, with the headline: 'Red Shadow stalks into the ring'. Moreover, the walls and shop windows of the seaside town seemed to be plastered with posters advertising the night's wrestling programme.

There, among the other names and faces, was our bout, promoted as the top of the bill. It read 'Bomber' Pat Roach (Birmingham, PWF heavyweight champion) and 'The Red Shadow', Ian Stafford (Bromley) v Dick the Bruiser (Holbeach) and Pretty Boy Stuart (Minster, Isle of Sheppey), together with a photograph of Pat looking suitably menacing. It resembled the kind of mock-up poster you can buy in Carnaby Street. I used to own one of those 'Wanted' posters as a child. This time, however, it was for real.

At the Brighton Centre that night the Charlatans were playing live in one of the halls, while Premier Wrestling Promotions took centre stage in the other. As I entered our hall the ring was being erected and all was relatively quiet. It gave me some time to mull over the official programme. It made disturbing reading.

'The tag match sees "Bomber" Pat Roach, the PWF heavyweight champion and, of course, the star from "Auf Wiedersehen Pet", teaming up with newcomer "The Red Shadow",' it stated on page one. 'They face a battle royal against two of wrestling's hard men, Dick the Bruiser and Pretty Boy Stuart, who are sure to give Roach's partner a real baptism of fire. Whether Roach can come to the rescue of his team-mate when the going gets tough remains to be seen, but it should be an intriguing contest.' Hardly a vote of confidence, then. The night's supporting bouts included names I was now familiar with. The Anarchist and Mr Vain were back on again, together with Kris Kay and Steve Grey. In the centre pages the full ingredients of an 'action-packed night of wrestling' were revealed. I'm not sure which caused me more anxiety: the line under 'tonight's main event, a special tag team contest' stating that there was a 'one hour time limit', or the fact that Pretty Boy Stuart came from the Isle of Sheppey. This, to my increasingly desperate state of mind, translated as 'one hard bastard'.

Slowly the other wrestlers traipsed in. It was another night and another dollar for these boys, wrestling's pub singers compared to the rock stars of the World Wrestling Federation. Goodness only knows what they earn, but it is not a lot, certainly not enough to make a living, but just about enough to warrant twenty minutes or so of hits and knocks, slams and falls. Tonight it's Brighton. In forty-eight hours' time it will be Hastings. A week earlier it was Eastbourne. And so they carry on, Doug Williams by day in Camberley, 'The Anarchist' by night; Peter Collins to his friends at work in Bristol, 'Mr Vain' to the blue-rinse brigade and the cocky kids at ringside; Ian Stafford to the media, 'The Red Shadow' to grappling fans. To these boys, to Pat Roach and to promoter John Freemantle, this is the business. You can keep your WWF, with its insultingly obvious plots and its glitzy entrances; this is good, old-fashioned wrestling, where what you see is what you get.

The crowds may be small – hardly more than three hundred people were there to see The Red Shadow make his debut – but they are loyal, and most vociferous in their support of or dislike for the wrestlers. Middle-aged women in the front row scream abuse and wave their programmes in a threatening fashion; young boys call out taunts from the comparative security of several rows back; and men with their pints cheer when a particularly painful move has been successfully completed on the bad guy in the ring.

John Freemantle seemed relieved when I arrived. 'You've turned up, then,' he said, with a wry smile. 'Now, don't forget, your tag bout will be decided by the best of three falls, three submissions, or a knock-out. In theory there should only be one wrestler from each side in the ring at any one time, and the time limit's one hour'. He took a quick glance at the gibbering wreck in front of him and added: 'Somehow, I don't see it lasting an hour.'

I asked him what he could tell me about my opponents, Dick the Bruiser and Pretty Boy Stuart. 'They're rule-benders,' John replied. 'They don't play fair. They're guaranteed to give you a hard time.'

With nervous laughter I tried to dismiss such comments as a wind-up, but John was not quite finished. 'Listen, Ian, this isn't theatre, you know. People can and often do get hurt. Don't forget, you asked for this. Well, one way or another, you're going to get it tonight.'

He was right, of course. I had asked for it. In fact, I had no one to blame but myself. Still, as I wandered up to the dressing rooms on the first floor of the Brighton Centre, I could not help wondering just what John meant by 'get it'. Pat and I would be sharing our own changing facilities, with our opponents next door in another. There was a window on the upper half of their door, and I decided to peer through to see what they looked like.

First impressions of my opponents were not exactly favourable. Pretty Boy Stuart was anything but pretty nor was he a boy: he had a large gut, a shaven head with a pigtail sticking out at the back, and a clutch of tattoos. As I stole a glance he was stuffing his flesh into a leotard. His mate, Dick the Bruiser, similarly tattooed but harder set, saw me looking and seemed to snarl in my direction. They looked like a couple of night club bouncers who were about to throw a tiresome drunk out of their premises and on to the street.

A disbelieving BBC producer friend of mine, Nick London, had come along to watch the evening's violence unfold, and he decided to have a chat with the two opponents. To his credit, what Dick and Pretty Boy told him he kept to himself until after the bout, which is just as well, because if I had found out before I may well have driven straight back to London.

'I gather he's a new bod, then,' Pretty Boy said to Nick. 'Well, I came into the business in the 1960s. It was hard for me and it'll be hard for him.' Dick the Bruiser expressed similar sentiments. 'I've had some hammerings in my time,' he added. 'Now it's our turn to hand some out. Rules are meant to be bent in wrestling and I win a lot more than I lose. I haven't come two hundred miles tonight to pussy around. He deserves what he's going to get.'

Pretty Boy wanted to know more about me. Nick explained my

masochistic desire to explore wrestling. The man from Minster's eyes lit up.

'A writer?' he asked. 'A writer?' He burst out laughing. 'Well, he's either brave or stupid. I'm going to play with him for a while, then go for his throat. I'll let him think it's not too bad, then go for the kill.'

Dick's plans matched those of his partner. 'I've been a wrestler now for over twenty years, so I'm not going to let him think this game's easy,' he said. 'It's going to be a good evening. At least, it will be for us.'

Pat Roach, meanwhile, had finally arrived, his unflustered demeanour in marked contrast to The Red Shadow who, by now, was in a state of near-hysteria. Pat was clearly out to enjoy himself tonight.

'If something happens to you it's me and my reputation that's at stake,' he told me. 'You'll be okay. You'll probably be unconscious and out of it. But it would reflect very badly on me, and I can't afford that to happen. So when you bleed tonight, bleed well.' He then made a point of looking me up and down before passing further comment: 'You should have worn brown shorts.'

All it required at this point was for a priest to appear to read me the last rites. Instead, Nick decided to chat merrily away to Pat as he began to change. 'What can you teach him in half a dozen lessons?' the Bomber said as he jerked his head towards me. 'Let's face it, he's absolutely insane. If anything happens to him, it's his own fault. The fact is, although he's shown a lot of guts and heart, he has no natural wrestling instincts. And although he's quite a fit man, his body is not hard enough. It takes many years of wrestling for the body to harden up. It means he won't be able to absorb the punishment.'

I was listening to all this while pacing up and down the changing room, as Pat warmed to his theme. 'You'll see tonight a raw person going head on in a situation totally new to him,' he said. 'The facts will be awful, bare and rare. He's probably a very silly person, but he's a journalist, and journalists by tradition have got no brains.'

Roach and I changed into our wrestling attire. Pat's was plain and simple. A black, single-strap leotard covered half of his oathouse torso as he enacted a series of stretching exercises. I pulled on black leather boots and somewhat unflattering wrestling briefs and continued to pace the room like a condemned man on death row, feeling slightly foolish as well as suicidal.

Only a few minutes now remained before it was our turn to enter the auditorium. Pat and I went through our gripping exercises to warm up. I decided to ask him how he had received the massive scar on his left arm.

'Dick the Bruiser,' he replied, with a loud guffaw.

The dressing room door opened and a man's head appeared. 'Gentlemen, it's time,' he announced rather grandly, and we made our way down a flight of stairs and to a corridor. Dick and Pretty Boy were already there, and when they caught sight of me they both grunted and snarled. Dick looked the more menacing of the two, especially when he started punching himself hard against the arm and chest, like a gorilla in *Tarzan*.

As they entered the auditorium you could hear jeers and boos from the crowd, no doubt egged on by the two bad guys. Pat and I waited patiently in the corridor for our turn, and I wrapped my 'Red Shadow' cloak around me to keep warm. Mr Vain and The Anarchist emerged to wish me luck. 'We'll be watching with great interest,' they informed me.

The thought flashed through my mind that there was still time to get out of this, even as we waited for the signal to enter the fray. Nobody could actually force me to do anything. I could just refuse point blank, and never be seen in Brighton again. But my chance went. The music from 'Auf Wiedersehen Pet' piped up, and someone shouted: 'You're on.'

As soon as Pat emerged he started cheering and clapping along to 'That's Living All Right'. The crowd stood up and joined in. I followed suit, walking behind Pat in my red cloak. As we approached the ring Dick the Bruiser leant through the ropes and kicked me on the side of my hip so hard that I fell into the first row of the audience. It prompted outrage from an elderly couple nearby who stood up and accused Dick of being a coward. 'Sit down, you silly old cow,' he shouted back.

John Freemantle was standing in the ring with microphone in hand. 'Laydeez and Gennelmen,' he shrieked. 'And now, the night's main event.' Dick and Pretty Boy's names were greeted with more abuse from the audience, while Pat received huge applause. When John then announced: 'Ian "The Red Shadow" Stafford' a somewhat confused applause followed.

The referee that night was Peter Szakacs, a former wrestler who came to Britain from Hungary during the 1956 uprising. His late brother, Tibor, was a famous heavyweight in the 1960s and 1970s. Peter tried to tell all four wrestlers to have a good, clean bout, but his efforts fell on deaf ears. When Pat and I stretched out our hands to shake those of our opponents, Pretty Boy laughed and Dick kicked me again.

I tried to appear calm in the face of such provocation, but I knew I would shortly be out there very much on my own. Pat and I alternated, as planned, in getting in and out of the ring, much to the amusement of the crowd. When I entered the ring both Dick and Pretty Boy were clamouring to face me. When Pat emerged on the scene, both could not remove themselves quickly enough.

Eventually I stayed put and stood facing Pretty Boy. Things went roughly according to plan at first. Pretty Boy grabbed me first by the arms, and then by the head before hurling me across the ring. This enabled me to employ my roly-poly tactic, and I sprung back on to my feet and gave him a look.

'Don't you get clever with me, boy,' he screamed across the ring amid jeers. He threw me a second and a third time, but I recovered sufficiently to wrap my arms around his shiny shaven head, and send him spinning to the canvas.

So far, so good. I was unhurt and into the bout, and the crowd were on my side. 'Get up slaphead,' someone shouted at Pretty Boy as he rose to his feet and gave me a withering look. Then Dick the Bruiser entered the proceedings, and at this point any script there might have been was torn to shreds. Within seconds he had grabbed me in a wrench-like headlock, dragged me down to my knees, and started to punch me in the stomach and forehead.

This experience was a great deal worse than what I had expected. Every so often he would pick me up, throw me down again, and follow through with another headlock and sneaky punch. Not content with this he then hauled me to my feet by grabbing my hair, dragged me across to Pretty Boy, and invited his partner to elbow me across the bridge of my nose. I had a fleeting glimpse of a large tuft of reddish hair lying on the canvas.

Pat Roach was standing helplessly in the far corner. Both Dick and Pretty Boy had made sure that I was unable to reach my partner in order to bring him into the bout. With hindsight both might well have handled me more roughly than they did, but at the time – as Dick held my head between his arms while his fist began to stuff itself into my mouth – I was growing increasingly concerned. All Pat could do was complain to the referee.

After ten exhausting minutes, Dick and Pretty Boy received their first public warning after sandwiching my head between the top and middle rope and repeatedly hitting me as I suffocated. 'Stop that now,' Szakacs shouted at the Bruiser. 'It's okay, ref,' Dick replied gruffly, as he tightened his grip around my neck. 'He's still breathing.'

This presented me with an opportunity to initiate one of the key moves learnt in Roach's Birmingham tent. I sent Pretty Boy towards the ropes, ducked under his arm as he flew back at me, and hit him with an uppercut on the rebound. I then ran across the ring, stiff-armed Dick who was standing in his corner, and high-fived Pat who tore straight into Pretty Boy. Having repeatedly slammed Pretty Boy, Pat made way for me again within a couple of minutes, and with my opponent clearly groggy from his meeting with Roach I was able to hurl myself horizontally at him, causing him to tumble backwards. I lay across him as the referee counted out the required three seconds for the first fall of the bout.

John Freemantle announced the fall, but as soon as he had left the ring all hell broke loose. The Bruiser threw himself at me, dragged me back on to the ropes, and invited his partner to take turns with him in punching, elbowing and kicking me. Amid the mayhem a second public warning was announced against the bad boys, but this had about as much effect on them as my attempts to prevent the assault. Dick finally picked me up, lifted me high above his head, and slammed me down on to the canvas before holding me down to record the equalising fall. I was so tired by then, and so winded by the slam, that a child could have finished me off.

At this point the referee suggested to a largely unemployed Pat Roach that I had received enough attention and that maybe he should call a halt to the bout. Pat was also concerned, but insisted we fought on.

One fall all, and still Pretty Boy and Bruiser were not finished with me. In the background I could vaguely hear the cries of 'Shadow, Shadow' emanating from the audience, who had obviously decided that anyone was more likeable than the two guys duffing me up. My body was drenched with sweat and my hair continued to be ripped from my head.

Occasionally I would get the upper hand and throw one of them into a corner, but more often than not I was on the receiving end of the pair's nasty calling cards. The sweat was now dripping off the tip of my nose, which itself had become clotted with my blood.

Tag bouts normally last no longer than fifteen minutes. We had entered the twenty-fifth when I managed to tag Roach. Acting as my knight in shining armour Roach flung himself at Pretty Boy, sending him flying to a neutral corner before picking him up and hurling him back down again with a furious thud. After the third consecutive body slam, and with Pretty Boy lying oblivious to the world on his back, the Bomber invited me to finish off the bout for good.

I had barely enough strength to re-enter the ring, but as I fell on top of Pretty Boy I realised that he, too, had been sapped of all his energy. 'One,' referee Szakacs uttered. 'Two.' I expected some kind of response from Pretty Boy, but he lay flat and motionless. 'Three.' The bell sounded, promoter Freemantle entered the ring, and I slumped to my knees, unable to celebrate through sheer fatigue.

To my astonishment, the vocal crowd went wild. Pat Roach bent over, hauled me back on to my feet and lifted up my sweat-drenched arm. Pat thanked the crowd over Freemantle's microphone as Dick and Pretty Boy stormed out of the ring arguing between themselves.

Suddenly hordes of children were clambering into the ring asking for autographs. For me this was a novel and somewhat embarrassing experience, but it seemed that these kids had really bought into the idea of 'The Red Shadow'.

Backstage, Dick and Pretty Boy were getting changed in their dressing room. Although they had hardly been gentle with me, I recognised that it could have been worse and went over to thank them for their efforts. 'I've been doing this a long time now, so there was no way I was going to let you walk into a ring and think it's easy,' Dick said, repeating the sentiments expressed earlier to Nick London.

Well, I didn't, and I don't. My bruised back, abdomen and jaw; my scratched neck and shoulders; my cut nose, ripped-out hair and whiplash injuries can all testify to this. It's a rough old game, all right, played primarily by some rough old people, but they are much fitter than one could possibly imagine – and far more professional, too.

The Anarchist and Mr Vain came down to offer their congratulations and were amused to see the desperately tired and shell-shocked state I was in. 'Now you know what it's like,' they said. 'Maybe next time you'll fight us?'

By the time I finally made my way back to our dressing room Pat Roach was all set to drive back to Birmingham. 'Well,' he said. 'It looks like you've come out of this in one piece. You did okay, and I'm not ashamed to tell people I trained you. In fact, given more time and experience, you could make it as a wrestler.' He smiled and gripped my hand firmly. 'So, our next match is at Morecambe on Monday night. I'll see you there.'

Funnily enough I received a call from John Freemantle the following morning, just as I lay in yet another hot bath filled with a cocktail of exotic oils. 'Do you fancy doing it again?' he asked.

'Are you serious?' I asked.

'Totally,' replied the man with the microphone and the bow tie. 'I've got loads of shows planned for the summer. Let me know which one you fancy and we'll put something on. We can't let The Red Shadow just disappear, can we?'

I told him I'd think about it. And that's what I'm doing. Thinking about it. Maybe the world has seen the last of The Red Shadow. Then again, perhaps he will return in the night, with his red cape and his black boots, his unbeaten record intact and his mission still to rid the ring of all the bad guys.

chapter three

 # EARNING YOUR STRIPES

The truth of the matter was that The Red Shadow had been hurt that night. He had managed to disguise this from both his adoring public in Brighton, and from Dick the Bruiser and Pretty Boy Stuart, but he spent the following week back home nursing a whiplash injury to his neck, in addition to a number of abdominal bruises. He needed also to return to his alter ego, namely me, pretty quickly. My wife and children, after all, had grown sick of my limp impersonation of the WWF's The Rock around the house. And so it was that the red cloak was returned to the fancy dress shop, and the black patent boots were hidden at the back of the wardrobe. It was time to move on.

I somehow doubt that the sight of a chap in a red cloak answering to the name of 'The Red Shadow' would put much fear into the hearts of the next bunch of sportsmen I was to spend time with. The Leicester Tigers had just completed their second successive league championship-winning campaign, and with a host of English and other international star names in their ranks and the biggest support in the country, they were clearly the best rugby union team to play for.

This was fine in theory, of course, but would the Tigers really be foolish enough to allow me not only to train with them but also to play in a real-life, full-on match? There was only one way to find out, which is why I found myself sitting in a conference room at Leicester's Welford Road Stadium in front of the team manager and former England player Dean Richards, Leicester and England captain Martin Johnson, and the club's chief executive, and yet another former England international, Peter Wheeler.

I had come to know Martin 'Johnno' Johnson well over the previous couple of years, boring him with accounts of my past sporting adventures in return for his long lists of sports trivia questions which often ruined my night's sleep as I puzzled over the correct answers. Johnson is the consummate player's player, a no-nonsense lock-forward who leads not so much by his mouth but by example on the field. His reputation comes before him on a global scale, enhanced by leading the British Lions to victory in South Africa in 1997, and England to the inaugural Six Nations title in 2000. Most fans have seen him emerge first from the trenches, forehead furrowed and eyes glinting with determination, but I have also witnessed the man pumping the air with delight after delivering the correct answer to a trivia question, or talking long into the day of his love for American Football and, in particular, the San Francisco 49ers.

Johnson knew of my intentions because I had already run the idea past him. He was all for it, suggesting that a week's pre-season training tour in Northern Ireland would be the perfect opportunity for me to become a Tiger, and for the rest of the Tigers to have some fun at my expense. 'The more distractions the better,' he said, cheerily. Yet he could not predict what Dean Richards would say about the idea. 'He's his own man, and not even the players know what's in his mind.'

I wasn't too confident myself. Although Dean and I were acquainted in a working capacity, we did not particularly know each other as people. All I understood was that the man is regarded as the focal point and heartbeat of the Leicester Tigers, a former captain turned manager, whose contribution to England during much of the 1990s was almost without equal. Like Johnson, Richards was always the first to place his body on the line.

As I presented myself and my proposal to Richards, a smirking Johnson, and an intrigued Wheeler, I studied Dean's expression in search of some kind of sign that might just suggest he would go with the idea. I saw nothing. Dean sat there impassive and expressionless, save for an incredulous look when I showed him a wrestling poster with 'The Red Shadow' topping the bill. 'Are you making all this up?' he asked, semi-seriously. I recounted my night in Brighton.

'And what position do you play?'

'Flanker, Dean,' I replied, puffing up my 5 ft 10 in, 175 lb frame.

'Hmm,' he replied, eyeing me up and down and appearing neither convinced nor impressed.

When I had concluded my speech Wheeler shrugged his shoulders, looked across at Richards and said: 'Well, it's Dean's shout.' Johnson, just four days away from his wedding, left in a wild hurry for a waistcoat fitting without further comment. After what seemed like an interminably long pause, Dean announced that he would sleep on the idea and call me in the morning.

On my way back home to London I managed to get hold of Johnson on his mobile telephone and asked how he felt it went. 'I really have no idea,' he admitted. 'I told you, Deano doesn't reveal too much. But if you want me to be honest, I think you're struggling. I'll see if I can put in a good word for you.'

I thanked him for his support, wished him luck for his wedding, and prepared myself for rejection. The call came from Dean, as promised, the following morning. 'Okay,' he said. 'Let's give it a go. You can come out with us to Northern Ireland and train for a week. If we think you're good enough, and assuming you can last the week – and that's a big assumption – then we'll give you a run out against Ulster.'

Richards had taken me utterly by surprise. The man had just told me that I could play for the English champions against the 1999 European champions. Okay, so he had also underlined the fact that I needed to survive the week first, but my pumping adrenalin had dismissed this immediately as I mentally pressed the fast forward button straight to the big match. Once I had gathered my composure I thanked him for his unexpected decision, attempting to sound calm and relaxed about the whole matter. 'Not at all,' he replied, chuckling at the other end of the telephone. 'I think the boys will enjoy having you on the field with them. It should be interesting to see what happens.'

Before I had time to enquire just what he meant by that last statement Dean informed me that the Tigers would be spending a week inside an army camp in Omagh, the troubled Northern Irish town whose centre had been severely damaged by a massive and senseless bomb two years earlier; the bomb had left an indelible mark on the community, and indeed on the people of Great Britain. The rest of the boys would be ferried across the Irish Sea, but due to existing family holiday commitments it was agreed that I would join them the following day.

A letter from Dean followed with a few last-minute instructions: 'Bring some boots and some trainers, and get yourself insured.' The insurance reference served as further warning that the week would be anything but easy.

Training in readiness for my time with the Tigers proved harder than I anticipated, a fact I put down to being on holiday and to my age which, despite my youthful delusions, was now veering towards my thirty-seventh birthday. I managed to run every day on holiday, and found a weights room in the hotel but, as I arrived at Birmingham Airport for the short flight to Belfast, I was not entirely convinced that I had done enough – especially when I bumped into an eager Neil Back and Adam Balding in the terminal building.

Back, the England flanker, is reputed to be the fittest player in rugby, and Balding, an England Under-21 player, was becoming an ever-present in the Tigers first team squad. Both appeared fresh, fit and confident.

'It's going to be a long, hard week,' Back promised, when we arrived in Northern Ireland. 'Especially for you.'

An Omagh Rugby Club official collected us from City Airport and then drove around the ring road to the international airport, where Leicester's new signing, Winston Stanley, was arriving. Winston had come to replace his fellow Canadian international, Dave Lougheed, who had retired from the game at the end of the previous season. For a man who had just flown from Vancouver and then Manchester he was in remarkably fine fettle, although after meeting me he must have wondered if he really had just joined the best club in England.

During the 70-mile journey across Northern Ireland, Back – squeezed with me and Stanley in the back of the car – provided some tips. 'If Dean takes his teeth out then you know you're in trouble,' he said, referring to his team manager. 'And watch yourself at all times. You're going to be an easy target this week.' With that in mind I was grateful when we arrived at the Lisanelly Barracks to discover we had just missed a particularly physical training session, the first of the week for the boys. A rather battered Martin Corry filled us in as we stood by the training pitch. 'It was a very good one to miss, believe me,' said the England international back row forward. 'It all went off.' By that he meant that a few of the front row boys, as is their wont, lost their tempers with each other after an hour or so of being battering rams. It all sounded horrendous to me and I was already asking myself just what I had let myself in for.

A welcoming Dean Richards took me to the officers' mess, where I found I would be staying alongside the Leicester team management. Dean introduced me to the rest of the back-up team: coach John Wells, assistant coaches Ian Smith and Andy Key, fitness coaches John Duggan and Pete Atkinson, secretary and kit-man Cliff Shepherd, and physio Chris Brooks. I made a special point of introducing myself to the physio. Past experience had taught me that Chris and I would be getting to know each other pretty well in the forthcoming week.

The fact that I would be staying in the officers' mess provided the players with some instant ammunition, for while they accused me of enjoying 'port and cigars' they were cramped into army digs elsewhere in the camp. Although my accommodation could hardly be described as luxurious, it seemed like the Ritz in comparison to the spartan environment the rest of the Tigers found themselves in. I thought about requesting a move to join the players in a show of team camaraderie, and then came to my senses. The week was going to be tough enough as it was, without making it any worse. Hooker Richard Cockerill had already greeted me with these comforting words: 'You're going to get so much stick this week.' The rest of the front row brigade seemed equally pleased to hear of my intentions when I explained them over a late dinner. 'Look forward to training with you,' announced a smiling Darren Garforth as he rubbed his hands together with glee.

I joined the management that evening for a game of snooker in the officers' mess, and a drink in the adjacent bar. 'What will you have?' Dean asked.

I wasn't quite sure what to say, bearing in mind that I was supposed to begin training in the morning, and was meant to be acting like a professional rugby player. 'Just an orange juice, please,' I replied. Dean gave me one of his disdainful looks. 'Okay, just a half of lager then,' I suggested, rather weakly.

'That will be a pint, then,' Dean said, as he poured the glass himself and signed a chitty. He watched me drink the glass until the last drop had disappeared down my throat. Then he shook his head. 'I have to say, for a professional rugby player, I'm a bit disappointed that you're drinking.'

It was a predictably troubled night's sleep. Not for the first time I had a feeling of impending doom. The bed itself was worse than a hospital bed, with every movement inducing a loud creaking noise. On top of this I found myself sharing with Cliff Shepherd. Cliff is a delightful man, and a former Leicester Tiger himself during the 1950s and 1960s, but it had been some time since I had last shared a bedroom with another man, especially someone in his sixties who had no inhibitions about wandering around the room stark naked. He also liked to have the windows and curtains open all night. The light from the army camp's lamp-posts and the cold from the unseasonal Northern Irish weather only made matters worse.

Still, in the morning I was prepared, like the man facing his firing squad, for whatever fate lay in store for me.

The day began after a high fibre, high carbohydrate breakfast. John Wells gave a team talk in the gym, housed in a bubble tent beside the training pitch, outlining moves from the previous season and new ones to be practised during the course of the week. Then it was all out on to the pitch for a two-and-half-hour training session, which began with a series of stretches and sprints. The backs trooped off to their corner with Pat Howard, the former Wallaby who had become player-coach at Leicester following Joel Stransky's departure from the position that summer. The forwards, including their new acquisition, got down to scrummaging.

At first it appeared too physical, especially when hooker Dorian West and Darren Garforth exchanged a couple of blows. To the outsider this would no doubt seem unacceptable, but in the context of a rigorous training camp – where physical contact is considerable and there is great pressure for places within the first team with the new season just a fortnight away – it is perfectly understandable. Dean Richards commented later that he is never too disturbed when a bust-up takes place, providing it is sorted out quickly and amicably. 'It shows the intensity,' he said. 'It proves they mean it.' Within moments the rest of the scrum were mocking Dorian West for his feeble attempts to hit his room-mate for the week's camp. West, or 'Nobby' as everyone called him, soon found himself re-christened 'Harry the Haddock', after his flapping fists. Within moments the two foes were laughing and hugging each other, as the rest of the pack made haddock impersonations.

Happily I managed to escape any violence by virtue of the fact that I remained in the back row, alternating between open-side and blind-side flanker, as well as number eight. The players were remarkably accommodating and supportive as soon as they could see that I was trying my hardest. Dean had warned me that some of the squad – especially the media-wary England boys – were a little sceptical about my presence in the camp, which was something I had expected. I was delighted to see how soon this attitude would change, with the likes of Back, Corry, Cockerill, Garforth and Lewis Moody readily offering me their much-needed advice. Although I had played much rugby in the back row, and at a half-decent level, it had all been a very long time ago, and seemingly minor but crucial pointers – such as where precisely to grip – had been forgotten.

I felt relieved when the first training session was under my belt, especially since I had emerged apparently unscathed, save for a bruise or two from a couple of rucks. I joined Cockerill and Garforth for the afternoon circuit session back in the gym, together with the other forwards. The backs had already been, and the 'PDCs' were still to come.

'What's a PDC?' I asked Cocker.

'The Prima Donna Club,' he replied, looking across at one or two of the better-known names. 'In other words, the England boys who toured South Africa. We never had it before, but one or two returned a bit lippy. It never lasts long here, you know. You're always brought back down to earth at Leicester.'

Keeping up with Cockerill and Garforth proved an impossibility when it came to lifting weights, due mainly to my comparative lack of strength but also to my lack of technique, which made it potentially dangerous. The boys looked after me, however, finding lesser weights and tutoring me in the correct procedures. When we emerged we found John Duggan and Dean Richards engaged in filling plastic wheely bins, first with cold water and then with enormous quantities of ice cubes.

'Get in,' Dean ordered, as I wandered outside.

'I'm sorry?' I asked.

'This will do wonders for your aching muscles,' he said, pointing to the bins. 'Now don't be a faggot, and get in.'

Peter Short, the young and promising lock-forward, joined me as we stripped down to our underwear and clambered gingerly into the two bins, gasping as the ice cold water hit our nether regions. Before long the rest of the Tigers were queuing up for this ten-minute form of sado-masochism.

John Wells stopped by for a brief chat as I froze in the makeshift plunge bath. Alongside Richards he was another man who, if cut, would bleed the green, red and white of the Leicester Tigers. An underrated back row forward, in my opinion, he had played for the club during the same fifteen-year period as Richards. As soon as Richards was appointed rugby manager he asked Wells to coach the side, and within a year both had steered the Tigers to their first league championship title.

Strangely enough, John Wells and I had come across each other long before, way back in the early 1980s, when we had faced each other on the school playing fields. He was hardly likely to remember me – I played for a Stamford school XV in which I was anything but the star – but I remembered him, a confident flanker whose combination of skill and guts made him stand out from the rest of his Magnus Newark team. 'You were the only side to beat us that year,' he recalled, before describing half the game.

Dean Richards and the players had given me the impression that Wells adopted the sergeant major approach as a coach, but I saw little evidence of this during my week with the Tigers. He was very precise in his work, and I would often pass his room and see him furiously writing up notes or discussing moves with his fellow coaches, once using his finger to draw on a steamed up mirror.

Being another no-nonsense character, I would not have been surprised if John had been nervous about my participation just a fortnight before the start of the new season – but if he was, he did not show it. Instead, like the rest of the management and playing staff, 'Wellsy' did his best with the lumbering addition to his forwards squad. 'I think you're slightly mad,' he added, studying my screwed up face as I jigged about in the wheely bin trying to find warmth.

The team had a public relations trip to Omagh Rugby Club that evening, but before then I thought I would discover a little more about the Lisanelly Barracks. Up until this point the Tigers had been left very much to their own devices, although the presence of the military was very much in evidence, and helicopters hovering above were a common sight. From time to time we would see squaddies being punished in the square, which normally took the form of high-speed marching coupled with abuse from a staff sergeant. It made most of the boys yearn for more training sessions out on the field.

The regiment stationed here in Omagh was the Worcestershire and Sherwood Foresters. After the 500 lb bomb exploded in the market town's bustling main street in August 1998, causing the death of twenty-nine men, women and children, the regiment and the then Royal Ulster Constabulary were heavily involved in the clear-up. One of the officers told me that the very gym we were using for our weights sessions and team tactics had been a temporary morgue that day. Even two years on, part of the main street remained a bomb site.

That evening what was to become a nightly game of cricket commenced in the main parade square. Players wandered in and out of the proceedings in-between calling home on their mobile phones or escaping the camp for a short while to shop at the nearby supermarket. This night the rules were one hand, one bounce, made harder for the batsman because while everyone crowded around him, he was not allowed to hit the ball hard. It resulted in a comical series of one-ball innings. Poor Paul Reeves, a South African centre who had come to Leicester on trial, scored six consecutive golden ducks. 'As you can see, it was a tough career choice for me between rugby and cricket,' he said, with a resigned shrug.

At nine o'clock what was to become a nightly highlight – and a rather quaint one – took place. Muffins, scones and tea were served, and the players, to a man, dropped everything for this. Their appetite during the week would be understandably ravenous, this being a collection of mainly huge men who pushed their bodies hard. Even the small guys, like Austin Healey, were bulging with muscles, and as a result a great deal heavier than one would imagine.

It was over a blueberry muffin that Leon Lloyd, the England centre, recalled the day he was told he had been dropped from the 1999 England World Cup squad. 'It was one of the worst days of my life,' he said. 'And then, to make it worse, Leicester had a club ladies' night that evening. I refused to go at first because it meant all the players had to dress up as women, but I was persuaded in the interests of team camaraderie. I sat in the corner all night like a transvestite, thinking this was a rather bizarre reaction to being dropped.'

The trials and tribulations of a rugby player. I would discover this for myself in the morning, following another very poor night's sleep. The other players fared little better than me in the sleeping department. Some complained that the beds were too small for their large frames. Others accused each other of snoring. And Martin Corry had to put up with Austin Healey's sleep-talking. 'He doesn't even shut up when he sleeps,' the big number eight said.

This was supposed to be the day for team building, when the squad and management left the army camp for a series of adventures and challenges designed to pull everyone together. We had been told that paint-balling, canoeing, abseiling and mountain-biking had all been arranged at another British army camp some ninety minutes away, although in the end only the paint-balling took place.

The squad was split into five groups that were to take turns to fire at each other, with one group defending a position from the others. We had two turns each, and although I emerged more or less in one piece from our first sojourn in the bushes and gorse, my inevitable comeuppance awaited.

My group, which included Leon Lloyd, Geordan Murphy and Ben Kay, was supposed to defend a flag on the top of a hill. I volunteered to take the front bunker. I knew I might receive some flak from an attacking force that included Neil Back and Martin Corry, but

I hoped that my show of bravery and team solidarity would be well received.

This proved to be a major mistake. When I managed to hit Corry full in the face mask with a sniper's shot I felt I was earning my stripes for my group, which was supposed to be directly behind me guarding the flag. It was not. In fact, my brothers-in-arms had scampered well behind their own lines, leaving me completely exposed. The odds were already against me without the double-crossing help of one of my colleagues: a vengeful Corry had managed to sneak up behind me only because my team had allowed him to pass. The first I knew of the big man's presence was when I felt a large, painful thud in my back. I turned around just in time to take another pellet in my chest, and a third on my shoulder.

I counter-attacked as I ran for cover, leaving Corry to advance to the flag. When I emerged from the undergrowth, with thorns embedded into the palms of my hands, I noticed Back stalking nearby. I rose to shoot him, but he declared: 'I've got no ammo. I've got no ammo.' The rule of the game, stated quite clearly at the start by the commanding officer, was that you could not shoot a defenceless man who was returning to the ammunition truck. If you did, then you would face a firing squad.

'Are you absolutely sure?' I asked the England flanker, not altogether believing the man.

'Yeah, yeah, of course I am,' he shouted back.

I turned round to search for Corry. A split second later a pellet thudded into my buttock, followed by a triumphant 'Yes!' from a gleeful Back, who then scampered off down the hill. 'I honestly thought I had no bullets left,' he explained later. 'Then I heard a rattle and I realised I had one remaining. It wasn't an easy shot, you know. You were thirty metres away, and there was a wind, so I had to judge it just right. It was a pressure shot, which is why I was so pleased when it hit your arse.'

Well, as you can imagine, I was so happy for Backy. 'But that was against the rules,' I protested.

'True, true,' he accepted. 'But you learnt one valuable lesson today. Never trust a rugby player.'

As I still possessed a number of pellets, and as I could neither see nor hear any of my other brave colleagues, I decided on a course of hara-kiri by venturing up the hill to take on my attackers. If I had been Clint Eastwood I might have taken them all out. Instead, five of them discovered my intentions and ran after me, firing at will and peppering me with pellets from head to toe. At one stage I took a spectacular tumble and rolled down the hill – to the great amusement of Back, Corry and company – and, as I raised myself back to my feet, another pellet slammed into the side of my head.

Back on the team bus my exceptionally bruised body proved to be one of the main points of entertainment. The players just could not get enough of seeing me lift up my t-shirt to expose my wounds. Another source of amusement were the antics on the back seat.

Cockerill, Corry, Garforth, West and prop Graham Rowntree sat proudly on their back-seat thrones that afternoon, and woe betide anyone who attempted to replace them. One after another they tried, from Peter Short to Austin Healey, Mark Meenan and Steven Booth, a rugby league player on trial at Leicester. At one stage half a pack of young forwards – including Adam 'The Beast' Balding and Ben Lewitt – piled in, but the result was always the same. Any ambitious back-seat challenger would return to his front-of-coach seat with his t-shirt ripped and his underwear torn away from his backside. The aisle soon became an underpants graveyard.

Pat Howard made the mistake of managing to slide his frame under a row of seats, emerging in the back corner as the occupants concentrated on fighting off their younger foes. On discovering Howard, whose whoops of joy were probably an error, they piled into the backs' coach to leave him as naked as the rest of those who had tried before.

James Overend – the centre, who was back from a long-term injury – and I sank our heads and hoped we would be ignored. My name was called out a couple of times, but I managed to fob off the back row boys with a promise that I would make an attempt later in the week. Poor Jimmy Overend was trying to read a book, but found his face pressed up against his own window as Peter Short's now bare buttock rammed into the side of his head. 'Nice, this,' he commented, as he tried vainly to push this mass of flesh away.

Short provided the other entertainment high spot of the day. To the obvious surprise of the rest of the squad he revealed himself to be a fan of WWF wrestling, and in particular, The Rock. As we waited for the bus to take us home the big lock from Liverpool treated us to an impersonation of some of The Rock's finest moves. 'He is the People's Champion,' he announced. 'And this is the people's elbow.' With that he lifted a willing Geordan Murphy off his feet, slammed him gently to the ground, and then proceeded to run first to his left, then to his right, before finally dropping his elbow down on to the Irishman's chest.

This, all conducted with an exaggerated raised eyebrow, had the rest of the players in fits. Perry Freshwater, the New Zealand-born hooker, decided to get in on the act with a move he termed 'The Worm'. While a bemused management squad observed from the bus, Perry slid along the ground face first before flopping on to Short. 'No one gets up from the worm,' Short announced, to more laughter.

Although a number of plans for the team-building day had failed to materialise, the combination of my paint-balling assassination, Short's WWF antics and the back-seat capers had left the squad in good spirits. A quick game of touch rugby took place on our return to the Lisanelly Barracks, providing a useful stretch for us all after three hours on a coach. I had survived two days now with the Tigers, although a collision with prop Ricky Nebbett in the touch rugby, in which I came off considerably worse, reminded me of what was yet to come.

That night I went out with Dean Richards, Ian Smith, Andy Key and my room-mate Cliff Shepherd to the nearby hotel bar. It was here, over a Guinness, that the importance of the following day

Everton sport their new signing

**Burnishing my
ball skills
before the
big game**

In the dug-out

In the thick of the action

About to go on and the
adrenalin is flying

An invitation to a
wrestling spectacular

Thrown by The Bomber
in training

Pretty Boy Stuart learns not to
mess with The Red Shadow

Feeling the full
weight of
Dick the Bruiser

Beaten up by the
bad boys

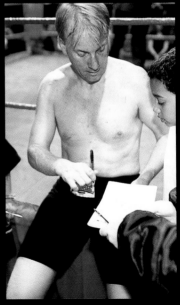

The Red Shadow and
The Bomber triumphant

An instant hero?

**Leicester Tigers
in training**

**Painful results
from paint-balling...**

**...and relief from an
ice-filled wheely bin**

**Called up for action
against Ulster**

Tigers trio: Stafford, Pat Howard and Louis Deacon

Launching an attack with a diving pass

Congratulations from Dorian West

Taking the strain
while Denis Betts
(left) and Gary
Connolly look on

Stretching point

Shoulder to shoulder
with Billy Boston

Gaining hard
yards...

...feeling
the force of
a tackle

Winning
Warriors

was spelled out to me. It was to feature a major defence and tackling session.

'We've got to see if you can take it,' Dean explained. 'It's not going to be very pleasant for you. You've done okay so far, but if we really are going to allow you to wear a Tigers jersey and play for us against a team like Ulster, I've got to know that you have the character to withstand the kind of hits you're going to experience tomorrow.'

Not for the first time, I attempted to appear calm as my manager continued to paint a horrific picture. Inside, meanwhile, my guts were churning. Ian Smith took some time to provide me with a crash-course coaching session in the art of tackling and making hits that would not result in decapitation. As we were in the middle of a hotel bar this proved a little awkward, but his potentially life-saving advice was received almost too eagerly by his pupil.

After a night haunted by images of my back being broken and my head being ripped off, I reported for an early morning team meeting in the camp's education centre. It was to give me quite an insight into what makes the Tigers the team, more than any other in English rugby, that simply refuses to accept defeat.

After Pat Howard and Leon Lloyd had talked through some backs moves on a blackboard, James Grindal, the England Under-21 scrum-half, stood up. He led a session designed to analyse both the Leicester Tigers' performance and the approach that other teams would take against them. What was particularly noticeable was how self-critical the team was, despite having won two back-to-back championships. 'We got dumped out of the Tetley's Bitter Cup last season, and we didn't even qualify from our group in Europe,' said Howard. 'We're really not that good, you know.'

Grindal wrote a series of headings on the blackboard. Interestingly, although the team identified three or four strengths, the column headed 'weaknesses' was far longer. Likewise, although a few opportunities were expressed, many more suggestions were accepted under the heading 'threats'. There would be clearly no room for complacency with this lot – especially after Neil Back delivered an impassioned speech on what he saw as the lack of professionalism in the club. A man like Back, with his England record, his long service at the club and his tremendous capacity for hard work, is held in the highest respect by all the other Leicester Tigers, so when he spoke his mind others listened. When eating some of the younger players would hide their mountains of food when they saw Neil approaching to avoid a reprimand from him.

The session ended on a lighter note, with everyone clamouring for Peter Short's 'people's elbow'. Again, with Geordan as his willing accomplice, Short reduced the players to giggles with his elbow-flaying antics, and the intensity of the previous moment was replaced with merriment.

Martin Johnson had emerged that morning after arriving at the camp the night before, fresh from his honeymoon in the Bahamas. Two days earlier he had been sunning himself on New Providence Island. Now he found himself slumming it in army digs with the young lock-forward, Chris Jones. I thanked him for having put in a good word to Dean as he had promised. 'It obviously did the trick, then,' I said, slapping him on the back.

'Oh shit, I forgot all about that,' he admitted. 'Sorry, my mind was full with the wedding. I see Dean let you come, though.'

Indeed he had, but without Johnson's input. I was even more amazed that the manager had decided to try me out.

A physical forwards' session followed, with a set of twenty-four line-outs and then a further twenty successive mauls in which, again, minor flare-ups took place. Having been trampled while following a line-out I came to the conclusion that the best way of surviving all this was to throw myself wholeheartedly into the fray. The results of this course of action included a streaming cut on my shin and a bleeding, swollen left ear. 'That's exactly how this started,' Garforth said, pointing to his own blown-up ears. My ear would remain swollen for the rest of the week. The line-outs were as confusing as they were treacherous: I was forever having to ask what calls such as 'Elephant 3' or 'Domino 1' meant.

After the tiring morning training we endured another weights circuit session back in the gym. Lunch was taken gratefully but nervously because, for all my efforts that morning, I knew that the big test – and the most frightening part of the whole week – was to begin that afternoon.

'Are you ready for this?' a smiling Paul Gustard asked as we trudged back on to the pitch a couple of hours later.

'Yeah, sure,' I replied, failing to hide my anxiety.

'Good luck,' he added. Others said the same as they trotted by – the same characters who would shortly be knocking lumps out of me. I appreciated their good wishes, but they also alarmed me. Why was everyone fearing for me?

My question was soon answered. After a few warm-up rucks and mauls we were split into two groups, one wearing rather flimsy-looking tackle pads, and the other ready to charge. The teams alternated, but this provided no respite for me: you either suffered a big hit from a defending Tiger, or you attempted to hit one of them yourself with a tackle designed to stop him in his tracks.

The latter, believe it or not, was marginally better. I was part of a straight backwards line, and when the converging pack had stormed past, each of us was supposed to stand on our spot. Of course, half the time I found myself clattering to the ground, especially when I was meant to stop Martin Johnson. In the corner of my eye I could see Richards and Wells standing on the touchline studying all this with considerable interest.

At one stage, in the heat of the battle I forgot about staying put and chased Derek Jelley after he and his colleagues had converged on my group-mate behind me. Throwing myself at Derek from behind, I brought him down and landed, clumsily, on top of him. Understandably, this produced a string of expletives from the prop. Sensing that he was close to punching me I apologised immediately. 'You were supposed to stay where you were, not come back and tackle me,' Derek explained later, when I asked him what I had done wrong. 'The fact that you brought me down like that embarrassed me, but seeing that you forgot, and you've apologised, we'll leave it at that.'

By such diplomacy battles can be avoided, but if I avoided a bruising from Derek, a worse one was about to happen. It was my group's turn once more to charge at the tacklers, and during the course of taking on eight tackle-pad clad warriors, we all managed to run with the ball. When Graham Rowntree popped the ball up to me, I found myself running close to the touchline. Perry Freshwater stood some 10 metres away, deep in concentration and intent on ensuring that on no account would a writer get past him.

I had already concurred with this, hence my pass inside to Garforth. My costly and painful error was this, however: not content with offloading the ball, I paused in admiration of my spinning effort instead of bracing myself for contact a split-second later. I might have argued that his hit was late, but I still should not have exposed my whole left side to the New Zealander. The force of Freshwater's hit was frightening. I flew across the pitch and landed with a hefty thud on the ground, with Perry's arms still clasped around my waist.

I was badly winded and, although desperate not to reveal my pain in front of the others, I remained on all fours for twenty seconds or so as I regained my breath. Perry had shot a quick glance up to the watching management, as if to say: 'Was that okay to hit Ian as hard as that?' Unfortunately, it was. As Dean Richards had already explained, if I was really hoping to play against Ulster I had to be able to take hits such as this. I rose to my feet and gave Perry a quick nod to show I was okay. 'Welcome to the office,' he replied, as he ran off for more mayhem.

The hits then started to come thick and fast. The usually friendly Chris Jones not only tackled me but also proceeded to lift me off the ground and dump me forcefully on my back. Short followed suit, his shoulder dipped and his expression full of competitive malice. Each time I managed to get up, like the knight with no limbs in *Monty Python's Holy Grail*, determined to last the session.

After the group tackling came the individual version, where one player had to tackle another who enjoyed the luxury of a support player to pass the ball to. It was just my luck that I had to face Gustard, Kay and Short. At least Jamie Hamilton was there too, the experienced but relatively small scrum-half. I found the fact that his club nickname is 'baby' to be encouraging. At least that was one less big hit to expect.

This proved to be a major misconception. Gustard, Kay and Short tended to splatter me, although I would on occasions hang on to them like a terrier as they dragged me across the pitch. It was Hamilton, though, who hit me the hardest. In hindsight, I made it easy for him. He was expecting a shimmy or a side-step from me, but instead found this now exhausted wannabe flanker trotting straight at him. Baby stopped me in my tracks, and then forced me first backwards, and then upwards with the force of his hit, before throwing me unceremoniously on to the ground.

The hour-and-a-half-long session of suicide ended with a fifteen-minute game of full-on tackling, by which stage my legs had turned to jelly and my body ached from head to foot. My contribution to this was negligible. I felt shot through. As I walked slowly back to the gym, where another, much-needed appointment with a wheely bin awaited, the players congratulated me on surviving. 'Still standing then,' Martin Johnson commented, with an approving nod. 'Sorry about that tackle,' Chris Jones said, making a point of running up to me. 'You all right mate?' Perry Freshwater enquired, with a wink. Then Baby Hamilton checked to see if I was really okay.

'You're supposed to be small and not so strong as some the others,' I complained to him.

'Yeah, but you made it so easy for me,' he replied. 'You didn't do anything. You just ran straight at me.' By the surprise in his voice, it was clear that it had been a long time since an opposing player had done this. If only all were like me.

A smirking Dean Richards and John Wells came over for a chat as I stood frozen in the wheely bin trying my hardest to look unperturbed. 'Well, what do you think, John?' I asked the coach.

Wells was smiling at the painful comedy that had just taken place. 'Well, you know, there were times out there when . . .' He paused, provoking my deluded hopes to soar. 'When you were a sodding liability.'

Dean laughed and added: 'But we saw enough to give you twenty seconds on Saturday.'

The relief was discernible. Somehow I had managed to do enough to convince Dean and John to select me, albeit reluctantly, for the final moments of the game. This had nothing to do with my ball skills, nor my running skills, nor my technique nor tactical nous. In fact it had nothing to do with any skills at all. It was due wholly to the fact that I kept on getting up. I had reached the painful conclusion – literally as well as mentally – that my qualities as a rugby player, if I ever possessed them, were consigned to the dim and increasingly distant past, and in any case would have been so far short of the level required at a team like the Leicester Tigers. This should have come as no surprise, but it depressed me nonetheless.

Much of my evening was spent in physio Chris Brooks's room taking up a bed that was also required by a good number of Tigers. This could, and probably should have annoyed them, but they were laughing too much at my discomfort to care. The physio is, of course, much more than merely a physiotherapist: he or she becomes the father confessor, the psychologist, and the Samaritan. The physio's room therefore becomes the social centre of wherever a team may be. It was no different in Omagh.

As I lay on the bed most of the squad seemed to come and go, helping themselves to bandaging and plasters, or strapping ice cubes to whatever bruises had emerged. Dorian West took a handful of Ibroprufen painkillers as though they were Smarties, suggesting I do the same before Saturday's game. Jamie Hamilton needed his ankle looking at. Martin Johnson stayed a while longer as Chris worked on his Achilles. His verdict on me that night was either a bruised or a fractured rib. Three of my fingers had also been damaged, although I had no idea how this had happened. They were probably trampled on during the defence session, but as I was too busy compressing my rib at the time, I failed to notice.

The rib was a concern, of course, and it would cost me another sleepless night as I failed quite miserably to find a pain-free position in bed, but I was determined to play against Ulster and dismissed it as an inconvenience. The prescribed painkillers helped me in this cause.

Having warned me that I would hardly be able to move in the morning, Chris suggested that I should have a couple of beers that night. 'Just to help you relax,' he said. Never has a suggestion been so gratefully and instantly acted upon. I joined the management for a drink back at the officers' mess, and Dean asked me what I had thought so far of the week.

I told him that what had struck me most was the sense of team spirit, evident throughout the squad. There seemed to be no real peer pressure nor, despite the PDCs, any superiority complexes, just a mutual understanding of every individual's vital role within the team. The lack of ill-feeling following bust-ups on the training pitch, the hunger for continued success revealed in the team meetings, and the general banter and sense of camaraderie all contributed to the conclusion that, while one or two other teams might match or even better the Tigers for star names, they could not equal them in terms of a collective force.

Dean nodded his head throughout this speech. 'It's the Leicester way,' he said. 'Always has been. That's how it was when I was playing, and that's how it is today. It's our greatest strength. Occasionally you do need to put a few of the players in their place, but in general we're all singing from the same hymn sheet.'

The next morning, as Chris Brooks had predicted, I was moving around like an old man. A hot bath made little impact, and when the forwards began the morning's proceedings with some line-out practice and moves, I was barely able to run at all. 'You're showing good mobility there, Ian,' remarked an amused Paul Gustard as he observed my fast hobble to the ball.

Funny though it was, I was concerned. It was difficult to see how I could play in a top match in two days' time. It was hard enough, of course, to imagine this even if I was fully fit, but virtually impossible with me in my current wrecked state. Another ice-cold plunge bath in the wheely bin followed a weights session, but what really initiated my recovery was Tim Stimpson.

Stimpson, the team's full-back and goal-kicker, had been watching my attempts to stretch in the gym. Eventually he ambled over and told me how my face had been contorted with pain almost before I had even begun a particular stretch. 'You've got to relax, be calm, think of something nice,' he said, putting on his therapist's voice and pushing my legs across my body for me. The England player turned out to be big on psychology, especially visualisation, which he said helped him no end in his place-kicking. 'You've got to shut out the noise and the pressure when you play, and especially when you kick,' he explained. 'That's where the visualisation comes into use. You just replay your best kicks in your mind, and then attempt to reproduce them.'

Although his initial pushes and pulls on my body were painful, slowly my arms and legs, back and hips, were able to rotate and stretch again. 'You must be the stiffest person I've ever seen in my life,' Stimpson commented, as he continued his good deed for the day. By the end of the stretching session he had transformed me from a tin man back into a flexible human.

By the afternoon I was able to run again as the team went through its specific moves for the game in forty-eight hours' time. As I was a last resort of a reserve, I played little part in the goings-on. No matter, I was just pleased to be mobile again. After dinner I joined the rest of the team for some firearms practice down at the barracks shooting range. Split into various groups of five, we all learnt first how to fire a range of shotguns and pistols. The firearms officers had rather thoughtfully stuck a picture of Jonah Lomu's head on the target, enabling thirty-odd rugby players to pepper the great All Black winger with a series of bullets. Then the groups took on each other in a competition to see who could score the most points. A £25 prize was on offer, although a collection of competitive men like the Tigers would never need any extra incentive to beat each other.

John Wells and Darren Garforth were on the same team as me, with Garforth unwittingly striking me on the head with one of his hot cast-offs as he pumped his shotgun at the selection of targets. We did well, but not quite well enough. The team that included Andy Key, Jimmy Overend and Adam Balding won, although controversy was to emerge later that evening when Jimmy revealed that they had been given more bullets than the rest of us. (The prize money was subsequently withheld amid mock acrimony.) Poor old Cliff Shepherd invited more amusement by first managing to miss his target, hitting the grassy bank next to it instead, and then emerging with a mighty bruise in-between his eyes, where the gun had slammed back into his face after firing. Fortunately Cliff, despite his age, was like everyone else in the Tigers squad: thick-skinned, and always ready with a verbal riposte.

The day before the big match was a time for those who were playing – and this included me – to take it easy. I undertook an early morning jog and stretch, and practised some ball skills with Matt Skinner and Lewis Moody in the gym. As I trudged back to the mess, a vanload of Tigers screeched to a halt. The door opened and Martin Corry shouted: 'Ian, quick, Johnno's down at the pitch and he wants you to join him for some training that will come in very useful to you.' I thanked Martin and dashed back down to the pitch in time to see an extraordinary sight. The England captain was dressed from neck to toe in so much protective clothing he looked like the Michelin Man. Over his head sat what looked like a birdcage.

He started to run away from me and down the pitch. A nearby dog handler let loose a big, snarling Alsatian, who set his sights immediately on a sprinting and rather comical-looking Johnson. Seconds before the army dog caught him, Johnson tripped over his own feet and landed on the ground with a crashing thud. 'I couldn't get up because of the weight of the clothing,' he explained later. 'Besides, the dog was on to me in a flash.' And so he was. From a distance it looked quite terrifying. There was the captain of England being savaged by a very angry dog. Yet a couple of minutes later Johnson emerged like a kid coming out of a candy store. 'That was great. Do you want to have a go?' I declined his kind offer. Having been gunned down by a paint-balling assassination squad earlier that week, and then relentlessly boshed by the Tigers pack for ninety minutes, the prospect of being half-eaten by an Alsatian certainly lacked appeal.

Besides, I was looking forward to the trip to the seaside that social secretary Richard Cockerill had organised for the team. The day out at Portrush was not compulsory, but most of the guys took the chance to escape from the barracks on the traditional day off before a match. After a ninety-minute minibus ride, in which we passed the time with various 'guess-the-person'-type games, we arrived in a dull and grey Portrush. Despite it being August, the town seemed half closed down. Cocker immediately received abuse from the rest of the team for arranging such a trip. 'It will get better,' he insisted, warming to his position as guide. 'Those on Cockerill's tours, follow me.'

The mood only brightened when a number of cafes were discovered on the promenade. We chose one and everyone piled in. In terms of lunch orders the players varied from the conscientious, who ate chicken and salad, to those who merely wished to redeem the day. 'Ah, seaside fish and chips,' declared a satisfied Dorian West, as he and his fellow front row boys tucked into huge plates of traditional seaside fare. 'And a cup of tea to wash it all down with. What could be better?' If only Dorian and company had seen the disapproving look on Neil Back's face at that moment.

A decision was made to journey on to the Giant's Causeway, the famous series of granite steps that juts out into the Irish Sea. The weather began to clear, and even the Leicester forwards appreciated the stunning beauty of a site described as one of the eight wonders of the natural world. Climbing up the natural staircase until sitting on top overlooking the sea, we all grew inquisitive concerning how all this took shape. Luckily we had young Harry Ellis among us, a promising scrum-half who had just taken his 'A' level in Geography. He promptly delivered a quick lesson on erosion to Messrs Johnson, Back and West, before Tim Stimpson telephoned his father for verification. 'He had a book on the subject right next to him,' he announced, to a somewhat quizzical bunch of team-mates.

Yet another team meeting was called that evening. Led by Pat Howard, with Dean Richards and John Wells observing, the Ulster team was dissected player by player. There was no doubt about it: although lacking a couple of their decent names, Ulster looked very strong, with a team that included international stars such as David Humphreys, James Topping, Niall Malone and Ryan Constable. It still seemed quite incredible that, at my age, I was about to make my debut for the Leicester Tigers – especially against this lot.

There followed more cricket, and another visit to Chris Brooks for strapping, treatment and painkillers ended the day. My plans for an early night were stymied by my inability to sleep. For the rest of the Tigers, although still important, this was just another pre-season game. For me, it was another journey into the fantasy world of my dreams. Excitement and nerves fuelled my insomnia. Would I make a complete fool of myself? And would my battered body withstand rugby at the highest level?

Match day finally arrived, and as far as I was concerned not a moment too soon. The week had seemed more like a month to me, not because I had not enjoyed the company of the Tigers, but simply due to the fact that, one way or another, I had suffered on almost a daily basis.

'Do you think you could do this week in, week out?' Neil Back asked me over breakfast. My answer was obviously negative, although maybe I could if I were fifteen years younger and filled with an ambition to be a top rugby player. Still, we would all be finding out a little more about my questionable prowess that afternoon. A brief line-out practice took place in the main square, before the team assembled for a final briefing and the chance to get their hands on the official kit for the match. Cliff handed me a pair of green socks, some white shorts bearing the Tigers emblem and that of sponsors Vauxhall, and the green, red and white striped jersey. It was the first time I had even seen the official Leicester jersey all week, and it felt surprisingly good. I was beginning to feel not just like a Tiger, but an accepted one at that.

It was time to go. We all piled on to the team bus and sat quietly as we made the ten-minute journey to the ground. When I had made a similar trip with the Springboks a couple of years earlier, driving to their Test match against the Irish, I had been surprised by the intense atmosphere on the coach. On this occasion I was perhaps even more taken aback by the silence. This, after all, was going to be a pre-season friendly match. It was in part experimental, with a number of younger, reserve players getting the chance to reveal to the Tigers' management what they could do, in a game that was going to consist of three half-hour sessions. Not a great deal hinged on the result. Yet still the intensity was there. For Winston Stanley, for example, the experienced Canadian international, this would be his Leicester debut. For James Overend, the jocular centre, this was his comeback match after over a year out with injury. For Paul Reeves and Steven Booth, this was their chance to extend their trial periods into permanent signings. And for the likes of teenagers Oliver Smith and Harry Ellis, this was their moment to become a Tiger. The friendly abuse that had flown around the coach all week was nowhere in evidence now. From time to time the quiet was disturbed by the odd murmur, but that was about it. It only served to heighten my own anxiety.

There was a carnival atmosphere at the Thomas Mellon Playing Fields in Omagh that afternoon. The crowd was not the biggest – maybe two thousand had made the journey to see two of the best sides in Europe play – but a combination of brass bands and busy marquees created a lively buzz. The fact that the proceeds from the game would go towards buying specialist equipment for the local County Hospital would, no doubt, have helped make Omagh the focal point of sport that Saturday afternoon in Northern Ireland. Inside the dressing room, however, the atmosphere was very different. Slowly and methodically, the players changed into their strips. Some enjoyed a final massage, others went to work on strapping their fingers and backs, ankles and shoulders, as if they were gladiators ready to do battle. Chris Brooks and John Duggan were hard at work preparing the players. Pete Atkinson would normally have been assisting as well but he, a former player for Nottingham, had been promised a run out in the game and was therefore changing with the rest of us.

Half an hour before kick-off the Tigers went through their warm-up practice. This instigated what looked like a major problem for me. Despite having spent much of the morning undergoing frantic stretches to alleviate any remaining stiffness, I felt a sudden pull in my right quad muscle. Although it caused no problems when jogging, as soon as I was required to sprint it hurt quite badly.

My timing could not have been worse, and as warm-up was concluded I was the first back to Chris Brooks for a large dollop of Deep Heat cream, rubbed furiously into my thigh. The smell and warmth of the cream eased the throbbing of the damaged muscle, and my hopes began to rise again.

Perry Freshwater had the honour of leading the Tigers out on to the field. A number of the well-known internationals, such as Johnson, Healey, Back and Corry, were sitting this game out, although they all came to watch with interest and to lend their support. Leicester still fielded a good number of famous rugby names, however, and the likes of Pat Howard, Darren Garforth, Graham Rowntree, Dorian West and Geordan Murphy, together with established first teamers such as Paul Gustard, Jamie Hamilton, Derek Jelley, Andy Goode and Adam Balding made it a strong-looking outfit.

Ulster followed suit, and although I failed to mention it to any of my team-mates, the size of some of them made me question, even at this late juncture, whether it really would be sensible to complete my plan. Dean Richards, John Wells and the rest of the management sat with the remaining squad players as the match got underway, and although Leicester enjoyed most of the possession, Ulster led at the first interval by twelve points.

During the interval Dean assembled everyone in the middle of the pitch. He was not unduly concerned by finding his team down, because he had seen many chances created and appeared confident that these would soon be converted. By the end of the second third, however, his mood had somewhat darkened. Despite first Pat Howard and then debutant Paul Reeves scoring tries for Leicester, Ulster had maintained their advantage due to a couple of breakaway tries from their centres. The message that a clearly perturbed Dean was trying to get across to his besieged men was that they had forgotten large chunks of the previous week's training, and that all too often possession had been kicked away. The use of various expletives underlined his frustrations.

As we jogged off the pitch again Dean revealed the line-up for the remaining half an hour. 'Ian,' he shouted out. 'You're on for the final ten minutes.' I had started to grow concerned that Dean had simply forgotten about me in the heat of the moment, or had looked at the losing scoreline and come to his senses. But this was not the case. True to his word, despite his team being on a losing ticket with just a fortnight to go before the start of its league championship defence, he was ready to throw me on.

With the clock ticking, I began to warm up along the touchline. Some of the Leicester players let out a cheer and shouted some words of encouragement. 'Don't forget, hit them low and from the side,' an injured Tristan Prosser whispered into my ear. Someone in the crowd recognised me from my previous book. Asking me to sign his programme he asked: 'You're not seriously going to go out there, are you, and play?'

I nodded my head grimly and continued stretching. As the clock read twelve minutes remaining, the crowd fell to a deathly hush. Jamie Hamilton had collided head-on with a kick from team-mate Ben Lewitt's leg. It was the kind of accident that is never far away in a rugby game, and now Jamie was lying prostrate close to the touchline – where I was standing in readiness to come on. Physios from both clubs rushed to the scene and when the seconds turned into minutes I could tell something was seriously wrong. Eventually a neck brace was produced, and Jamie was stretchered off in front of me. It emerged later that he had fractured his cheekbone and eye socket. He would be out of action for two months.

As sorry as I felt for Jamie, I have to admit that I felt even more sorry for myself. This was the situation. Leicester had just lost their experienced scrum-half to a horrendous injury. They found themselves 31–12 down, with just ten minutes remaining. What, then, could they do? The answer was simple. Throw Ian Stafford into the fray. Harry Ellis sprinted on to the pitch to replace Jamie, and Dean asked me to take over from Peter Short. 'Ian,' he shouted out, as I began to run towards my team-mates. 'Don't let me down, now, you hear?'

I nodded my head and positioned myself for the restart. As with my time on the Goodison Park pitch, the following ten minutes flew by. Unlike my time playing for Everton, however, I found myself continually involved in the game. The strangest thing of all was that I not only forgot about my injured rib, fingers and thigh, but at no time during my Leicester debut did I feel any pain at all – despite having genuine injuries that would cause me much discomfort later. 'Strangest thing, adrenalin,' Martin Johnson would remark later.

Within a minute I found myself tackling one of their big forwards. It was not exactly a textbook move, but a desperate leap on to his back managed to bring him down. A surprised yell of approval from the Tigers ranks on the bench served to motivate me still further. A pass followed to Pat Howard, and then another, from the floor, to Winston Stanley. I played a hand in another tackle, and then set up a ruck in which the ball was retained.

Then came the moment that would be replayed later in many a daydream. After some concerted pressure the Tigers set up a ruck some 20 metres from the Ulster try line, and 8 metres from the left-hand touch. It was probably the case that I was the last forward to arrive at the scene, for when Harry Ellis grabbed the ball I emerged on his left-hand shoulder to take the pass. I looked up and realised that there, in front of me, lay the Ulster try-line, with absolutely no player from either side in my vision. The thought that I was about to score one of the most unlikely tries in the long and successful history of the Leicester Tigers flashed momentarily through my mind as I tried to sprint for the line. Within a couple of seconds, though, the dream was shattered. From seemingly nowhere an Ulster flanker bore down and tackled me into touch.

I have thought of those few seconds ever since. Should I have attempted a dummy pass inside? Maybe I could have linked up with a colleague? Should I have at least attempted to brush off my assailant with a forceful hand-off? I wish I had attempted all three now, but at the time all I could think of was to put my head down and run for the line. The problem was, the week's training had taken its toll. My speed was already close to negligible when I arrived in Omagh. By the Saturday afternoon it was non-existent. It was first-hand proof of how a rugby player at this level needs the ability to make an instant – and correct – decision. What looks easy from the stand is anything but on the pitch.

The final whistle blew moments after the subsequent line-out. Leicester had lost, 31–12, but I was content, nevertheless, not just to have survived without any further injury but also because I believed I had not made a complete fool of myself. If anything, I wanted the game to continue a little more, just in case another scoring opportunity should fall on my lap.

We shook hands with our opponents, forming the traditional arch for the players and then with each other. John Wells was the first of the management to reach me. 'I would have been very happy for you if you had scored,' he told me, with a beaming smile. Dean was close behind, and he, too, was laughing. 'Bloody hell,' he said. 'You nearly did as well.' Others later offered their views. 'It was like one of those nightmares, when the true moment of horror turns into slow motion,' Lewis Moody recalled. 'We all thought you were going to score, and we all thought, "No, no, no".' Martin Johnson was in a purposefully deflating mood. 'Cardinal sin,' he said, shaking his head and tut-tutting. 'You lost possession, and you allowed yourself to be bundled out into touch. Big mistake, that. Big mistake.'

There was little point protesting. If I wanted to taste rugby at this level, then I had to adopt the same standards as the best, and this meant not missing tackles, not conceding tries or turnovers and, in my particular case, not losing possession, even in attempting to score.

My flight back to London was due to leave a couple of hours later, so I had little time to savour the moment at Omagh. Martin Johnson and I were driven together to the airport, stopping briefly at Omagh Hospital to check up on Jamie. Martin Corry and Perry Freshwater had left the match early to be by his side, and it was clear on seeing Jamie that he was in a bad way. I wished him luck, and thanked him for his help during the week, but I was sure little if any of this registered. It was a numbing reminder of how sport can so quickly turn against you, and I counted myself rather lucky not just to have played for Leicester, but also to have emerged in one piece.

This wasn't strictly true, as the following morning spent in casualty and an X-ray department verified. A fracture of my number ten rib and a broken tip of my right ring finger were revealed, which made me wonder how on earth I had managed to play ten pain-free minutes for the Tigers the day before. My wife was horrified, too, to see my bruised body. I was black and blue, partly through the various knocks picked up in training, but primarily due to the paint-ball bruises that had exploded all over me. The results of Neil Back's direct hit on the buttock and Martin Corry's close-range assassination were now plainly in evidence. 'It looks like someone's set upon you with a baseball bat,' she remarked, as she ran me a hot bath filled with yet more soothing oils.

Dean Richards had promised to deliver a brutally honest verdict on my week's endeavours with the Tigers, and when we spoke a couple of days later this is precisely what he proceeded to do. 'Good points,' he began. 'Grit and determination. What surprised me and the boys was that we thought you'd get battered and wouldn't be fit enough for the Ulster match. But you got stuck in, took the hits, and kept coming back for more.' He continued: 'As for the match, well, we're still laughing about that. By what must have been total fluke, you kept turning up in the right place at the right time. In fact, on three occasions you popped up with lines that any player would have been happy with. Yes, you did well.'

I was relieved and taken aback to receive such a verdict from the great man himself, but I remembered this was how Walter Smith started his report on me with Everton. His took a definite turn for the worse, and Dean was about to follow suit.

'Having said that, when you had the chance to score you didn't because you didn't possess the pace, and you allowed yourself to get munched. I'm not sure if you showed any skill whatsoever, either with your defence or your ball-handling. I'd have to be mad to think about signing you for the Tigers.'

Why that last comment should have hurt so much is a mystery to me. What else was I expecting? Did I really think Dean was about to invite me to join Neil Back and Martin Corry in the back row, at the expense of the likes of Paul Gustard, Adam Balding and Lewis Moody? Still, as I pointed out in a rather fruitless attempt to defend myself, Leicester did not concede any points when I was on the field.

'So, Dean,' I enquired, in the vain hope of some final comforting words. 'If you add up everything you've said, what's your final conclusion?'

There was a deep sigh on the other end of the telephone line. I took this to be a good sign. Dean was clearly gathering his thoughts and about to deliver a concise and encouraging finale.

'Well, Ian,' he replied finally, after an interminably long pause. 'All in all, I'd have to say one thing.'

Again, he paused, toying purposefully with me in the knowledge that by now I was hanging on to every word he was saying in the vain search for compliments.

'You were a bag of shite, Ian. A complete bag of shite.'

chapter four

 OUT OF MY LEAGUE

The broken rib sustained during my Leicester Tigers adventure took an eternity to heal; the broken finger likewise. Although both fractures were technically mended six weeks later, any subsequent knock to the damaged areas – either while in training or at the hands of my rough-and-tumble son – reminded me that my body was growing increasingly fragile as a result of all this fantasy chasing.

What concerned me even more was the next sporting episode that loomed menacingly ahead. I recalled the reaction of the Leicester Tigers' Martin Johnson when I informed him that the alternative rugby code would be my next port of call. 'Rugby League – well. There's no hiding place in that game. I'm not sure I'd fancy that myself.' Coming from one of the hardest and most fearless union players in the world game, this was hardly comforting to hear. My optimism was hardly bolstered by the fact that I had turned thirty-seven years of age shortly after being mauled by the Tigers, but for some sado-masochistic reason, I was determined to give league a shot.

My experience of playing rugby league amounted to two days spent training with the Sheffield Eagles back in the early 1990s, when the then top division club had among its ranks the likes of Garry Jack, Mark Aston, Mick Cook and Anthony Farrell. It was for a television film, and my efforts resulted in two cracked ribs courtesy of some eager tackling at my expense. Most of the time this was when I had possession of the ball. Once, when I chipped the ball over a couple of Eagles players, mainly to avoid more contact, I was flattened regardless. Time, happily, had eased the painful memories of my short stay with Sheffield but, as I was planning to do it all over again, they came flooding back.

I had set my sights on Wigan, or rather the Wigan Warriors as they are now called in these super-professional days of summer rugby. Although my earliest recollections of league were the Leeds and St Helens sides of the 1970s, I was aware not only of some of the great names that had plied their trade for Wigan before then, but also of the dominance that the Lancashire club held over the sport during the late 1980s and for most of the 1990s. The names, even for a southern-based, union-playing, football-loving sports nut such as myself, tripped off the tongue: Edwards and Bell, Clarke and Offiah, Hanley, Gregory and Robinson. Today it is little different: Farrell and Betts, O'Connor and Radlinski, Connolly, Renouf and Dallas.

In September 2000 I travelled to Warrington to watch the Wolves take on the Warriors in one of the last games of the Super League. In front of a full house at the Wilderspool Stadium I observed Warrington putting up a determined fight, at least for fifty minutes of the match, until Wigan decided enough was enough and, like a racing car finding an extra gear, moved effortlessly away to end up with a handsome victory. It was as if, almost cruelly, the Warriors had been toying with their opponents. Bearing in mind that Warrington themselves finished sixth in the Super League that season, and had turned over the likes of St Helens and Leeds in the process, this dismantling by Wigan was breathtaking to watch. The speed of the game and of the players was impressive. The high-impact collisions were simply disturbing, as was the stream of players – notably wearing the blue of Warrington – that kept hobbling off the pitch. 'We did our very best,' Warrington's Allan 'Alfie' Langer told me afterwards. 'But Wigan take some stopping.'

Having been bruised and battered during my training with the Leicester Tigers – resulting in my far from fit and fresh performance against Ulster – I decided this time to improve my physical state. A new Holmes Place gym and leisure centre had recently opened close to my house, and I decided it was time to turn my back on my muddy trainers and the sub-standard equipment in my garage. In the afternoons, therefore, I would take my place on the rowing machines and treadmills, and in the evenings I would return for a double dose. The evening was when the really serious exercisers turned up. I preferred the afternoons – they made me feel fitter.

There was, of course, the small matter of persuading Wigan to let me join them, train with them, and play in one of their end-of-year matches. There was one match, in particular, that I had in mind: Wigan versus St Helens, the Boxing Day derby. This was a game that I had been aware of since my first appreciation of sport: an annual clash between the deadliest of rivals, one that shaped how the Christmas holiday itself would fare not only to both clubs but also – especially – to both sets of supporters. Those who follow Leeds and Bradford may argue that their West Yorkshire derby is the main match, but history, tradition, and the very fact that Wigan and St Helens have been slugging it out for most of the honours over the past ten years, insist that there is no bigger rugby league game in the northern hemisphere than the Warriors versus the Saints.

True, what was once a vital part of the league fixture list has now become a friendly, but try telling that to the clubs – especially now that St Helens has held the upper hand over Wigan for a couple of years, following Wigan's earlier domination. Indeed, prior to Boxing Day 2000, the last time these two sides would have met was in the Super League Grand Final two months earlier at Manchester United's Old Trafford stadium, when the Saints emerged as champions for the second successive year. So, it may have been a friendly in terminology, but it was most definitely not in deed.

So how did I manage to become a Wigan Warrior? The answer is, remarkably easily. I had become friends with Phil and Andy Clarke in an association with their website company, Rugbee.com. Phil used to be the Great Britain and Wigan captain during part of their 1990s heyday, that is until he broke his neck playing for South Sydney in 1995. His elder brother, Andy, had a few run-outs for Wigan reserves, but had made his name partly through his own health and leisure company and also through being the conditioning coach for a host of sports teams, including Liverpool FC, Manchester United FC and the Irish national rugby union team.

It was Phil who volunteered to be the mediator. Given the choice of an approach from me, or one from a former captain, hero, and even one time chief executive, the conclusion was obvious. Phil suggested that he would give Maurice Lindsay, the long-serving Wigan chairman, a call on my behalf. I had once interviewed Lindsay back in the mid-1990s, when he was the chairman of the Rugby Football League, but I doubted whether he recalled the day, or me.

It turned out he did. In fact, he also seemed to be aware of my earlier participatory sporting adventures, too, and when Phil called me a few days later he announced that it was looking good. I was to contact Maurice at home that night to discuss the idea further.

That evening I prepared myself for the hard sell. I worked out the reasons why Maurice Lindsay and Wigan should agree to allow me not only to spend some time with them but also to run out at the superb JJB Stadium on Boxing Day and face St Helens. I was barely convinced myself, and despite Phil Clarke's reassuring tone, I was far from hopeful when I picked up the telephone and dialled Lindsay's number.

'Hello, Ian,' Lindsay's cheery voice sounded down the line by way of an introduction. 'Yes, we'll do it. Would the St Helens match on Boxing Day be okay with you?' His instant approval took me aback completely. I was just about to launch into a speech full of phrases such as: 'I know it's preposterous, I know you think I'm crazy, but just hear me out.' Instead, Maurice carried on. 'I'll get the relevant people to get in touch with you shortly. Congratulations. You've just joined Wigan.'

Well. As I replaced the receiver I was once more overcome by a range of mixed emotions. First came excitement. Bloody hell! I was going to play for Wigan! Then came fear. Bloody hell! I was going to play for Wigan! It was fantastic news. It was also terrible news. I had felt like this before, notably when Steve Redgrave had informed me a couple of years back that he would ensure that my week spent with him and the Great Britain coxless fours would be the worst of my life, and also when Roy Jones Jr had sent notice that he would fight me in Florida. Now I had subjected myself to all this again. It was bad enough being boshed by the Tigers, and then by Ulster, yet the general feeling from everybody I spoke to was that this was going to be a whole lot worse.

A week later I was driving in my car when the mobile telephone rang. Pulling over to the side of the road I pushed my receive button and heard a New Zealand accent on the other end of the line. 'Afternoon, Ian,' said a chirpy voice. 'Frank Endacott here.' I sat up in my seat, ready to receive the Wigan coach who had just coached New Zealand to a rugby league World Cup final defeat to the unstoppable Australians.

'Delighted to hear you're joining us,' Endacott announced. 'I've heard all about you, and I think it's great you're going to play for Wigan. I have to say I think you're also completely mad.' Frank went on to inform me that he would not be there for either the pre-match training or the Boxing Day derby, preferring a break back home in Auckland before returning in January to prepare Wigan for a serious assault on the Super League and Challenge Cup. Instead his assistant coach, Billy McGinty, would be in charge, with help from Dean Bell, the former Wigan captain. 'But I'll make sure I see the match video,' Frank promised, ending the conversation. 'And if I like what I see, I'll sign you.' I thanked the Kiwi for his support, and informed him that I wouldn't be cheap.

We were now into December and my training was being hampered by my frustratingly familiar right calf muscle that, once again, was playing up. A tennis match against Bjorn Borg in London – for my column, 'The Player', in *Esquire* magazine – had resulted in a minor tear, and I faced yet another race against time to regain full fitness in readiness for Wigan. My long-suffering physio, Sarah Connors went to work on the calf and also my back, which was now rock solid in stiffness as a result of my earlier sporting exertions. Sarah had given up advising me against such activities long before, although as she manipulated my pained body she couldn't disguise a disapproving expression when I told her I was going to play rugby league for Wigan.

Although the injury was clearing up, I was desperate to prevent it from happening again, hence my interest in a newly developed healing device called a Skenar. The device had apparently cleared up a long-term groin problem that had troubled Dan Luger, the England international rugby union winger, for eight months. I went to see Dan at his Chiswick home. He produced what looked like a portable men's shaver. 'You place it on your skin and it sends electrical impulses via the skin and nerves to the brain,' he explained. 'Biofeedback provokes rapid recovery. It's a way of using your natural pharmacy to re-energise your body.' In other words, it prompts the brain to release its natural self-healing chemicals.

It turned out that his girlfriend, Jerilee Bonner, was a trained instructor with the Skenar. She offered to provide me with a session, which is how I found myself half-naked inside Dan Luger's flat one afternoon with his girlfriend. The results were stunning. Apart from a few headaches, I suffered no side effects. Once Jerilee had gone to work, my calf, back and neck felt remarkably free again. In turn this gave me a renewed confidence in my ability to train. With just a fortnight to go before I was due to report for duty at Wigan, the timing could not have been better.

The following day Billy McGinty contacted me. A second row and loose forward, he had retired five years earlier and had since become Wigan's reserve team coach. Like Maurice Lindsay and Frank Endacott before, Billy was immediately friendly.

'Here's the plan,' he announced. 'You report for training on Monday morning, that's December 18th. Bring your boots, your gum shield and, most importantly, yourself. We'll be doing speed and agility and skills in the morning, and weights in the afternoon.'

Right.

'Tuesday. Conditioning and attacking in the morning. Weights in the afternoon. Wednesday. Conditioning and defence work, then weights. Thursday, more conditioning, team runs and weights. Friday, team runs and weights. Saturday off.'

I managed to cut in. 'Thank God for that, Billy.'

'Sunday, Christmas Eve, more team runs in the morning. You can have Christmas Day off with the rest of the team, then Boxing Day's your big moment. All right?'

'Sounds good, Billy.'

He sounded a little out of breath as he was talking. 'You're lucky you're not with us now, Ian. We're doing the dreaded hill runs. It's not nice, and the boys don't look too pretty doing it.' He ended the conversation with a repeat of Frank Endacott's assertion. 'Anyone who's fought Roy Jones Jr, and who now wants to play for Wigan without any experience of playing rugby league at the highest level before, must be off his head,' he said, with a laugh. 'But we're looking forward to the challenge of turning you into a Wigan player.'

On a trip to Manchester I thought it might be worth talking to Jason Robinson and Apollo Perelini, formerly of Wigan and St Helens respectively, who had just crossed the great rugby divide and joined the Sale Sharks rugby union team. Both put me straight on an early misconception I had made that the Boxing Day derby game was now, after all, just a friendly.

'There's no such thing as a friendly,' insisted Robinson, the former Great Britain, England and Wigan winger. 'Wigan and Saints are arch rivals. The fans can't wait to get back to work or go home and gloat if they win, or go into hiding if they lose.'

Perelini, who played against Robinson in the grand final win for St Helens in what was, for both of them, their last rugby league game, agreed. 'I've never played in a friendly against Wigan because they don't exist,' he said. 'When I first arrived at Saints the fans told me, "We don't care if we lose every game of the season, as long as we beat Wigan in the league, and on Boxing Day." It's always one of the hardest games of the season. It's going to be physical. Very physical.'

Coming from a large slab of Samoan mountain, this was not exactly what I wanted to hear. Neither, for that matter, was Robinson's next offering. 'There's nowhere to run in rugby league,' he promised. 'Both teams have the firepower to do a lot of damage. On the field there's no love lost between the two sides. Apollo and I are good mates, for example, but on the pitch he'll try and run straight over me. I can assure you that wherever the weak link may be in the team, the opposition will find it, and then run at it.' Jason was giving me a knowing look at this point.

I don't know why I even bother talking to these people. One day someone might just fill me with hope, even if it is false hope. These sportsmen are just too damn honest. Why couldn't they just have told me it would be a complete snip? Instead, I left Sale's Heywood Road ground convinced that I had just agreed to my own suicide, played out in front of a large and passionate crowd at the JJB Stadium.

The week before I was due to join Wigan, I found myself in a couple of bizarre situations. First, I received through the post an official Rugby Football League registration form. It emerged that I had just a couple of days to beat the governing body's deadline if I wanted to play rugby league. It made interesting reading, especially the part that stated: 'Please indicate the country or countries for whom you wish to be considered for international honours.' I ticked the box marked 'England', much to Billy McGinty's later disgust. McGinty, who had played for Scotland as well as for Great Britain, was none too impressed by my allegiance. I assured him that my playing for England was fairly improbable.

Under the registration status section, from a choice of professional, amateur or trialist, I chose trialist, and then added 'Wigan' next to the club I wished to be registered with. Embarrassingly, the large section provided for 'career details' remained blank. What the Rugby Football League thought of this when they received my signed registration form, a document confirmed by Wigan's stamp of approval, heaven knows. What Wigan must have been up to, signing a 'trialist' whose date of birth was clearly marked 16/9/63, and who wished only to be registered with the club, from the 18th to the 26th of December, was probably a question asked within the halls and corridors of the RFL headquarters in Leeds.

The second strange situation was that I ended up spending most of my final days before the Wigan encounter in the winter sunshine of Barcelona, in the company of the Jaguar Formula One racing team and Eddie Irvine. I was with them as part of an ongoing sporting adventure described elsewhere in this book, but aspects of the conditioning that Eddie and his fellow driver Luciano Burti had to follow fitted in nicely with my preparations for Wigan.

And so it was that I found myself on the rowing machine inside the Jaguar motor home or, under the supervision of Jaguar fitness adviser Nick Harris, producing a series of hill sprints interlaced with press-ups and star jumps, backward runs and jumps to my feet from a lying position. On my return home I continued this short-lived but intense training, either at my new gym or outside on an uphill street, where I would drop to the floor before sprinting 200 metres uphill. As it was mid-December, and cold, I certainly turned a few heads.

Having assured my family that there was nothing to worry about – something I had difficulty believing myself – I packed my bag with my boots and the gum shield that had faithfully seen me through training with the Springboks and fighting Roy Jones Jr, plus a bottle of arnica capsules for the inevitable bruising I would endure, and left for Wigan. It was 5.15 on a dark December morning, and a four-hour drive northwards was perhaps not the best way to prepare for my first training session with a bunch of supremely fit and strong athletes.

Training would begin at the impressive Soccerdome, an indoor sports centre found next door to the JJB Stadium, within Wigan's Robin Park complex. There, by way of a reception committee, stood McGinty and Denis Betts, Wigan's colourful loose and second-row forward, who had played during most of Wigan's successful years in the 1990s, as well as for Great Britain and England. Still just thirty-one years of age, Denis remained a key player in the current side. Both looked me up and down for a while, obviously wondering just what possessed a person of my appreciably smaller stature to undergo such a week.

Billy had left some of the Wigan training kit at home, so I emerged in my Leicester Tigers shorts and a sports t-shirt and was introduced to the rest of the team by Billy and Denis. We began training indoors. After a series of sprints and jogs, and practice in ball-passing skills, I teamed up with Brian Carney, Wigan's new recruit from Hull, who was signed to fill the considerable hole on the wing left by the departure of Jason Robinson. He, like me – for what it was worth – was going to make his Wigan debut in eight days' time, so he was keen to make a good first impression. This included, when we took turns running away from each other using a large expanding rubber belt called a 'viper', hauling me to the floor which, at least, provoked some merriment from the rest of the watching squad.

Some of the big names currently at Wigan were not training that week. Kris Radlinski, Steve Renouf, Terry O'Connor and captain Andy Farrell had all been given extra time off after having featured in the World Cup, although I would get to meet O'Connor and Farrell later in the week.

In charge of the session – and indeed, for all the fitness and conditioning periods that week – was Nigel Ashley-Jones, an Australian who had left St Helens in rather acrimonious circumstances just two months before. 'It was a week before the play-off semi-finals when I told

Saints I would be joining Wigan,' he explained over lunch. 'They told me to leave immediately, which wasn't the way I wanted it to end. You could say, as a result, that I'm very much looking forward to Boxing Day.'

Nigel was probably in the minority. With the League having done away with winter rugby – moving instead to the fast, dry pitches of summer with the creation of the Super League – the Boxing Day derby, although a big match, now falls a few weeks after the start of the pre-season training period. Denis Betts found my initial enthusiasm for the forthcoming game amusing. 'You must be the only person at Wigan who really wants to play next week,' he said, with a laugh.

The other topic of interest over lunch was Billy McGinty. Billy's career was spent for much of the 1980s with Warrington and then, between 1991 and 1995, with Wigan, before ending with one season at Workington. It was at Wigan where he became a Great Britain international, as well as a triple league champion and double cup winner. It was with Scotland – by which time he was a Workington player – that he sustained his career-ending injury. The bang on his head was so severe that he was advised that any further collisions could result in terminal damage. 'It was a good enough reason to quit,' he explained. Billy's injury story was one of many I would hear, to my discomfort, over the course of the week.

Yet alongside his successful career there is something else that has kept McGinty's name written indelibly in the annals of rugby league folklore. It concerns a piece of foam made to look like a pineapple ring, the Prime Minister, and a key component of Billy's private parts. It is probably best if McGinty tells the story.

'It was just after we'd won the 1992 Challenge Cup final at Wembley,' he began. 'We'd beaten Castleford and for me, having also been called up for the Great Britain team just a fortnight earlier to tour Australia that summer, I had fulfilled two of my dearest professional dreams. I hadn't won much at Warrington, and I'd always wanted to win the Challenge Cup.

'A week earlier I had sustained a cut on my leg which kept opening up. In order to protect it I cut a hole in a large piece of yellow foam, strapped it around my leg, and wrapped it up in bandaging. When I came out of the showers I was obviously in high spirits and, for want of finding a better place to put the foam ring, I hung it on my didgeridoo. [That's Billy's terminology, not mine!] At that moment John Major walked in and almost bumped into me. I was a little lost for words, especially when he looked down my body and saw what must have been a pretty strange sight.'

I pictured the scene, as Billy continued: 'I told him, "It's a pineapple ring", for some reason. I'd always thought John Major seemed a bit dull and grey but, quick as a flash, he replied, "Well, that's the last time I'll eat pineapple." That was it. He walked out, and I reflected that my first ever conversation with a prime minister might have gone better. Two weeks later, when I was with the GB squad in Papua New Guinea en route to Australia, my hotel bedroom phone began to ring in the middle of the night. The British tabloid press had just seen the whole episode on a BBC documentary. I'd forgotten that some TV cameras had been recording inside the dressing room. You didn't exactly see what John Major saw, but it was pretty obvious what had happened.'

There is a footnote to this bizarre story. 'In 1997, when Major lost the general election, there was an article somewhere that named the ten people he was most likely never to forget,' McGinty added. 'Nine of the names were household names, and mostly world leaders. The tenth name was Billy McGinty. That's my little claim to fame.'

That's not strictly true, of course. McGinty played his part in Wigan's success in the first half of the 1990s, and was a member of the Great Britain team that won a historical Test victory against Australia in Melbourne in 1992, but it is doubtful that anyone, let alone the Prime Minister, would forget meeting McGinty in such circumstances.

That afternoon I teamed up with Denis Betts and Mick Cassidy (Wigan's other long-serving forward, who was enjoying his testimonial after ten years' service) for a ninety-minute weights session in the bowels of the JJB Stadium. Of course, in their company I felt extremely weak. After they had lifted 120 kg they would kindly pull off half the weight for me to reproduce the same exercise. Their fitness, and their strength, was quite staggering. For those few who may still believe that rugby league players drink beer and eat steak for England, and remove all their teeth before playing the game, I have some news. They are – or at least the Wigan players are – supremely fit and athletic, and it was as much as I could manage just to maintain half the weights that my more illustrious colleagues were able to pull, jerk, lunge and heave.

Betts and Cassidy have had their fair share of injuries, too. 'Most recently,' Betts announced, sounding as if he couldn't be bothered to list them all, 'a dislocated shoulder and snapped cruciate ligaments.' Having played for Wigan since he was seventeen years old, save for a two-year sojourn in Auckland, it is a minor miracle that the man is still standing, let alone still playing the sport at the highest level.

Cassidy gave it some thought, too, dismissed a whole catalogue of setbacks, and plumped for a shattered elbow. 'That's probably been my worse one,' he decided. 'But I've had a fair few.'

Cassidy would not be playing on Boxing Day, but Betts would, indeed as team captain in Andy Farrell's absence. 'Used to be the biggest day of the season,' he reminisced, as we rolled backwards and forwards on large inflatable balls during a spot of pilates. 'That, and to a lesser extent, Good Friday, which was always the other fixed day of the year when we played St Helens in the league. It meant that every Christmas Day we had to go easy, very easy, with the food and drink. I remember once training with the team at Central Park on Christmas Day morning.'

Betts had invited me back to his place for a cup of tea and a chat, but before then I had been asked to pay the Wigan administrative offices a visit by the main entrance of the JJB Stadium. Wigan's chief administrator, Mary Sharkey, was waiting with a waiver for me to sign. Now, over the past couple of years I've been forced to sign a number of waivers, to the extent that you might think I would have become immune to the message they conveyed. This is not the case. Each one is clearly designed to scare the living daylights out of you, and Wigan's was no different.

'Dear Sirs,' it began. 'I, Ian Stafford, understand the nature of rugby league and the tactics which are a characteristic and normal part of the game. I further understand that I have been expressly put on notice that I undertake this activity at my own risk and in participating in the game on the 26th December, I accept the risks involved. Yours faithfully.' In other words, if you kill yourself, it's not our fault. I duly added my signature at the bottom and went off to meet Denis Betts and his family for late afternoon tea before spending the evening at Andy Clarke's house where I watched a couple of videos that McGinty had lent me of Wigan at their best last season. 'Just study the defence, the running back, the angles of running, and the way gaps are found,' he had advised me. I did, and came to the conclusion that my debut for Wigan was a ridiculous notion.

In the morning the newspapers were beginning to grow excited about the forthcoming game on Boxing Day. In particular they focused on the fact that St Helens were likely to be fielding the Australian forward, Peter Shiels, just signed from the Newcastle Knights, and hoped also to be including Mick Higham, who seemed to be in the middle of a tug-of-war between Saints and Halifax for his services. There was, thankfully, no mention of Wigan's surprise decision to field a new player with negligible talent and advancing years.

Before training began Billy McGinty took me aside and informed me that I would be playing in the second row on Boxing Day. This surprised me. I was expecting to be selected on the wing, although McGinty's reasoning made sound sense. 'You might not be involved much on the wing, and then, suddenly, find yourself exposed,' he explained. 'At second row, though, you'll be in the thick of the action. You'll also have the likes of Denis Betts and Simon Haughton close by to shield you.' I informed Denis of the news. His response, as usual, was reassuring. 'I hope your insurance is good,' he said.

This particular morning's training was the most challenging of the week. Indeed, Nigel Ashley-Jones would admit later that he had his own term for the session: 'The bag drill of death'. By now the cold snap had hit Britain hard, but it was not the fact that the temperature had hit freezing point, nor the gusting winds that produced a wind-chill factor of well below zero that hurt us, rather the drill we were ordered to perform.

We split into twos, with one holding a tackle bag and the other lying face down on a line, 20 metres from the try line on a rugby pitch. My partner was Simon Haughton, the England second row forward, who had missed much of the previous season with various injuries. 'Bet you can't wait to play on Boxing Day, then?' I asked him as we prepared for the exercise.

'I'm raring to go,' he answered, with a big smile.

Nigel explained the drill. 'You start by running backwards to the try line,' he shouted. 'Then it's down on to your stomachs, and up again. Sprint to the tackle bag and tackle. Then run backwards back to the middle line. You have to do this in fifteen seconds, then swap with your partner. Then repeat this exercise twice, making sure you complete in thirty seconds. Then it's three times, four times, five and finally six times, all keeping to fifteen seconds each time. That means that your six in a row must be done in one minute thirty. Got it?'

He blew the whistle, and we began. The first time was not too bad at all. I quietly thanked Nick Harris, the Jaguar conditioning coach, for those hill sprints in Barcelona the week before. Simon took his turn, and then it was back to me for two in a row. And so we went on until, by the time we reached the fourth attempt I was beginning to huff and puff. To my encouragement, so were a few others. Simon started to shout out words of support as I stumbled my way through five, and finally six times, collapsing at the end, lying sprawled on my back and sucking in oxygen. Billy and Nigel had allowed me a slight dispensation. I could run forwards on occasions, and did not necessarily have to fall completely on to my stomach.

'Thank God that's over,' I whispered hoarsely to Simon as he came forward and picked me up from the ground with a hefty tug of his paw-like hand.

'Okay guys,' Nigel shouted. 'Well done. Now we do it again, this time starting at six, and working your way down to one.'

My heart sank. It reminded me of Archie Knox at Everton, when he tricked us into believing we would be undertaking three sprint-based exercises around their Tuscany training pitch, only to then land a fourth on us just as some of the team began to retch. By the time we had completed all six again – now with everyone shouting encouragement to each other's partners – the Wigan squad as a general unit were exhausted, but there were still some basic ball-handling skills to undertake. We split up again into groups of seven and four, with the seven attacking the four in a touch rugby game. Afterwards Dean Bell, the former Wigan captain and now the club's 'rugby executive', ambled over for a few words of advice.

I had been introduced to him briefly in the gym the day before, but this day he appeared much warmer. 'Try not to run too laterally with the ball,' he suggested. 'You tend to be running as far as you can, and then simply passing to someone else who has the whole opposition defence on him. Try not to drop your team-mate in it.' He was right, of course. Instead of creating holes in the defence, I was merely dragging the whole defence alongside me, and then popping the ball up for a colleague to have to face three opposing players.

He had some words of encouragement for me later that afternoon in the gym. I needed them, too, because the morning's exertions had taken a lot out of me. Some of the more basic weights exercises were not too difficult, but where I really exposed myself was when it came to the chin and body dips. At one stage, alongside my usual partners of Betts and Cassidy, I was made to wear a weighted waistcoat and then tie a belt around my waist with a weight hanging between my legs. The object was to perform ten dips, but I sank heavily as soon as I attempted the first. Mick Cassidy fell about laughing when he saw this. 'Ian went down faster than the *Titanic*,' he shouted.

The inevitable trip to the physio's couch followed, the first of what would be a number during the week. Wigan's physiotherapist is Alan Tomlinson, who formerly looked after the Sheffield Eagles and, before that, Yorkshire miners. As soon as he placed his hands on my back he commented on its stiffness. 'No wonder your calf muscle's always getting injured,' he said. 'I can't remember the last time I felt a back this stiff.' I informed him that Tim Stimpson had said the same thing at Leicester, as well as, it seemed to me, half the world's top physiotherapists before him.

Brian Foley was also in the treatment room that late afternoon. Foley, who looks a little like the late wrestler and actor Brian Glover, is the club's youth development officer and one of the most colourful characters at the club. A former policeman Foley had played a part in both the Moors Murders and Yorkshire Ripper cases, as well as being a former SAS member. Last year he made the papers after extinguishing a fire he discovered at the JJB Stadium during a match. The averted disaster made him something of a local hero.

Foley took me into his corner of the Wigan coaching office, set up beside the weights room, and handed me a couple of pieces of paper. One was entitled 'Inspirational Reflections'. It turned out to be a poem Brian had written to motivate his youngsters, many of whom progress to the Wigan first team. The other was John Wooden's 'Pyramid of Success'. Wooden was an American high school coach and teacher in the 1930s, who developed his 'pyramid' in a search for self-improvement in his role.

It made interesting reading. The base line of the pyramid featured five ingredients: Industriousness, Friendship, Loyalty, Co-operation and Enthusiasm. Each had messages underneath. Under Industriousness for example, it read: 'There is no substitute for work. Worthwhile things come from hard work and careful planning.' Under Loyalty, came: 'To yourself and to all those dependent upon you. Keep your self-respect.'

The next line up in the pyramid featured Self-control, Alertness, Initiative and Intentness. The next Condition, Skill and Team spirit; above that Poise and Confidence; and at the top of the pyramid, Competitive greatness. Surrounding the pyramid were yet more components of the complete sportsman: Ambition, Adaptability, Resourcefulness, Fight, Faith, Patience, Reliability, Integrity, Honesty and Sincerity.

As if all this were not enough, the paper also featured two further texts. One was an extract from George Moriarty's poem, *The Road Ahead or the Road Behind*.

> Who can ask more of a man,
> Than giving it all within his span.
> That giving all, it seems to me,
> Is not so far from victory.

The other offering simply read: 'Success is peace of mind which is a direct result of self-satisfaction in knowing you did your best to become the best that you are capable of becoming.'

It was an extremely detailed and impressive sheet of paper. Indeed, as I was to discover during my stay with Wigan, mental strength and belief in oneself were the ingredients that the management wanted to drum into their charges more than anything else.

In my time I have been fortunate enough to have been in a number of professional dressing rooms, and the sight of a few motivational messages is not that unusual. Never have I been surrounded by them so much as at Wigan, however. Wherever you turned in the weights room and offices at the JJB Stadium, there would be a stirring message, usually on the theme of winning and losing. 'A winner listens. A loser just waits until it is his turn. A winner feels responsible for more than his job. A loser says, "I only work here".' And so on, with many variations.

Another source of motivational messages is Vince Lombardi. The guru of sports motivation, Lombardi was the man who transformed the lowly Green Bay Packers into Superbowl winners in the late 1960s. Everton's Walter Smith, for one, swears by him, having spent much of his time in Tuscany engrossed in Lombardi's book. It seems the Lombardi magic has weaved a similar spell on Wigan. My favourite Lombardi message was pinned up in Dean Bell's office: 'I firmly believe that any man's finest hour is the moment when he has worked his heart out in a good cause and lies exhausted on the field of battle victorious.' I challenge any sportsman, indeed anyone at all, not to be motivated by that.

I stayed at Andy Clarke's house that night, once more immersing myself in a bath filled with bubbles to ease my fatigue from a day that had even the Wigan players gasping for air. I was keen to meet Phil and Andy's father, Colin – who had played for Wigan and Great Britain from the early 1960s to the late 1970s, as well as later coaching the club – so when he and his wife, Margaret, invited me over for dinner, I readily accepted.

Colin, by his own admission, was not the cleanest of players. 'Played as a hooker between 1962 and 1978 and got sent off thirteen times,' he informed me, reliably. This reminded me of what Andy had said earlier in the day. 'I'll always remember Eddie Waring, the BBC rugby league commentator, saying those immortal words during a live, television game: "And Clarke takes another early bath." And I used to think, "Oh Dad".'

Colin laughs at this, especially as he is now part of the three-man Rugby Football League disciplinary committee, which meets whenever foul play takes place in order to mete out punishment.

I mentioned that this was akin to asking the late Oliver Reed to chair Alcoholics Anonymous.

'I'd say it's worse than that,' Colin replied.

He even missed the 1967 Cup Final after receiving the red card the week before. Admittedly this had been for a technical offence, which hookers often fell foul to, but it was hardly a good game to miss. 'It used to be a lot more physical than it is now,' Colin explained. 'There's no doubt they're better athletes these days, fitter, faster and stronger, but thirty years ago the discipline wasn't quite as rigid. For example, if someone hit you, the ref would pull you over and say, "I saw that. You can get him back with one, but then leave it at that." You couldn't do that today.' He seemed quite saddened by this advance in the game.

The subject then moved on to Phil, his younger son, and that near fatal day in Australia back in 1995 when a broken neck ended his career, and almost his life. 'We were actually in the air when it happened,' Colin recalled. 'When we arrived at Sydney airport there was a reception committee waiting for us. I thought the club didn't have to do that, but then I found out why. When we got to the hospital the first thing Phil did was to wriggle his fingers to show that he was not paralysed.' Colin shook his head at this point and stared, rather pensively, ahead. 'He was lucky, I suppose. Very lucky.'

Later on I would speak with Phil about this, a subject he was perfectly comfortable talking about. 'I was playing for the Sydney City Roosters at the time,' he said. 'I was so caught up with the game, and with the adrenalin, that I was ready to go back out on to the pitch. It was the club doctor who saved me. He just had a hunch that I wasn't right, and refused to let me back. Later it was explained to me that one collision might well have killed me.'

It was a cruel blow to a young man, just twenty-four years old, and at the height of his sporting prowess, but Phil does not see it this way. 'I was fortunate to have enjoyed the career that I'd had, captaining Wigan and Great Britain, and winning trophies,' he insisted.

'Moreover, I was very lucky that the injury was recognised, and that it was not another inch or so away from the damage. I could have easily ended up paralysed.' Phil took a refreshingly positive view: 'Although the injury caused my premature retirement from rugby league, I see my sporting career as merely the first in hopefully many chapters in my life.' It was a strangely moving sentiment, and I wondered how many others would be able to take the same view. There was, of course, one other thought that crossed my mind at the end of this conversation. The man had broken his neck playing rugby league. I, too, would be playing rugby league very shortly.

On day three of my time in Wigan, the squad underwent more conditioning in the morning. It was another cold and blustery day and most of us were now wearing woolly hats. I trooped off with the front row and second row forwards for our own conditioning, under the watchful eye of Billy McGinty, which featured a series of ten 40-metre sprints, with a thirty-second recovery period. Once this was completed, we repeated the exercise before rejoining the rest of the squad for attack and defence work.

What was especially noticeable was how we would run for 10 metres backwards and forwards three, four and sometimes five times before enacting a move with the ball. This, of course, was to make us well rehearsed in the practice of getting back 10 metres when defending at a play-the-ball. In my case, it was extremely useful to have such an alien rule drilled into my head.

In-between the morning skills and the afternoon weights, McGinty informed me that he had decided exactly when I would be coming on to the pitch during the St Helens game. I had assumed that he would repeat Dean Richards' tactics with Leicester, and save me for the final ten minutes. This, though, would not be the case.

'You'll come on with around five minutes remaining in the first half,' Billy said. 'Then you'll start the second half for five minutes or so. That way, you can't lose the game for us.'

'Or win it,' I added, tongue lodged firmly in my cheek.

'True,' Billy answered back. 'But I wouldn't want you to be blamed for missing a tackle in the last minute that cost us the game. In any case, it means that there will be plenty to play for when you are on because I'm sure the outcome won't be decided.'

Fair enough. Although he hid them well, Billy's concerns were later revealed when, after the weights session had ended, he ran through with me a number of key areas of the game. This I think, was as much for his peace of mind as mine.

There were three key points that he wanted to get across. Firstly, possession. 'Never lose the ball when you're tackled,' he insisted, before showing me the proper way to hold the ball. Secondly, running at your opponent: 'Never run straight at him. It's not advisable for anyone, and especially not for you. You don't want the full force of your opponent's body weight hitting you. So, make a slight jink and go for the small gap to his side. He'll still get you, but it will be with his arms. That's not likely to injure you so much.' And thirdly, drift defence: 'Move with your fellow defenders in whatever direction they may be moving, so that you're not leaving a gap for the opposition to exploit.'

Brian Foley was watching all this with great interest. When Billy had finished, Foley produced a pair of boxing gloves, for me, and a pair of pads, for him. 'Come on, then,' he said, to a man who had already completed two training sessions that day. 'Let's do a bit of sparring.'

He proceeded to chase me around the weights room bellowing out instructions. 'Jab, jab, two hooks,' he'd shout, enjoying every minute of it. 'Now give me six straight jabs.' Fifteen minutes later, by which time I was drowning in perspiration, the session ended.

'Just as well I've had an easy day,' I quipped.

'Thought you'd enjoy it,' he replied.

Terry O'Connor had shown up, too, just to pump a little iron and say hello. 'Now I know that in my absence we're in safe hands,' he announced, shaking my own hand and smirking. 'Just make sure you're still standing by Boxing Day, eh?'

I just about had time for a quick shower before meeting up with one of the true greats of modern rugby league, Shaun Edwards, for a coffee. Phil Clarke had earlier fixed us up. 'Are you in the Holy Land at the moment?' Clarke had enquired over the telephone to his former team-mate, referring to the small rugby league metropolis otherwise known as Wigan.

'He has to be one of the hardest and most committed players I've ever known,' Phil had added. 'Especially for someone as relatively small as he is.' He began to reminisce. 'I'll never forget one of his first games for Wigan. It was the old Lancashire Cup final, and St Helens were the opposition. Mal Meninga [the former Australian captain] was playing for the Saints at the time. Shaun ran at him, and Meninga picked him up, turned him upside-down and threw him into the ground in one of the worst spear tackles I can recall. It must have hurt like hell, but Shaun just picked himself up and played the ball.' There was more to come: 'Then there was the 1990 cup final win over Warrington. Shaun dislocated his cheekbone early on, but he went on to complete the rest of a game that Wigan won.'

When I met Edwards I was keen to hear about his experience playing for Wigan versus St Helens. He had played in quite a few such matches during his fourteen-year career, most notably the 1989 cup final, when Wigan ran out winners by 29–0. 'It was the nil that made it so special,' he recalled, with a gleam in his eyes. 'That's what got everyone going. Stickers were made and you'd see them stuck to car windows for years afterwards.'

So when defeat came, it was a terrific blow. 'When we lost, it was terrible, just terrible. It affected my life to the extent that I rarely showed my face after a defeat to St Helens. The thing was, the fear factor was always so prominent. You'd get to the ground an hour and a half before kick-off on Boxing Day, and already the crowd would be milling around in anticipation. It all added to the occasion, and to the pressure. I took it as a personal insult if I ever lost to Saints. I mean, they even speak differently to us over in St Helens. The humiliation of losing was always a far deeper emotion than the ecstasy of winning.'

I asked him for any useful tips before my Wigan debut. 'Don't get worried about the occasion,' he instructed. 'The first time I played in a Wembley cup final I was so in awe of the place and the occasion that the game passed me by. So play your own game, stay within the team structure, and don't let anyone bully you.'

Anything else? 'Just one thing,' Shaun added. 'Don't try anything clever. If you do, you'll look a complete prick.'

The chances are I was going to look like one in any case, but I thanked him for his time. 'Good luck,' he added, as he wandered off into the night. 'I'll be there, and I'll be watching you with interest.'

The following morning's training consisted of yet more conditioning work – forward and backward skips, forward and backward lunges, forward and backward sprints, a series of jogs and sprints, and so on – and more team runs, with the emphasis on defensive lines, attacking angles, and the 10-metre rule. George Unsworth, the kit-man, trotted over to say his greetings, a man who has followed Wigan avidly for the best part of forty years. He promised me that he would prepare my own shirt, with my name on the back, plus ensure that on the day of the big match there would be a skull cap and shoulder pads ready for me. 'You're going to need them, my lad,' he added, with a knowing expression on his experienced face.

Dean Bell had again spent the morning on the touchline, observing carefully the goings-on. He invited me back to his office during the lunch break and, over tea, wanted to know a little more about my motives, aims and background. I, in turn, was fascinated to learn more about the man known in some quarters as 'Mean Dean' – a reference to his uncompromising approach to the game. Bell captained Wigan during part of their unprecedented run of success in the late 1980s and early 1990s.

'He would never ask you to do anything in a game that he wasn't prepared to do so himself,' Billy McGinty had commented earlier. 'Dean would give one hundred per cent in every game, no matter how important it might be.' And according to Phil Clarke: 'Dean just didn't know when to leave the pitch. It didn't matter what injury he picked up, he'd be back on again as soon as he possibly could.'

Dean pulled down his badly scarred bottom lip. 'It took twenty-four stitches once during a game,' he recalled in his slight New Zealand drawl. 'A few days later it burst when I tried to eat a chicken sandwich. The doctor couldn't anaesthetise the area because he couldn't find enough remaining flesh on the lip, so I had to have more stitches put in without an anaesthetic.'

I asked him if it hurt, which just might have been the most stupid question out of a fair few I asked anyone all week.

'Just a bit,' he replied. 'I was a very committed player, because I was very proud to be at Wigan.'

What, even as a Kiwi? 'When I was a kid back home in Auckland I used to get up in the middle of the night to watch the Challenge Cup final,' he recalled. 'Wigan, more often than not, would be in it. When I came here I was already aware of the tradition, and it took me no time at all to become immersed in it and what the club means to the town. I was lucky to have played in a truly great side, too – so good that even when I went and coached at Leeds for a while I would receive abuse at matches from St Helens fans. I can understand it. It must have been terrible following the Saints when we were winning everything.'

Like Shaun Edwards, Dean Bell admitted that the fear factor was always his dominant emotion. 'It stems from my childhood,' he explained. 'When I was a kid and had just had a good game of rugby at school, on the journey home my father would never mention the two tries I'd scored, but the one missed tackle I'd made instead. It's stuck with me.'

Having spent much of my time that week in the company of people who had been badly injured plying their trade, I felt it necessary to run through some tackling again, albeit with the man who broke his neck playing rugby league. And so that night, in Phil Clarke's kitchen, we went through a few moves. 'Don't keep your head up too high when you're about to be tackled,' Phil suggested, as I sped past his fridge. 'You're likely to get it knocked off your shoulders by someone's straight arm.'

I attempted a second run, this time past the cooker. 'Mind you, don't get too low either,' Phil added. 'That's how I broke my neck, after all. The most important thing is never go into a tackle, or make a tackle, half-heartedly. That's the most likely way to pick up an injury.'

There was one person in particular I just had to meet in Wigan before donning the famous red and white stripes. Billy Boston is probably the most famous man ever to play rugby league – 'our sport's Pele' as Phil Clarke put it. Cardiff-born Boston joined Wigan as a teenager and, 485 games later, the Great Britain winger's 478 tries still stand as a club record. Awarded an MBE in 1996, and a member of the Rugby League's Hall of Fame, Boston had just been made a freeman of Wigan for helping put his adopted home town on the sporting map.

Colin Clarke, who played with Boston towards the end of the great man's career, fixed up breakfast between us three days before Christmas. 'I was eighteen when someone from Wigan came down to my house in Cardiff's Tiger Bay,' he told me. 'I didn't even know where Wigan was. I was playing union for Neath and the Welsh youth team at the time. I remember my mother telling the Wigan party, "Offer him £2,000." I took her into another room and told her I didn't want to go to Wigan. She went back to them and said, "Give him £3,000 and he'll sign right now." And that's how I came to play for Wigan. It was the best mistake I've ever made in my life.'

Boston proved to be an instant hit. 'I must have been the first coloured person in Wigan,' he continued. 'But I never had, and to this day have never had, any racial problems at all. Within six months of joining Wigan I was playing for Great Britain in Australia.

'My name started appearing on local buses: "Billy Boston is playing for Wigan today." I couldn't believe how much the town took to me. I was just a member of a really fine side, but I suppose I got more of the limelight because I scored the tries. And you know something? Playing for the club never leaves you. It stays in your blood forever. That's why I'm envious of you right now. You'll be playing for Wigan on Boxing Day. I wish I could be.'

I asked whether the obvious rivalry between Wigan and St Helens had always been evident. 'Oh yes,' Billy replied. 'The rivalry is unbelievable. We didn't like losing to them, especially if 47,000 had turned up to Central Park to watch. It's an amazing thing, this rivalry. We're talking about two small towns, barely six miles apart, in a corner of Lancashire. Yet the match between them and us takes on a global interest.'

After training that morning I had another session with Alan Tomlinson, who put all his strength into manipulating my now solid back. Brian Carney was in for some treatment on his shoulder, too. Barely three years earlier he had been studying law in Dublin and playing league for a pub team; now, having played for Ireland in the World Cup, he was about to make his debut for Wigan. 'I still find it hard to take it all in,' he admitted.

I told him that I'd heard on the grapevine that one of the Boxing Day debutants would probably be playing his last game for Wigan. 'It might be me, not you,' he replied, with a smile. 'Just remember, don't kick the ball, and when you're in possession of it, just stick it up your jumper and run.'

Thanking Brian for his advice, I thought it might be the done thing to pay Maurice Lindsay a quick visit in his office at the JJB. He was about to leave for Australia, so I caught him just in time. 'We'd better discuss your contract for next season when I return,' he said, enjoying the joke.

'It'll cost you,' I retorted.

'Whatever it takes,' he replied. 'Good luck.'

Five days of training had now passed, and although I felt dreadfully tired, I was also encouraged that I had lasted the distance. My calf muscle was holding up, my muscle soreness and stiffness was nowhere near as bad as it was during the week spent with the Leicester Tigers and, although nobody's presence in the Wigan side was remotely threatened by my challenge, I felt that I had not been too badly shown up or exposed either in conditioning or when the ball was in hand.

That night Phil Clarke added his own remembrances to the long list I had accumulated over the week concerning the big derby. 'For the sake of the family you'd try to enjoy Christmas Day, but your mind would forever be thinking about the next day's game,' he recalled. 'Even when you did succeed in forgetting about it for a minute or two, someone in the family would bring it up. You just couldn't escape from it.

'Wigan versus St Helens was one of the most intense games I ever played in. The win bonus always used to be bigger for beating St Helens, because there was nothing better than to beat Saints. I remember sitting on the team bus once when a Saints fan caught my eye. He screamed at the top of his voice: "Fuck off, you Wigan bastard." And I sat there on the bus wondering what could possibly have incited him to behave like that. He had pure hatred written all over his face. So it's going to be passionate on Boxing Day.'

Phil added some useful advice for when I came on to the pitch. 'When Saints reach their fifth or sixth tackle they'll kick the ball down-field,' he said. 'Most of your team-mates won't chase it because they know someone will collect at the back. Try and get back there so that you can receive the next pass. Also, if there's a break on the wing, the ball will probably end up back in the middle of the park where the tries are mostly scored. If you're up there, you just might be the one on the receiving end of the final pass.'

Anything else? Phil nodded his head, and smiled. 'Just be lucky,' he added. 'I got knocked out once for ten full minutes in the Boxing Day derby. I just got my tackle all wrong.' It was always good to end a conversation on a positive note, I felt.

The morning of Christmas Eve was spent back at Wigan, although the forty-five-minute training session proved to be very light. 'We want all your energy preserved for Boxing Day,' Nigel Ashley-Jones explained. Meanwhile, one of the high-profile stars due to play alongside me reported in injured that morning.

Gary Connolly, looking suitably sheepish, had fallen off his bicycle the night before while taking his dog for a walk. He now lay in the physio's room sporting a sling protecting his damaged shoulder. 'They'll never believe me,' he kept saying, referring to his suspicious colleagues who queried the way Gary tended to contract injuries mysteriously close to Boxing Day.

Denis Betts gave a candid response. 'I've tried everything to get myself injured or sick,' he admitted, standing in the cold and now snow-flecked training field. 'I've been falling over, I've been going outside in just my underwear, but I'm feeling fine. In fact, I've never felt better. I can't bloody believe it!'

At the end of the official training session Billy McGinty read out the starting thirteen. Brian Carney and Francis Stephenson, in particular, received ovations from the rest of the squad after their debuts were confirmed. 'Now guys, don't overdo it tomorrow over Christmas dinner,' Ashley-Jones shouted. 'You've got to be supreme athletes the next day.' In a rather touching finale, almost everyone shook hands and wished each other a very happy Christmas.

My training had not quite finished, however. In Andy Farrell's absence, Phil Jones would be the place kicker in two days' time. I had been dropping heavy hints all week about the possibility of kicking a conversion if Wigan happen to score near enough to the posts when I was on the pitch. It was a long shot, but I was living in hope. Phil and I made the short journey from the training pitch beside the Soccerdome to the JJB Stadium, where we were joined by Brian Carney and the brilliant Australian three-quarter, Brett Dallas. The two backs wanted some practice receiving high balls punted by Phil and myself, followed by some low, grubber kicks, where the ball would bob and weave, skid and bounce along the JJB turf. Although both Brian and Brett were too nice to say anything, their patience must have been tested by my ability to send both types of kick in any direction except theirs.

It was good, nevertheless, to be finally out in the middle of the

25,000-capacity all-seater stadium. Built only two years earlier to house both the Wigan Warriors and Wigan Athletic Football Club, it is yet another fine example of the modern stadia that have been cropping up all over the British Isles in the past five years.

It was even better to be sharing the place kicking with Phil Jones, whose accuracy in finding the middle of the goalposts from any angle was impressive. He'd managed to play for the first team on fifteen occasions the previous season when Farrell was absent injured, and seemed to be champing at the bit to get out and take his chances against St Helens. Unhappily for me, having found the target consistently, my radar suddenly lost direction just as Billy McGinty and Nigel Ashley-Jones sat down in the stands to watch us at work. It soon became obvious that the only conversion I had even a chance of taking in the match would be one 10 metres out, straight in front of the posts, and when the game, if it was to be, well and truly won.

Tea and toast was taken at Phil Clarke's house, where Andy Farrell joined us for a chat. At twenty-four years of age, 'Faz' has already achieved most rugby-playing goals in his career, captaining both Great Britain and an England team that made it to the 2000 World Cup semi-finals. 'Wasn't much fun being murdered by the Australians,' he remarked, referring to the rather one-sided semi-final defeat.

Farrell had come primarily to lend his advice. We began with kicking, just on the off-chance. 'Once you know where the posts are, keep your head down and keep your eyes on the ball. Try and shut out the crowd. Just think it's a training kick, out on a deserted field somewhere.'

What about the rest of the game? 'Possession is the key,' Farrell explained, his eyes peering out from beneath a baseball cap as he sipped his tea. 'Either pass as soon as you get your hands on the ball, or run at their defence, but don't run then pass. And keep your head down in readiness for the collision.'

I looked across at Phil Clarke. 'I was just unlucky,' he insisted, guessing my thoughts.

Farrell had not finished. 'You'll find the pace of the game incredible, especially as you're coming on mid-way through. The others will be up to speed, but you'll just have to pick it up quickly. You'll be knackered just running backwards and forwards all the time.'

Did he feel the game would be intense? 'Definitely, yes. It's Wigan versus Saints, after all. Also St Helens are playing the Brisbane Broncos in the World Club Challenge soon, so they'll be looking for a good performance. I promise you, if you touch the ball twice and make a couple of tackles in the ten minutes you're on you will have done well.'

It was, to say the least, an unusual Christmas Day. Apart from the fact that I consumed just the one glass of wine, and just the one extra portion of turkey – something that's unheard of in my household – my thoughts often strayed to the events looming largely on Boxing Day. My ability to put on a brave face was severely tested by a number of text messages I discovered on my mobile telephone from some of my so-called friends. 'See you in Wigan General,' read one. 'Prepare to meet your doom,' said another. 'You're going to die,' announced a third. It was just possible that one of these statements would be proven correct.

It wasn't my best-ever night's sleep, either, but having landed myself in this mess I only had myself to blame. A couple of Christmas present CDs helped to concentrate my mind as I drove across the snow-covered Pennines to Wigan on Boxing Day morning, in time to meet up with the rest of the team ninety minutes before kick-off. Crowds were already gathering around the stadium concourse, waving their scarves, blowing their trumpets, and buying hot dogs and burgers from the various stalls.

Billy McGinty had just begun his warm-up talk in the home dressing room as I sat down and gave him a quick nod. 'Now's your chance, boys,' he kept repeating. 'They beat us last time. Don't let them do it again. We've worked hard all week for this. For the youngsters in the side, this is the moment you've been waiting for. For the experienced ones – Denis, Brett, Chris Chester, Simon – you know what it's like to beat Saints.'

The team members were slowly changing into their colours as this went on. Denis, as captain for the day, would add his own words of encouragement as the familiar dressing room smell of Deep Heat started to pervade the air. Brian Carney and Francis Stephenson performed stretching exercises on each other; Mark Smith, the young hooker, stretched out on the floor; full-back Wes Davies – Billy Boston's grandson, no less – received a rub from Alan Tomlinson; the highly regarded David Hodgson exchanged passes of a ball with a number of his young colleagues; and Simon Haughton, making his long-awaited comeback, appeared alone with his thoughts. Once again I was in an environment that had changed immeasurably overnight – from general chatter and banter to quiet intensity. Nobody inside the Wigan dressing room saw this game as a friendly.

Most of the boys took some time reading the match programme, too. The St Helens team may have been missing Sean Long and Tommy Martyn but, with eight of their Grand Final starting line-up from just two months before, it still seemed pretty formidable to me. Among an impressive line-up the Saints boasted Anthony Sullivan, Paul Newlove, Paul Sculthorpe, Paul Wellens, Kieron Cunningham and Sonny Nickle. This, I concluded, was not going to be nice. Interestingly, Wigan named seven substitutes, plus a mysterious 'A.N. Other'. I have been called this a number of times now, and am seriously considering adopting it as a permanent pseudonym.

Meanwhile, Billy McGinty and Nigel Ashley-Jones made a point of talking individually to each and every one of us. 'You've been caged up, and now we're ready to unleash you,' Nigel said to young Ricky Bibey, the big, friendly prop-forward. Nigel had this particular way before a game. 'Good luck, big feller,' he said to me, shaking my hand and slapping my back. I was one of the smaller players in the team that day, but Nigel was trying his best to make me feel a little larger.

I had my own peg that afternoon in the dressing room. Number 21. There, hanging from it, was my own kit. The white shorts; the cherry and white stripey socks; and, best of all, the famous cherry and white hooped shirt. 'A lot of great men have worn those colours,' commented George, the kit-man, as he saw me staring at my kit. 'So do us proud today, eh?'

With half an hour to go before kick-off we ran out on to the pitch for some warm-up exercises, taken by Nigel. Sprints, stretches, passing moves and tackle bags were all used to pump the lungs and heat up the body. Meanwhile St Helens carried out almost identical practices on their half of the pitch.

The ground looked only half-full – the official gate would later be confirmed at 11,197 – but it seemed atmospheric enough to me. The more avid followers of Wigan may have been wondering what this ageing redhead was doing running about with their boys on the pitch. There were a few unfamiliar faces around him, but they were clearly academy players, some fifteen years younger. Could this be Wigan's secret weapon?

We ran back into the dressing room and prepared ourselves for the grand entry. Almost everyone felt the need to visit the toilet. One of the youngsters admitted to me that he was petrified. 'Me too,' I told him. Denis Betts made a point of coming over to say a few, final words. 'Remember, keep hold of that ball, don't kick it, and stay in line in defence,' he said, before shaking my hand. 'You'll be fine.'

The other players followed suit, lining up and shaking each other's hands and slapping backs. 'Let's go to war, boys,' shouted Nigel Ashley-Jones. 'Let's go to war.' I slipped my shoulder pads on under my jersey, held my skull cap in my hands, and walked out of the dressing rooms close to the back of the Wigan line-up. The reserves took their seats in the dugout, wrapped up to protect themselves from the biting cold, and waited for the all-girl cheerleaders to finish their act, and the game to begin.

The match began reasonably well for Wigan. Simon Haughton marked his comeback with a try after just six minutes when he went over from Francis Stephenson's pass. Anthony Sullivan hit back for Saints with a try in the corner before David Hodgson outpaced four chasers to run the length of the field to score for Wigan.

Meanwhile their new recruit began to warm up on the touchline, sprinting and jogging, skipping and bounding, and wondering whether Messrs McGinty and Bell might get cold feet over me. They did not. After thirty-six minutes I was given the nod to emerge from the reserves' seats behind the Wigan bench, and prepare myself.

Unbeknown to me at the time Dean Bell had informed the St Helens coach, Ian Millward, that I would be playing. Billy McGinty had also mentioned this to match referee Ian Smith. 'When the touch judges heard they started to laugh,' McGinty revealed later. 'The referee said, "I can't give him any special privileges, you know." And I replied, "I understand that. All I'm asking is that you are aware of this if you find him a metre offside."'

There had already been a number of bone-crunching tackles and nerve-jarring big hits, and with Wigan just eight points ahead the match was hardly sewn up in favour of the home side, but this was the moment when I would be making my official debut. Stuart Jones was summoned off, and on I ran, adjusting my Springboks green and gold mouthguard and moving my skull cap into a more comfortable position on my head.

During the commentary on the official match video I was presented with afterwards, the TV commentator is heard to remark: 'On comes number 21. We don't know his name, but we've heard he's Wigan's secret weapon.' Within moments the secret weapon found himself scrumming down alongside Simon Haughton. Within a few seconds more Martin Aspinwall's cross-field run had added a third try to Wigan's score. I tried to keep up with him, in the faint hope that he might look to his left and pass inside, but the young player had only the line in his sights. By the time he rose from his triumphant dive, Brett Dallas and I had arrived to congratulate him.

'Through the introduction of number twenty-one things have turned around for Wigan,' announced the commentator on the video, sounding suspiciously as if he was enjoying the joke. As Phil Jones converted the half-time hooter sounded and we jogged off to enthusiastic applause.

'Wigan brought on number twenty-one to immediate impact,' the commentator added.

In the dressing room most of us gulped down energy drinks, ate bananas, and stretched. Both Dean and Billy made a point of informing me that I had been offside as I prepared to defend at first, something I had to keep an eye out for in the second half. Other than that, they were happy with my performance so far. Bearing in mind that all I had achieved up to that point was to run on to the pitch, escape having been given offside, push in one scrum, and congratulate the try scorer, this was nothing to crow about. It would change in the second half, however.

As we ran back out on to the pitch, I noticed that the tannoy system was blasting out the theme tune to the film, Gladiator, Vangelis's 'Conquest of Paradise'. It seemed a fitting piece of music to play. Denis Betts gave me a reassuring wink as we prepared for the Saints kick-off. 'Come on, Ian,' he shouted. 'You're doing well.'

A minute into the second half I finally got to touch the ball. As I was under orders to simply make some hard yards, I ran towards the Saints defence, making sure I jinked at the last second to avoid maximum impact. The impact, I have to say, still felt pretty maximum to me, as three of the opposition piled first in to me, and then on top of me. The adrenalin hid the pain of the hit, although I would feel it the next day, and as the three Saints players lay on top of me, I enacted the rugby league wriggle on the floor, trying for a quick restart. This achieved little, but I felt it was the least I could do. Laying the ball back I quickly surveyed the ground I had made in the cause of the Wigan Warriors. It must have been at least 12 to 15 metres, I reckoned. Later, when Billy McGinty sent me the match statistics, I was stunned to discover that my efforts had counted for rather less. '4 metres', the stats read, although this referred to the point at which the passer released the ball, rather than the point from where I caught it a few metres further behind.

Moments later we had scored again after Hodgson intercepted a sloppy pass to touch down close to the posts. 'Once again, who was involved but number 21,' announced the match commentator, by now surely finding it difficult not to laugh out aloud. 'He's adapting well to rugby league. Maybe he could solve Wigan's propping problems.'

Straight from the restart Wigan gained possession, and promptly lost it after I dropped a pass that had been directed behind me. Only the referee will know how he judged this to be a knock on, but St Helens had the ball back in their hands. 'Make up for it with some big hits,' Denis said as he ran past me. Later Billy McGinty exonerated me. 'Wasn't your fault,' he said, rather kindly. 'The pass was too far in front of the guy next to you, and too far behind you.'

Nevertheless, St Helens came running at us. You might have expected them to have directed their attacks straight at the weakest link. After all, Ian Millward knew I would be playing. McGinty admitted later: 'If the roles had been reversed, I would have instructed my players to have tested you out.' The bizarre fact was that no Saints player ran directly at me. It meant that I became involved in two consecutive tackles, which later went down on my stats sheet, but the truth is that they were 'assists', where I came in to help the initial tackler haul the man down, rather than face one-on-one hits.

Shortly after my second tackle, and eight minutes into the second half, I was replaced. Added to my first half contribution, that totalled eleven minutes of rugby league for Wigan. 'Stuart Jones substitutes number twenty-one, the influential replacement,' chirped the match commentator. 'The secret weapon's off.'

Within a minute St Helens scored their second try of the afternoon. 'And as soon as Wigan sub secret weapon number twenty-one, Saints come up with the points,' the match video pointed out. A second Saints try followed two minutes later, making the score now 22–14 in Wigan's favour. 'Wigan's falling asleep since number twenty-one's gone off,' the commentator added, pushing irony to a new extreme.

For a while it was looking anxious from Wigan's point of view, but a close-range drive from Mark Smith, followed by two further tries from Chris Irwin and Stuart Jones, settled the matter in convincing style.

The clock read five minutes to go when I leapt up from the bench in the hope that McGinty, sitting high up in the stands, would allow me on for the final few minutes, safe in the knowledge that I could not, single-handedly, lose the game for Wigan at this late stage. Nigel Ashley-Jones encouraged me to perform some rather ostentatious warm-up stretches in front of McGinty in an obvious attempt to catch his attention. It worked. Billy confirmed my reappearance over his walkie-talkie radio, and back on I came for the last four minutes.

'The secret weapon's back,' chuckled the commentator, who must have mentioned me more than any other Wigan player by now. 'I gather it's his first experience of rugby league.' I was rather proud of my record so far – in that the team had not conceded any tries when I had been present on the pitch, and had scored two themselves – but this would be marred in the dying seconds when John Braddish went over for St Helens for nothing more than a consolation try.

Later, in the club bar, Gary Connolly was to remark that I had missed the last tackle on the Saints substitute half-back, but on studying the match video both McGinty and I came to the conclusion that by the time I had arrived on the scene Braddish was already in mid-dive. I landed on top of the Saints player and then, seeing that the ball was barely touching the line, attempted to drag it slightly back in the vain hope that the referee would rule that Braddish had failed to reach his mark. It didn't work, and my efforts were rewarded with a hefty shove in the shoulders from a rather irate colleague of the try scorer's. 'You've lost,' I commented, rather bravely, as my attacker was almost out of earshot.

Any chance of some 'afters' was dissipated by the sound of the end-of-game hooter. Wigan – indeed 'we' – had won by the commanding scoreline of 40–20. Everyone shook hands with each other, slapping backs, patting heads and giving each other appreciative nods. I'm not sure if the St Helens players knew of my true identity, because most seemed to treat me like any other of the Wigan players as they acknowledged our victory. I joined my winning colleagues as we applauded the stands in the JJB Stadium packed with home supporters, before making a point of shaking Denis Betts's hand and thanking him for his help during the long, fraught but ultimately rewarding week. 'I still think you're nuts,' Denis commented, with a broad grin.

As I ripped the skull cap from my head the club mascot, Kelvin the Gorilla, ran up to me and draped his large, furry paw over my shoulder. 'Are you the bloke who played for Everton, then?' a voice asked from inside the gorilla suit. 'Did you enjoy that, then?' he followed up. 'What's it like to play for Wigan, then?' came a third question. In a perfect world it would have been nice to have been carried off the JJB pitch high upon the shoulders of Denis Betts and Simon Haughton. Instead, I left in the company of a large gorilla, although we would return for a celebratory team photograph.

'Not great, but not bad,' was Shaun Edwards's summing up afterwards in the bar. 'You did all right, considering,' added Colin Clarke, as he bought me a much-needed pint of lager. 'You didn't look out of place,' was how Phil Clarke put it.

Billy McGinty had promised me a more considered verdict on my fifteen minutes of play the following day, once he had slept on his team's victory. I woke up in the morning with a throbbing pain to the left-hand side of my face and my nose, where I had been hit in the tackle, and my neck felt incredibly stiff, too. Clearly, the effects of my adrenalin rush the previous afternoon had worn off.

I telephoned Billy. 'To be honest we were all worried that you might get yourself seriously hurt,' he admitted. 'And I was also concerned that you might let the team down. You did well to get through the week's training, and you gave it your all in the game. You showed lots of bottle, and you weren't found wanting.' All right so far, I thought. He continued: 'If you were going to take a knock it was when you took the ball up, so I was pleased to see you play the ball. You were hungry for it, and you were prepared to go into the tackles. So, in short, you did your best, and you didn't do anything wrong.'

Well, that was fantastic to hear. I could boast a hundred per cent winning record playing for Wigan, I had emerged largely unscathed, and the coach was paying me compliments.

'If that's the case, what's the chance of me playing for Wigan again, then, coach?' I enquired. 'You may well have an easy Cup game coming up in February against lower league opposition.'

For the first time all week Billy McGinty was lost for words. 'Well, Ian,' he began, before stopping his sentence and rethinking his line.

'Yes?' I asked, with hope now rising in my tone.

'You see, Ian,' Billy said, attempting another slant.

'How about it, then?' I cut in, now filled with anticipation.

Billy probably realised by now that his post-match verdict had perhaps been a little too lenient. 'Let's put it this way, Ian,' he announced. 'Please, don't call us. If we need you, we'll call you. Okay?'

It was a nicer way of putting it than Dean Richards's more forthright verdict at Leicester had been, but it amounted to more or less the same thing. It was, in some respects, a reflection of how the two rugby codes worked. In union, still in a toddler stage of professionalism, every minute counted, and every act in training, especially when it came to the physical side, had to be conducted with maximum intensity. By contrast in league, comfortable with a professional approach that had been developed in the course of a hundred years, contact was for when it really mattered on the field during the game, and training was short, sharp and to the point.

Each method clearly works respectively for Leicester and Wigan, judging by the success both teams have seen in recent years, although neither would adopt each other's way of doing things. The league boys consider Leicester's training injuries and punch-ups to be insane; the union boys would see a forty-five-minute conditioning and skills session as merely a warm-up. There is one element, however, that they do, clearly, agree on. Neither sees Ian Stafford as their next big signing.

chapter five

 ## 'DASH FOR GLORY'

Maybe Wigan should have signed me, after all, for in the first round of the Challenge Cup they drew St Helens. As any Warrior fan or statistician will tell you, Wigan never lose when I'm playing for them, especially to their dreaded rivals Saints, but Wigan chose nevertheless to travel to Knowsley Road without my dubious qualities and promptly got knocked out of the cup. Still, there's always the Super League to win.

By then I had committed myself to another fine mess of Stan Laurel proportions. Despite never having boasted speed as one of my sporting strengths – and it is growing increasingly difficult to find any ingredient to support my claim to be one of this country's wasted sporting geniuses – I had decided to sample British athletics at its cutting edge. In years now past the Brits could boast mastery in middle-distance running or the decathlon, occasionally in long-distance running too, but only in recent times has it been possible for a whole group of our sprinters to be taken seriously at a global level.

Of course the British sprinter Allan Wells did become Olympic champion at the 1980 Moscow Olympics, but with the Americans boycotting the Games over the Soviet Union's invasion of Afghanistan the victory had always seemed a little hollow to me. Linford Christie, by contrast, mastered all before him during the early to mid-1990s, becoming Olympic, World, European and Commonwealth 100 metres champion.

John Regis, to a lesser extent, also shone in the 200 metres, but that was more or less it. That is, until now.

The generation of British sprinters that followed Christie and Regis – many of them motivated by seeing Christie beat all before him in Barcelona and Stuttgart – have now grown into a force that has even the Americans looking hard over their shoulders. Darren Campbell, for example, is the current European 100 metres champion, and took a silver medal in the 200 metres at the 2000 Sydney Olympics. Dwain Chambers won a bronze in the 100 metres at the 1999 World Championships in Seville, and was genuinely disappointed with taking merely fourth place in the Olympic final at Sydney. Jason Gardner – who, like Chambers, is a sub-ten seconds man over 100 metres – became the European indoor 60 metres champion and record holder. Christian Malcolm is the European 200 metres indoor champion and former world junior 100 and 200 metres champion, as well as recording fifth in the Olympic 200 metres final. Mark Lewis-Francis is the current world junior 100 metres champion. And so the list goes on. Julian Golding, Commonwealth 200 metres champion, Marlon Devenish, Allyn Condon. It seems that, after a long wait, our sprinters have all arrived at the same time.

These young men – all of them British, all of them world-class athletes – are together chasing the dream of becoming the fastest on the planet. It was to these high-flyers that I intended to turn, assuming I could find a suitable race to test myself at their level.

This proved to be something of a problem for many months. Perhaps unsurprisingly, it took a while for British athletics to warm to the idea of a pasty-skinned, red-haired bloke in his late thirties chugging along among a world-class field of athletes and in front of a paying crowd. My first efforts to feature in a major athletics meeting failed dismally. I hadn't recorded the necessary qualification time to enter any of the races at the summer's Amateur Athletics Association (AAA) meeting in Birmingham, explained one administrator. If they let me in, the floodgates would open. And, with the best will in the world, I would look rather stupid lining up alongside world and Olympic medallists. The AAA had a point, I suppose.

After many months of unsuccessful lobbying I had one final wild card to play: Alan Pascoe. The former European and Commonwealth 400 metres hurdles champion, Pascoe now headed Fast Track, the commercial arm of UK athletics that provides marketing and sponsorship event promotion, and generally organises the sport. Pascoe, with a good track record in this area following his success with Pascoe-Nally, Alan Pascoe Associates and other similar companies, had taken over the reins of British athletics in 1997 just when the sport was limping its way into obscurity. In debt, and in gloom after the Atlanta Olympics of 1996, the sport had lost its way since the halcyon days of the late 1980s and early 1990s, when a British team featuring the likes of Colin Jackson and Steve Backley, Linford Christie and John Regis, Sally Gunnell, Roger Black, Kriss Akabusi and many other household names took team and individual honours worldwide.

I had long known that Pascoe was a visionary in a sport that, at least until recently, has had a reputation of being bogged down by too much red tape and too many blazer-wearing amateurs. And so it was to Pascoe that I turned, with some desperation.

We met at Pascoe's Sloane Street offices, and it turned out that he already knew of my earlier sporting exploits. This was just as well, as my attempt at a professional presentation floundered when my portfolio of publicity for my first participatory book collapsed, spraying laminates all over his carpet. But it seemed that Pascoe had already made up his mind. 'I'll have to clear a few hurdles first,' he said, presumably unaware of the pun.

Such as what? 'Well, I'm thinking of the Norwich Union Grand Prix at the National Indoor Arena in Birmingham on February 18th,' he explained. 'So, there's the small matter of the sponsors, Norwich Union, the British Athletics Federation and, most of all, the BBC. They'll be covering it live that Sunday afternoon. I have to run past them the notion of you appearing in the 60 metres.'

Norwich Union, the NIA and the BBC would, after all, be promoting world-class athletics, exclusive to nine thousand paying customers at the arena and millions of television viewers. Having to watch me feature in the 60 metres would be like visiting the Louvre and seeing a work painted by Norman, my local decorator. Nevertheless, one week later, Pascoe telephoned me with a positive response.

'We're on,' he announced, unsuccessfully attempting to stifle his laughter. 'You'll be in the line-up for one of the two 60 metres semi-finals in what is the best indoor meeting in world athletics. It'll be a full house at the NIA, and I understand that the BBC will be covering the event live. So, we're talking about two million television viewers as well. That all right with you?'

Oh Lord! For probably the first time since I started out on this long voyage of sporting self-discovery, I felt profoundly unsure. At least with football, rugby and cricket I had played the games to a reasonable amateur level and could always hide behind a combination of my far superior team-mates and my own self-delusion. Here, however, in front of potentially millions of people, I would be exposed.

'That's fantastic news,' I lied.

'Now, a few rules,' Pascoe continued. 'Whatever else you do, don't false start. A couple of years ago we endured six false starts. I don't want to see your false starts causing one of the big name stars to false start as well and end up being disqualified. With respect to you, the public won't be coming to watch you come last.' This was true, I had to admit.

In preparation for my training regime I first called Annette Quarry, at the sportswear company Reebok, on Fast Track's suggestion. To my surprise Annette was greatly supportive and a couple of days later there arrived at my home a huge box full of training shoes and spikes, tracksuits and hats, leggings and pants, and even an all-in-one green and white outfit. 'It's our latest state-of-the-art gear,' Annette explained. Cramming my body into this I realised that a little working out would not go amiss if I really wanted to line up against finely honed athletes and not look completely ridiculous.

At the 'Back on Track' sports injuries clinic in Catford, Sarah Connors, my physio, and Amanda Lee, my masseur, failed miserably to hide their amusement at the prospect of my lining up at Birmingham. For over two years now Sarah had been nursing my battered body back to some semblance of fitness following my various sporting exploits, but this next feat was particularly close to home.

As one of the official GB athletics team's physiotherapists, Sarah had spent part of the previous summer out in Sydney working on our athletes at the Olympics. Indeed, it was Steve Backley, the multi-medal-winning javelin thrower, who had first recommended her to me. I had grown used to seeing some of the country's top athletes visiting Sarah's practice.

Now she and Amanda had the novel experience of preparing 'the old soldier', as they liked to refer to me, for a sprint race of the highest standard. While Amanda gave me a light sports massage, Sarah wrote down some basic training on a piece of paper. Week one would consist of speed endurance work, including sessions of six times 150–300 metres. Week two would concentrate on speed, with six to eight 100 metres races; and week three would focus on acceleration and speed from the blocks.

A serious bout of flu, the kind that sends you to bed for four days with aches, shivers and fevers, then delayed my training for over a week. That left me with just eight days, but I hoped that the general level of fitness I sustained from having played rugby union and league with the Leicester Tigers and the Wigan Warriors respectively would at least provide me with a decent base. I would soon be finding out.

Eight days before D-Day I reported for duty at the New River Stadium in Haringey, North London. Some twelve years earlier I had frequented the same track and worked out with the likes of Daley Thompson, Mike McFarlane, Donovan Reid and Clarence Callender, all in the cause of journalism. Now it was all in the cause of sport, and 'Mac' McFarlane, now one of the best sprint coaches in the country, had agreed to help prepare me for the following Sunday's race in Birmingham.

Among McFarlane's training group were Dwain Chambers and Julian Golding, but they failed to appear that Sunday morning. Tony Jarrett did, however, among a small group of younger athletes, and the man with a large collection of global silver and bronze medals in the sprint hurdles, as well as a Commonwealth gold, couldn't contain himself when I told him of my plans. 'One week's time, hey?' he repeated to me as his grin spread from ear to ear. 'You'd better get some training in, then, boy.'

And so I did, under the barking orders of Mike McFarlane. A two-lap warm-up jog was followed by a series of exercises involving hurdles; these included stretching the legs over the barrier forwards and backwards, then hurdling with one leg at a time, and finally ducking under the hurdles. All the exercises were designed to stretch the muscles in the hips and back – 'the control room', as McFarlane put it, of sprinting.

It was a typically cold and blustery February morning, and much of the conversation centred around warm-weather training. For all, whether it was Joyce Maduaka travelling to South Africa, or the boys going to Irvine, California, it could not come quickly enough. 'If the Olympics were held in Antarctica the Brits would clean up in the athletics,' Jarrett reasoned. He's most probably right, too.

The stretching over the hurdles was followed by some 'plyometrics'. The casual observer would have witnessed a small group of athletes bounding and hopping up a series of stone steps on the far side of the track – like a cluster of newly emerged frogs plus one, heavier toad, clumping his body upwards and downwards. Six triple-jump sprints followed, all in an exaggerated bounding style to accentuate the spring in the strides, before we drove in a small convoy of cars to nearby Alexandra Palace.

'What are we doing?' I asked Mike McFarlane, as we trudged through the park for five minutes before turning a corner and staring up towards the old Palace, which sat at the top of the steep hill in front of us.

'This, my friend, is the hill of death,' he replied, sounding like a trailer for a Hammer Horror film. 'And you're going to sample it.'

In other words, McFarlane's training group – including his latest recruit – would be sprinting up the hill for around 200 metres, with the recovery period being just the time it took us to stagger back down to where we started. The others would have to perform this eight times, in two sections of four sprints. 'You can do two times two,' Mac told me. 'I'm not going easy on you, but if you run it eight times I promise you that you won't be able to walk, let alone sprint, come next Sunday.'

Attempting it four times was certainly hard enough for me, and by my fourth attempt the others were beating me by a good 20 metres. Even they seemed close to death, however, by the completion of the eighth sprint. As casual Sunday morning walkers passed by with their children, Tony Jarrett and company were collapsing on the grass or a bench moaning in pain, the lactic acid inside their legs now burning in response to the intense workout. 'It's fuel in the tank for the summer,' Jarrett kept saying. 'I'll appreciate this come the World Championships. But not right now. Not now.'

As we drove back to the New River Stadium, Mike McFarlane and I talked of days past and present. During the 1980s Mike had been a Commonwealth 100 metres champion and European Indoor 60 metres gold medallist, as well as finishing fifth in the 1984 Olympics 100 metres final (won by Carl Lewis). 'I'd like to think I broke a few ground rules, because there were no black sprinters coming through in London at the time,' he said. 'And my coach, John Isaacs, was the only black coach I'd ever seen. I'd played football first for QPR juniors, but back then the game didn't believe that black guys could cut it, and racism was rife. Things, thankfully, have improved.'

Things have changed in athletics, too. 'I would be awesome now if I was a young sprinter,' Mac continued. 'I wish Mike McFarlane the coach could have had the chance to have trained Mike McFarlane the sprinter. I could have done with the knowledge I have now about attitude and diet, and commitment to training. Now, says McFarlane, he does it for the love of the sport. 'The boys, such as Dwain, Tony and Julian, look after me well, but I've known them since they were schoolkids. It frightens me that they entrust their talent with me, but we've become a family, our training group. If someone bleeds we all bleed. If someone underperforms we all help. And if one of them returns with a medal, then it is a group triumph, and an achievement that spurs everyone else on.'

The next morning another of Jarrett's predictions that my muscles would feel a response to all the stretching was proved correct. It took a telephone call from Andy Kay at Fast Track to haul me out of a hot bath. The ever-helpful Andy had phoned to inform me of two matters: the press conference I was expected to attend the next day in Birmingham, in my capacity as an athlete; and the likely line-up for the 60 metres on the Sunday afternoon at the Norwich Union Grand Prix.

'We're talking about Christian Malcolm, the current European indoor 200 metres champion and former 100 and 200 metres world junior champion,' Andy reported, with a distinct smattering of mirth in his voice, 'Mark Lewis-Francis, the current world junior champion at 100 metres: Jason Livingstone, the former European 60 metres champion; Leonard Myles-Mills, the overall winner of the four indoor sprint race series in Europe last year: Olympic finalist Coby Miller, an American, and his fellow countryman Brian Lewis, an Olympic gold medallist in Sydney with the American sprint relay team. Need I go on?'

So, no pressure there, then. I thought I should contact Linford Christie after this to glean some advice and comfort. I had known Christie for many years – our relationship has had its ups and downs, but today was a good day. He was keen to talk. Christie began with his trademark tip. 'You've gotta go with the "b" of the bang,' he insisted. 'Especially in the 60 metres. Even if it's the "a" you'll be left for dead. But there's a lot to do even before the sound of that gun, believe me.'

Like what, exactly? 'Ensure you have a good stretch, jog a little and sweat a little bit more. Do your drills – high knees, kick backs – and then, when you're out in the middle of the arena, get your measurements right with your starting blocks.'

Christie didn't know this at the time, but he was speaking to someone who had never used starting blocks in his life. As for measuring the distance between the line and the starting blocks to best suit your personal needs, this was all news to me.

'If you don't get those measurements right you'll be like a woodcutter without his tools,' Christie continued, warming to his theme. 'Then practise a few starts just to control your adrenalin. That's going to be difficult, too, because sometimes my heart's been pumping so much before a race I've felt as if I was about to die.'

His next piece of advice was particularly interesting to me. 'You may not end up running like a top sprinter, but there's no reason why you can't at least look like one before the start of the race,' Christie said.

He paused sufficiently long for me to provide the rather obvious retort. 'How, exactly, do I achieve this, then?'

'You've got to walk the walk. Look serious. Watch how the others do it. Sway from side to side, be prepared to eyeball anyone who tries to intimidate you. You can tell a guy who can run under ten seconds in the 100 metres just by their demeanour. Likewise, you can tell if someone's not really a serious player almost instantly. You'll have your work cut out in this department.'

Finally, lest we forget, he moved on to the actual race. 'Stay low and drive, and gravity will gradually pull you up. If you come out too low you'll fall flat on your face, so keep using your arms and your legs will follow. Don't dip at the end but run through the line. If you get anywhere close to eight seconds you will have done well.' There was a pause as Linford burst out laughing – it was not the first and most definitely not the last time a top British athlete would split their sides in front of me that week. Eventually he controlled himself enough to pronounce his shattering conclusion. 'But I wouldn't count on it, Ian. I wouldn't count on it.'

* * *

Tuesday, six days to go, and counting. I drove up the motorway to Birmingham for a midday press conference. Goodness knows how many press conferences I have attended over the years as a working journalist, but I have never found myself as one of the conference subjects. That is, until now.

The World Indoor Championships in Lisbon loomed in early March, and with the AAA's indoor 60 metres champion, John Skeete, having already bagged one of the two GB places, there was just one place up for grabs. The race was billed by Fast Track as a showdown, therefore, between Christian Malcolm and Mark Lewis-Francis, who were both in Birmingham to help promote the Norwich Union Grand Prix.

I told the local press, radio and TV crews that such talk only served to motivate me, that it suited me fine to be written off, and that I was at my most dangerous when not considered a threat. Christian and Mark, who had been given all the background to my participation, were keen to play the game, too.

In fact, they suggested that we should attempt a few starts on the track at the NIA for the benefit of the photographers. On the count of three we sped away, with me claiming a win over 15 metres on account of a blatant false start. 'We've got to watch this fella,' Christian said to Mark. 'He looks hungry, and he looks like a fast starter.'

We ended our mini training stint with three laps of the track, all at jogging pace. Both Malcolm and Lewis-Francis were soon complaining about the distance of 600 metres. 'My lactics are flying,' Christian said at the end, as he lay down on the track and rubbed his legs furiously.

The NIA looked resplendent. The three of us inspected the sprint track, situated inside the oval-shaped 200 metres track with its steep banks at either end. The eight lines of the 60 metres were in alternate light and dark blue stripes, and at the end of the track, high on one of the banks, were padded railings designed to prevent the sprinters from hurting themselves if they failed to apply the brakes in time after the completion of the race. 'It's my home track,' the Wolverhampton-based Lewis-Francis said, with a smile. 'Don't you go taking my place in that GB team, now.'

Both turned out to be interesting and affable characters. Malcolm, from Cardiff, talked of his disappointment at finishing fifth in the Olympic 200 metres final five months earlier. I asked him how he could possibly be upset over such an achievement at such a young age.

'It wasn't the position,' he explained. 'It was the fact that I was the thickness of a vest away from winning a bronze medal. I've thought about it often since, but I think I've reacted in the right way. I'm so hungry now to win senior medals.'

Lewis-Francis – described by double Olympic sprint champion Maurice Greene as 'the most exciting young sprinter I've seen – had his chance to compete at the Sydney Olympics, too. Revealing a wise head on such young shoulders, however, he opted for the World Junior Championships in Chile instead – and promptly won. His ambition was no less than Malcom's, but Mark was not in so much of a hurry.

'I've got time on my hands,' he told me. 'Anything I do at the moment at senior level is a bonus, and all good experience. Even racing against you can only add to my knowledge.'

I assured him that it was unlikely he would glean much from my challenge that Sunday. 'Ah, but you can't say that,' Mark replied. 'I haven't got a clue what you're going to do, nor how you're going to do it.' He gave me a long look before adding: 'I bet you haven't, either, have you?'

We bade each other farewell until the Sunday and left having made one final agreement. Mark agreed to be my pacemaker for the first 20 metres of the final. Christian would then take over for the next 20 metres, with me moving sharply up on to his shoulder. I would then burst away in that final 20 to take the line first. Somehow, come Sunday, I doubted they would stick to their promise.

The next day would prove to be crucial in my development as a world-class sprinter. Not, it has to be said, in terms of my speed so much as just knowing what to do and how to look the part. Malcolm Arnold, the former GB head coach and the man who has trained sprint hurdler Colin Jackson to world titles and records, had invited me to the University of Bath, where he took charge of one of the country's elite groups of athletes.

Jason Gardner had just completed his morning's workout when I arrived, and Alison Curbishley, the 400 metres runner (whom I knew from time I had spent earlier with Sally Gunnell and her husband, Jon Bigg), was sweating in the weights room. Jason seemed a particularly apt person with whom to discuss my forthcoming race, given that he was currently the European Indoors 60 metres champion and record holder with a time of 6.46 seconds. His recovery from a trapped nerve in his lower back meant that this indoor season did not feature in his plans, but his intention was to return to full fitness come the summer. 'Of course, it's really because I didn't fancy coming up against you in Birmingham,' Gardner joked as we sat down in the University café. 'But don't tell the others.'

If his body had been up to it Gardner would quite possibly have been lining up against me that Sunday. The previous season he had remained unbeaten in twelve races. But, I asked him, isn't indoor athletics the poor relation of its outdoor version?

'Not any more,' Gardner insisted. 'At the very least it breaks up the monotony of winter training, and it helps people like myself who like to compete. Any competitor would find it frustrating if they were prevented from competing from October through to May each year. The indoors gives me the chance to test myself against the best in a period of the year otherwise given up purely for training. It's the same for the others, too. After all, you never hear Maurice Greene saying indoors isn't important.'

Another myth is that most sprinters excel at either indoors or outdoors, and rarely both. 'I tell you, most of the guys in the world who can run a sub-ten-second 100 metres race are also very good indoors,'

Jason explained. 'I don't care who you are, even Greene, if you can't run a fast 60 metres, then there's no way you can make up in the last 40 metres of 100. The start may be crucial in the 60, but get a bad one in the 100 too and you've got no chance.'

As for my race Jason's advice was simple, but important. 'Block out everyone and everything,' he said. 'You might find that some of the other athletes try and ruin your attention. Just ignore them. And come the race, don't chase the line. The line will come to you. Keep your shoulders down and stay relaxed, especially if, or rather when, the others pass you and create a gap. Any athlete finds it difficult to accept someone passing them in a race, but you must keep smooth and relaxed.'

Much of it, then, is in the mind? 'It's an incredibly insecure sport. That's one of the many reasons why I'm so glad to have 9.98 seconds next to my name in the 100 metres. It not only tells me that I'm fast, but also tells the guy next to me. For the opposition, having just one digit less against my personal best preys on their mind at the start of a race.'

The conversation might well have continued like this all morning, but Malcolm Arnold came looking for me to start work. After a couple of circuits of the 400 metre track, and then a stretch back inside under the guidance of Alison Curbishley, Malcolm took me back out on to the track again, and to the start line.

'We've got to get the basics right,' he announced, rubbing his chin in a quizzical manner and eyeing me up and down. 'Let's see your starting position.'

Rather self-consciously I went down on all fours and placed my hands alongside the line that denoted the start. 'Move your thumbs across and lean forward so that your shoulders are level with your hands,' Arnold suggested. 'That's the position you need to be in after the starter has announced 'on your marks'.

From this position I had to raise my backside upwards and lean even further forward on the command of 'set' from the official starter. This was extremely uncomfortable when I first tried it out. It felt as if most of my body weight was being pushed down on to my fingers and thumbs, and as I waited for Arnold to shout out 'go' I was praying that he would hurry up. Much more of a wait and my fingers and thumbs would have buckled, making me fall flat on my face.

'Ever seen that happen?' I asked my coach for the day.

'I've seen athletes fall over because their blocks have slipped on impact, but never because someone's fingers have gone,' Malcolm replied. 'Still, there's always a first time for everything, and unless you redistribute your weight when you're down in the set position, you'll be seen making an even bigger idiot of yourself than I expect you to do in any case. Don't worry how long you take at the start of the race, at least within reason. Take your time and make sure you're comfortable before you commit yourself by remaining motionless.'

After these fundamental words of wisdom Malcolm trotted across the track, collected some starting blocks, and placed them down before me. 'Right then,' he announced. 'Let's see you in the blocks.'

I returned to my position on all fours, placing the sole of my right foot in the nearer block and then wedging my left foot in the other part of the block further behind. Malcolm moved both blocks around until we felt they were in the best position for my height and the length of my legs. Producing a tape measure he proceeded to mark out the distances between the starting line and the position of my right and left feet. 'That's 107 centimetres for your left foot, and 70 centimetres for your right foot,' he announced, before writing down both measurements on a scrap of paper. 'Keep these, and don't lose them,' he said. 'You'll be needing them for Sunday. Make sure you measure your blocks in Birmingham. If you can get them to meet these requirements, then your start shouldn't be so bad.'

The first time I attempted a start using the blocks, I managed a quick reaction but a less than explosive first few metres. Indeed, it was more the stagger of a drunken man than a sprint. 'Those first five paces are so crucial to the race,' my coach explained to me. 'Push off with your lead –

right – foot, and then push equally hard with your first step on the track, which is with your left foot. Keep your head down, and concentrate on one step at a time, making each one count.'

Like so many of my earlier participatory sports experiences – whether sculling with Steve Redgrave or throwing a jab at Roy Jones Jr – what appeared to be a relatively straightforward exercise turned out to be a highly technical affair, in which one error amid a host of otherwise correct ingredients could provoke a below-par outcome. Over the course of the next half hour I must have made twenty starts, and almost every one of them had at least one fault that prevented my fulfilling the requirements of the textbook start. Sometimes it would be my backside not being raised high enough in the set position. At other times I would fail to push out sufficiently hard with my lead foot. Then, having got this element right, I would stutter, using absolutely no power, with my left foot in taking my first, real step. Eventually, I produced something close to what Malcolm Arnold was asking for.

'Now that's more like it,' he said, clapping his hands and looking a little less weary. 'There's a danger you're beginning to look like a sprinter,' he added.

I knew that the start and those first few metres were better than before because they felt good – in the way that a golfer knows the ball will find the middle of the fairway by the nature of his swing and connection with the ball. It seemed to me that the only aspect still lacking was a truly explosive attack in those first few metres.

'Oh well, if you care to come down here for, I'd say, the next three years, we might just find that for you,' Arnold replied, when I shared my thoughts. 'That's why athletes train so bloody hard each winter. The power, and the explosion, doesn't come overnight.'

As we made our way back to his office inside the University of Bath sports centre I asked Arnold how he felt I would fare on Sunday. 'Well, let's put it this way,' he replied. 'What's Jason Gardner's European record time? 6.46 seconds, isn't it? I wouldn't have thought you're in much danger of beating that, are you?'

Waiting patiently inside was the Welsh 100 metre hurdler Colin Jackson. He had just driven over from his Cardiff home for some afternoon training and was in characteristically chirpy form, even more so when his coach explained the reasons for the performance he had just witnessed out on the track. I had forgotten the fact that, amid all Jackson's triumphs at the hurdles – world titles and records, European and Commonwealth golds, and a silver and bronze in the Olympics – he had embarrassed the sprinters back in 1994 by becoming the European Indoors 60 metres champion in a highly respectable time of 6.49 seconds. 'Sprinters consider hurdlers to be failed or frustrated sprinters,' he explained. 'The truth is that it's the other way round. Mind you, with a best time of 10.29 seconds in the 100 metres, that makes me the slowest hundred metre runner ever to become the European indoors sixty metres champion.'

Incredibly, Jackson was entering his fifteenth season in senior athletics, and in nearly all of them he had picked up some kind of a medal in a major championship. I asked him to run through his career and medals. It took the best part of a quarter of an hour, from his bronze at the 1987 World Championships to his second world title in 1999. Only the Olympic title had eluded him, although he had been close on a couple of occasions. At the age of thirty-four he had come to terms, quite happily, with the fact that he would never become an Olympic champion.

'It wasn't meant to be,' he said, with a philosophical shrug of his shoulders. 'And there's not a chance of me making it to the 2004 Games in Athens. I'm not complaining, though. I've achieved far more than I ever imagined I would. And now I'm just out to enjoy the sport and make a right nuisance of myself.' Indeed, Jackson seemed to relish the position he was now in: 'I remember when I was in my twenties thinking that there was no way someone in the mid-thirties could beat me. That's why the American, Greg Foster, who was in his mid-thirties, used to piss me off. Now I've reached that age, and I kind of like the notion of being awkward and rewriting the rules. You see, if I can stay fit and healthy this year, then anything's still possible come the World Championships this summer.'

Malcolm, Colin and Jason had all predicted that I would feel the effects of all those starts, and all those strains on parts of my body unused to such taxing exercises. They were right. As Jackson said: 'If you're not sore, then you haven't been doing it correctly.' This was of little consolation the next morning when I woke up feeling like the Tin Man in *The Wizard of Oz*. Just three days to go now, and I could barely move.

Yet this day would represent another important step in my transformation into a sprinter. I spent the morning watching a BBC videotape of the 60 metres in the AAA Championships held in Birmingham a couple of weeks earlier. 'It's all about starting, and all about power,' announced the BBC's athletics commentator, Stuart Storey, as he and I watched John Skeete power himself to a surprise victory. A few weeks later Skeete – despite protesting his innocence and claiming that his cough medicine had been tampered with – was to be stripped of his title and his place in the GB team for the World Championships after a banned substance called stanazolol was found in his urine. At the time, however, he was the very model of peak sprinting performance, seeing off both Christian Malcolm and Jason Livingstone, the former European 60 metres indoors champion.

As he burst out of the blocks Skeete's head remained downwards for a good 25 metres of the race, with his arms and legs pumping furiously like pistons on an engine. In common with everyone else his biceps and quads were bulging from the effort and power put into this exercise, but by 40 metres it was clear that Skeete would win. He appeared to have reached top speed just as he crossed the line, before hurtling into the padded railings up the steep bank on the curve of the 200 metre outside track.

It was now time for me to give my tactics some thought. The way

I saw it I had four options. The first was to false start twice and be disqualified. That would not only prevent the subsequent embarrassment of me trailing in last by some distance but would also provide me with the opportunity of 'doing a Linford'. I had been sitting close to the finish line at the Atlanta Olympics in 1996 when Christie, the defending Olympic champion, was disqualifed after two false starts in the 100 metres final. Even though Canada's Donovan Bailey went on to win gold and break the world record in the process, Linford still managed to steal much of the spotlight by strutting around the stadium, leotard pulled down to his waist, indignant after receiving such treatment. A repeat performance by my good self at the NIA would at least leave the question open: could I have been a contender?

Option two was inspired, I thought, but tricky. It went like this. The first three in each of the two semi-finals would qualify automatically for the final of the 60 metres at the Norwich Union Grand Prix. The two fastest losers would then make up the final eight. As it was highly doubtful I would qualify as either a top three sprinter or a fastest loser, my cunning plan was to twitch on the blocks just enough to provoke a false start from someone else, but not enough to disqualify myself. By my reckoning I had to remove five other sprinters from my semi-final, which meant ten twitches. Somehow, I couldn't imagine pulling this stunt off.

And so on to option three. This was another attempt to copy a former British athlete I had witnessed at an Olympic Games. Derek Redmond was one of our unluckiest athletes throughout the 1990s. Many felt that, amid the likes of Roger Black, Kriss Akabusi, Brian Whittle and other one-lap specialists, Redmond was the most naturally talented of the lot; however, he was also the most injury-prone. At the Barcelona Olympics in 1992 he seized up in agony as he rounded the final bend of a 400 metres semi-final and collapsed to the ground. Although he knew that both his race and his Olympics were over, he staggered to his feet, waved away officials, and was helped by his father to limp and hop to the finish line. Both were in tears, as was half the Olympic Stadium, but Redmond's determination to finish his race became one of the most memorable images of those Games. So, after 20 metres of the 60 metres semi-final, I would clutch my leg in obvious pain and fall to the floor. Raising myself back to my feet, with all the unsteadiness of a new born giraffe, I would somehow, bravely and heroically, crawl my way to the finish line. Sure, I would finish last by a long, long way, but the nine thousand-strong crowd would have witnessed one of the most emotional sporting scenes of the year.

Then again, my questionable acting skills might not be convincing enough – and instead of a standing ovation my efforts might be met with the sound of thousands of athletics fans jeering. Maybe this was not such a good idea after all.

And so I was left with my final option, which was just to run the damned race. This, clearly, was the least attractive plan of the four, but the one, nevertheless, which I knew I could carry out. So that was that. I would be running my race, and I would finish it.

That decided, the next aspect to attend to was my demeanour at the start. I had taken on board Linford's advice about at least talking the talk – even if I then failed to walk the walk – but should I be myself, or copy someone else? There were, again, various options. I could reproduce the Christie stare, the one in which his eyes seem to be on the verge of popping out of their sockets as he stands, motionless, on the starting line, apparently oblivious to everything that is going on around him. Alternatively, I could adopt the Dennis Mitchell 'mad minute', in which the American sprinter goes absolutely bananas on the line, jumping up and down, punching the air and slapping his own face over and over again. Or perhaps the Maurice Greene prowl could do the trick? Greene, the main man of sprinting right now, paces up and down his lane and around the general starting area, lolling his tongue and looking like a leopard sizing up a herd of gazelle before pouncing. Darren Campbell kisses his crucifix and crosses himself before slotting into his blocks. Colin Jackson stretches out way beyond the start line before walking back on his hands. And so on.

Eventually, I decided to aim for the 'complete sprinter' look. I would begin with the Linford stare, just to intimidate the others. Then I would produce the Greene tongue. Finally I would mimic the Jackson contortion as I made myself comfortable on the blocks. Three world champions, blended into one dream athlete – me.

I mentioned all this to John Regis when I paid him a visit that afternoon at his new offices in London's West End. Regis had just become head of Stellar Athletics, a new arm of Stellar Management which was run by an old friend of mine, Jonathan Barnett. By now all hell had broken loose in the world of British athletics, and most of it was centred around Linford Christie.

First Sebastian Coe, who needs no introduction, wrote a damning article in the *Daily Telegraph*, accusing Christie of being a poor team man when he was running and an even worse role model for the young wannabe athletes of today. Predictably, Linford hit back later in the week at Coe.

Meanwhile, three of Christie's high-profile clients at the former sprinter's 'Nuff Respect' management company, had announced that they were jumping ship and joining Regis at Stellar. Suddenly Dwain Chambers, Julian Golding and Tony Jarrett found themselves in a tug-of-war between two of the most high profile sportsmen of the early and mid-1990s.

No wonder John was pleased to talk about athletics, and in particular, my forthcoming sprint challenge. As a co-commentator at the BBC, and a man who would be sitting in the broadcast area at the NIA on Sunday right above the finish line of the 60 metres track, he was also keen to be filled in on what this was all about.

'Drive low, chop your stride and pump your arms and knees like there's no tomorrow,' John advised. 'And remember, the guy who stays within his own game plan will win. That means you must not panic, even when your game plan is under pressure. You'll find it difficult, though. Before the race, when you're down below in the warm-up area counting the minutes, you'll feel nerves like never before. It's how you handle them that will go a long way to deciding how you fare.'

I had known John for many years now, and had even massaged his legs once – in Irvine, California, when he collapsed to the ground, consumed by the burning sensation of lactic acid after a series of 300 metre sprints. Despite his recent retirement, and his failure to have ever claimed a global individual title, I had never seen the man more content.

'It's because I've finally got athletics out of my system,' he explained. 'I had planned to compete in last summer's outdoors AAA Championships in the hope that I had recovered from injury sufficiently to qualify for the Olympics. But the week before, in Budapest, I ran 21.65 seconds in a 200 metres race, and as I crossed the line I realised that was it. I imagined that coming to the AAAs as a spectator and commentator would be the hardest day of my life, but it was one of the best.'

Why was that? 'Because I felt no pressure on me at all,' Regis replied. 'You forget how much pressure there is hanging on you to produce your best, to qualify for major championships, and then to win medals. You take a close look at sprinters as they're lining up. Never mind the facade, look into the whites of their eyes. They're scared, I can promise you, because I've been there many times myself.'

Regis, like Jackson, has acquired a large haul of medals over the years, including a world gold in the 400 metres relay and in the world indoors 200 metres, plus Olympic relay silvers and a world individual silver, as well as European and Commonwealth golds. 'It's far more than I ever expected,' he explained – despite the lack of a world outdoor individual title. 'I remember when I started out in 1985. I said to myself: "If I ever win a medal in a major championships I'll be happy." My goal was to enjoy the experience of standing on a rostrum.'

So, no regrets, then? 'Only one,' he replied. 'The 1992 Olympic 200 metres final in Barcelona. For some crazy reason I decided to re-focus on my race as I was getting down into the starting position. In fact,

I was concentrating so hard on what I was intending to do, I only half-heard the starter's instructions. My ultimate time was far worse than my semi-final performance, and the fault lay with myself. Apart from that, I'm happy with what I've achieved, and happy to accept that now my natural, God-given ability has gone.'

That night I returned to the New River Stadium in Haringey to train once more with Mike McFarlane's group. Dwain Chambers and Julian Golding had this time turned up and, already acquainted with me from the 'Back on Track' sports clinic, seemed keen to help in any way they could.

After jogging a couple of times around the track with Patrick Stevens, the top Belgian sprinter, we returned to the warmth of the changing room and a stretching session on the floor and benches. This was a cold February night, and to make matters worse a dank, freezing fog was beginning to descend on us. We all wore bobble hats and kept on our running coats and tracksuit bottoms, our breath emerging as streams of condensation in the chill of the night. 'It's cold, and I'm getting cramps, but when you're standing on a podium receiving a medal, nights like these are worth it,' Dwain said, as he rubbed his legs following a particularly taxing 300 metre sprint. He, Golding, Jarrett and the others were performing a series of 200 and 300 metre runs, working on their stamina and endurance. McFarlane, thankfully, had other designs for me.

First, though, I had to throw off my trainers and replace them with spikes. I was a little concerned about this. The last time I had worn spikes was when I was training in Kenya with the country's long- and middle-distance runners prior to racing in a 3,000 metres steeplechase in Kapsabet. They pulled so hard on my already well-worn calf muscles that I decided to discard them for my dependable pumps. This time, however, I had no option. No sprinter, and certainly not one featuring in the semi-final of the Norwich Union Grand Prix at the National Indoor Arena, would be seen dead in simple trainers. So I would have to get used to them.

My remit that night was to sprint in short bursts, a move encouraged to improve my starts and my initial impact in the race. On McFarlane's shout I would produce a fast jog for 20 metres, and then a flat-out sprint for a further 50 or 60. It was a little unnerving performing this in front of some of the world's top athletes, but I realised it was nothing compared to what was to happen three days later.

Invariably, I would fail to produce one, crucial ingredient in the sprinting recipe. For example, I would be concentrating so much on my running that, unwittingly, I would be holding my breath. 'Breathe, breathe,' McFarlane would shout. 'Have you ever seen a sprinter not breathe in a race?' Next I would be gulping large mouthfuls of oxygen as I burst down the track, looking more like a goldfish than a runner, but failing to pump my arms with any kind of conviction. 'Pump those arms,' came the instruction. 'And those knees.' Finally I managed a 60 metre sprint that more or less resembled one completed by an athlete. 'Good, good,' a calmer McFarlane said. 'Run like that on Sunday and you won't let yourself down.'

Dwain Chambers was already inside, his night's work finished, when I joined him following my sprints. My right calf, the same muscle that had troubled me throughout most of my other sports, felt tight again after being subjected to my spikes, and my quads and hamstrings also pulled. Compared to Dwain, though, I looked in good shape. Dwain was prostrate on the floor, breathing heavily and rubbing his cramp and lactic acid reaction to what he termed a 'sadistic' training session.

Back out on the track the conversation turned to Maurice Greene, the man Chambers, Gardner, Campbell et al have set their sights on. Dwain recounted an interesting story about him during the Olympics.

'It was just before the 100 metres final,' he recalled. 'The thing about Maurice is that you're not supposed to look at him before a race. You see, people try and figure out his running and, don't get me wrong, he is a great runner. But it's not his strides, his power nor his strength that win him races. The truth is that most of us in that final possessed equal, physical attributes. With Maurice it's mental. He appears cool in warm-up, but he's very focused on the track. Most people make the mistake of looking at him and then crumbling.'

He continued: 'It is my belief, though, that I'm one of a very select few sprinters whom Greene reckons can beat him. We were below the track in the Olympic stadium in Sydney waiting to emerge for the final, and I found myself sitting directly opposite Maurice staring right at him. This turned into some kind of an eyeball match, but I refused to relent. Eventually, Maurice rose to his feet and walked away. I saw that as a significant message.'

It did not work out that way come the final, however. Greene confirmed his pre-race status as favourite by becoming the Olympic champion, and Dwain had to make do with fourth, having won a bronze in the World Championships the previous year. 'I learnt a valuable lesson that day,' Dwain explained. 'Instead of running my own race, I ran Greene's. There was a lack of focus on my part when it came to my race and, as a result, it became an uphill struggle for me. The year before, at the Worlds, I was relaxed and won a bronze medal. A year later, when I had developed into a better athlete, my mental weakness on the day cost me a podium place. I'll never make that mistake again.'

I was going to ask him about my tactics for Sunday's 60 metres, but before I could do so Dwain had moved seamlessly from his experiences to my forthcoming one. 'There's a link between what happened to me in the Olympic final and what will probably happen to you in Birmingham,' he said.

'There is?' I asked, somewhat surprised by the proposed similarity between Dwain Chambers, the current European number one at 100 metres, and Ian Stafford, who is just about ranked top in his own household.

'Yes, there is. You've got to run your own race, and not worry about the others. I was concerned about Maurice Greene and it cost me an Olympic medal. You will be affected by the speed that the others leave their blocks on Sunday and by the way in which they run away from you. You must try and look ahead always, and never sideways. It's a difficult thing to master, even for an experienced athlete, but as soon as you see others leaving you behind you panic and tighten up. Sprinters who try harder to run fast end up losing their smoothness, which kills their speed.'

As I drove home that night my mind was full, perhaps too full, of advice. But no one could question the quality of my advisers, and if I remembered even half of it I would be doing well. For the time being, however, I had been instructed by Mike McFarlane and the boys to rest. 'You're going to need all your energy in Birmingham,' Mike had insisted.

I settled for a gentle workout in the gym the following day, and then a trip to the physio for some treatment on my calf and quad muscles. The BBC's Mark Butler had left a message for me to contact him when I returned home. Butler is the man who provides the athletics commentators with all the background information concerning the athletes. Beside Christian Malcolm's name, for example, Butler would write: 'Former world junior 100 and 200 metre champion; current European Indoor 200 metres champion; fifth in the 200 metres final at the Sydney Olympics; aged 21, from Cardiff.'

He had never needed to write up someone like me before. So, for example, when he asked what my personal best time was for the 60 metres, the answer he received was: 'I haven't a clue. I've never timed myself before.' Indeed this was true. I suppose this could have been rectified during the week that had just passed, but I considered that recording a slow 60 metres time would have been damaging, psychologically. Much better, I reasoned, to enter the race in the naive belief that I might surprise someone. Still, after twenty minutes on the telephone, Butler had enough information to provide the likes of Stuart Storey, Steve Cram and John Regis with what they needed in the commentary box.

Another call followed; this time it was Fast Track's Ian Hodge. He had drawn up the two line-ups for the semi-finals at the Norwich Union Grand Prix, and was calling me to share the good news.

'You're in the second heat,' he informed me. 'This is at 2.38 pm. And you're in lane eight.'

I protested at this. 'I'd stand a much better chance in lane four or five,' I reasoned.

'No, you wouldn't,' Hodge replied. 'Anyway, here's the line-up. Lane one: Kevin Williams. Lane two: Jason Livingstone. Lane three: Coby Miller. Lane four: Gregg Saddler. Lane five: Chris Williams. Lane six: Mark Lewis-Francis. Lane seven: Tim Benjamin. Lane eight: Ian Stafford. Okay?'

Well, not really, no. This was, by anyone's standards, a world-class line-up. Williams, from Cardiff, is a former European indoor finalist. Livingstone, of course, is a former European indoor champion. The American, Miller, had made the Olympic 200 metres final, while his fellow countryman Saddler was no slouch either. Williams, from Jamaica, is an Olympic bronze medallist in the 400 metres relay, and Benjamin, just inside me, is the world under-18 200 metres champion. And then we had Mark Lewis-Francis, the guy who had agreed to be my pacemaker if we both made it to the final. It seemed to me that the other seven sprinters in my race were all capable of running close to 6.5 seconds. Still, I had the element of surprise at my disposal. After all, nobody in that race had a clue what time I was capable of producing, least of all me.

After a restful Saturday, but a restless Saturday night, I drove back up the motorway to Birmingham on the Sunday morning, having made sure my sports bag was packed with spikes and tracksuits, water, socks and my skin-tight all-in-one. Approaching the city centre I noticed numerous banners advertising the day's athletics meeting: 'The Norwich Union Grand Prix', it read. 'World-class athletics'. That statement, I knew, was not wholly true.

The first port of call was the athletes' hotel. The foyer of the Crowne

Plaza in the city centre was teeming with athletes from all over the world, checking the start-time lists and shuttle bus times pinned to a Norwich Union Grand Prix noticeboard, or swiping the bananas, bottles of water and isotonic drinks that were available on a nearby table. Ian Stewart was there, too, the former Scottish Commonwealth 5,000 metres champion who was now responsible for organising all the athletes for the meet.

I had come here to collect my accreditation, but was told instead to pick it up from the stage door of the National Indoor Arena.

Inside the NIA the auditorium was empty, save for some officials and television technicians. There were still nearly two hours to go before the start of the afternoon's action, but Mark Lewis-Francis turned up with his cousin to check out the track. 'I'm up for it today,' he told me. 'I really am.'

'So am I,' I replied. It was a comment that failed to work in the intimidation department.

Mark accompanied me down to the warm-up area directly below the track, a large, sports hall that resembled a school gym. Beside a table athletes queued to receive their numbers. I was designated No. 43, and when it was my turn to report to the officials I was presented with two number 43s and eight safety pins, to fix the numbers on to the front and back of my all-in-one.

In the sports hall could be seen some of Britain's finest athletes, all looking a little tense and all running through their own warm-up routines. Jonathan Edwards, the Olympic triple-jump champion, was there, walking round and round the hall alone with his thoughts. So, too, was Katherine Merry, the bronze medallist in the women's 400 metres at Sydney behind Cathy Freeman. Katherine's manner was more relaxed. She seemed calm and confident, and would later post the fastest indoor 400 metres of the season. Du'Aine Ladejo was there, too, the former European 400 metres champion. The past few years had not been kind to a man who had dithered over what should be his best event, even to the extent of experimenting with the decathlon. We exchanged pleasantries, and continued with our stretching.

A small group of Kenyans arrived, including Daniel Komen, the former multi world record-holder, with whom I had trained in Kenya a couple of years ago. They stuck together, jogging around the hall. Jason Livingstone, all fire and brimstone, glowered as he strutted up and down the centre of the hall, honouring me with a nod and a 'Whassup?' Somewhere else in the hall a mobile telephone rang out the theme tune to 'Mission Impossible'. Under the circumstances, it seemed rather apt.

Fully stretched, and with my numbers pinned to the front and back of my all-in-one, I practised a few starts myself, and then a few more sprints, creating a slight sweat without tiring myself out. I then sat down to flick through the programme on sale to the public. My name really was there in the line-up, alongside number 43 and the letters, GBR. There was also a list of the prize monies. Should I win the final, for example, I would be awarded 5,000 euros. Second place earned 3,500 euros, third 2,500 euros, and so on, right down to sixth, which commanded 500 euros. Birmingham was the second indoor meet out of four (the others being Stockholm, Gent and Liévin) that made up the Energizer Euroseries Meetings. The overall 60 metres champion, a verdict taken from a sprinter's three best results out of the four meetings, would return home with 20,000 euros in their pocket, on top of whatever funds he might have won in the individual races. I did check to see if finishing eighth in a semi-final resulted in a token prize, but realised this was wishful thinking.

Not long before we were due to be called up Christian Malcolm arrived, his demeanour serene and relaxed. Seeing me he ambled over and shook my hand. 'You've been drinking plenty of water, right?' he said, sounding like a concerned parent. 'And some isotonic drink, too? Make sure your muscles are stretched and warm.'

During the warm-up period I was forced to make my customary five visits to the toilet. I found that I was not alone. In and out the others followed suit, all trying but failing to disguise their anxiety. The minutes seemed like hours as we waited for the countdown to begin. 'It's the waiting that gets you,' Malcolm said, when he saw me staring at the clock on the wall. 'That's why I arrived here no earlier than I had to.' On my final visit to the lavatory I took off my t-shirt and tracksuit bottoms, and stepped gingerly into my all-in-one. 'Could be worse,' I thought, staring at the apparition in the mirror. Then I compared myself to some of the other sprinters who were also changing into their costumes. 'Could be a lot better, too,' I concluded.

The eerie silence in the hall was shattered by a tannoy announcement calling up the first-heat semi-finalists. 'See you in the final,' Malcolm said as he walked out of the hall and towards the athletics track. Shortly afterwards it was our turn. Mark Lewis-Francis, still keeping a watchful eye over the sprinter in lane eight, just prevented me from leaving the hall before confirming my existence to the organisers. Without a tick next to my name I might well have been disqualified before even reaching my blocks.

It was at this point that I remembered Linford Christie's advice about talking the talk and strutting my strut. All eight second-heat semi-finalists piled into an elevator to take us up to the entrance to the track. All I could do was attempt to act like an athlete, which meant looking unconcerned and confident. Occasionally, in the corner of my eye, I could see some of the others staring at me. God only knows what they were thinking. 'Well, he sure doesn't look like one of us,' was the likeliest verdict. In time-honoured fashion, however, not a word was spoken in the lift.

Assembling beside the corner of the track, but hidden from the spectators, we sat down on a bench and dumped our sports bags into crates placed beside us by a group of teenage boys designated to look after us. One of them will have returned to school the following morning with the boast that he looked after the world junior champion. Another will have to say he was in charge of me. Our names were taken again, just to ensure that the eight semi-finalists who should have been racing had turned up.

Mark Lewis-Francis caused a minor flutter in the organiser's hearts when he arrived late. 'Sorry,' he said, looking a mite bashful. 'Been in the toilet.'

We watched the first semi-final on the big screen hanging on one side of the arena wall. Nigeria's Deji Aliu won, with Christian Malcolm second and Ghana's Leonard Myles-Mills third. No sooner had they crashed into the barriers at the far end of the track and sauntered off than we were summoned to appear before the crowd, now packing the NIA to the rafters. There were a number of people I knew personally in the crowd that afternoon, not only from the world of athletics but also from other sports, or socially. There were many more at home watching all this on their television sets, who no doubt would soon be creased up with laughter on their sofas after a good Sunday roast. Somehow, I managed to cut this out of my mind and concentrate on the job in hand.

Having arrived at lane eight my first, all-important action was to measure the distance between the starting line and the blocks. I noticed that all the other semi-finalists produced rather fancy-looking metal tape measures, with automatic spring reactions. By contrast, the only tape measure I could find in the house the previous day had been one that had fallen out of a Christmas cracker. It was this I used at the NIA.

Having marked out my measurements, I rose to my feet, pulled off my tracksuit bottoms, then my top, and finally revealed my body to the world. I glimpsed Roger Black giving me the thumbs-up from his BBC TV pundit's position high above the start of the track. Roger, judging by his expression, seemed to be looking forward to this race in particular. Looking further across I could see John Regis sitting in the commentary box as well, wearing a wide grin.

It was time, as they say, to focus. After a couple of practice starts I lined up in my lane and stood, waiting to be introduced. Jon Ridgeon, the former sprint hurdler and world silver medallist, now working for Fast Track, was making the announcements from the arena floor. Stuart Storey was doing likewise for BBC Television.

Slowly a BBC TV camera spanned the line-up, pausing at each lane while the athlete was introduced. Eventually it came to me. As I attempted my complete athlete routine – the stare, the tongue movement, the contortion – Ridgeon explained to the crowd what this was all about. He concluded his introduction by stating: 'He's very brave to come out here and do this.' It was a nice thing to say, but something I hardly needed reminding of at the time. Meanwhile, as I discovered later when I watched the event on tape, Storey was making a similar point on television. 'I just wonder what thoughts are going through his mind,' he said, as the camera panned on to a figure crammed into a green all-in-one. 'He's practised hard, but it will still be a shock to him when the gun goes. Whether he false starts, or whether he'll get more experience than that, we'll just have to wait and see.' At this point, as Ridgeon announced my name, I waved limply to the crowd, rather self-consciously. I realised that there was no turning back from a situation I had wholly created but which had an inevitable outcome.

'Now that,' added Storey, 'was a nervous, a very nervous, look.'

Too right it was. Forrest Gump had come to Birmingham. Walter Mitty was in lane eight. This, surely, wasn't for real.

It was. 'On your marks,' the announcer shouted from right across the track close to lane one. I was determined to take my time over this, so I nestled my feet into the blocks, placed my fingers and thumbs gingerly on to the starting line, and wriggled my now crouched body from side to side until I felt completely at ease. Staring ahead at the light blue line of 60 metres that lay before me, I noticed in the corner of my eye that I was by no means the last to settle. Down there, resting myself on the track, 60 metres suddenly seemed like a fair old distance to me.

'Set,' the starter shouted. Lifting myself off my knees and on to my haunches, my fingers and thumbs felt far better thanks to Malcolm Arnold's advice concerning weight distribution. Even so, it seemed like a dreadfully long wait before I heard the sound of a gun.

'BANG!' We were off. I say we, because as the race began I felt as if

I'd made a quick start. It reminded me of Jason Gardner's assertion that a multitude of thoughts flash through your mind in the time it takes to cover just a handful of metres. This belief lasted a split second, the time it took the rest of the field to move away from me. This, for all the pre-race warnings, stunned me. I genuinely believed that I was running fast in those first 20 metres, but in that distance the seven others had left me for dead. I felt like a Hillman Imp that has the temerity to take on a Ferrari at some traffic lights, with similarly predictable results.

As a consequence I fell into the trap that others, notably Dwain Chambers, had warned me about. I couldn't help but glance across in desperation as I saw the other seven disappear ahead of me. Indeed, when reviewing the run later that night on television, I disappeared from the TV screen around the 40 metre mark, lagging behind while the seven others fought for supremacy.

What made matters worse was that I tried even harder to run faster, which was the second mistake Dwain and Jason had predicted I would make. Instead of running my own race I lost what ever looseness I possessed and tightened up horribly as I attempted to squeeze more speed out of my body. My legs seemed to be moving quickly, but my fellow semi-finalists appeared to be using their legs at twice the speed, as if someone had pressed the fast-forward button on the other seven, leaving me at normal speed.

As the seven crossed the finish line with less than two-tenths of a second between them, I had just passed the 40 metres mark. At least in this instance my humiliation would not last long. There was no case of two laps by myself here, or the even worse scenario of being lapped by everyone else in the race. It was just the small matter of 20 metres, just a couple of seconds more. As I crossed the line I produced what looked later to be an exaggerated dip. To this day I do not know why I did this. If I was hoping it might just push me up into seventh place, then I would have needed to have made up 20 metres – which would have taken some doing, or some neck.

The second rather embarrassing fact about the finish is that while the seven others hurtled up the steep bank to crash into the padded barriers on the outside of the 200 metres track, I did not possess enough speed to make it to the barriers. Aware of this I did something that I expect no athlete has ever done before, nor will do again. I continued running at the same speed once I had crossed over the finish line just so that I could be seen to be hitting that padded barrier hard.

As a host of girls handed each of us an isotonic drink, the results flashed up on the large screen that hung from one end of the arena. Coby Miller won the semi-final with a highly acceptable time of 6.66 seconds. Mark Lewis-Francis was second, and Gregg Saddler third. As this was marginally the slower of the two semi-finals, the top three from the first semi, plus the fourth- and fifth-placed sprinters from that race, would qualify for the final, together with Miller, Lewis-Francis and Saddler. Interestingly, there was then a lull in the results. The time for lane eight was yet to be revealed to the sell-out crowd. After what seemed like an interminable wait, the time of 9.14 seconds came up next to my name.

9.14 seconds. That was a second slower than I thought I could run. I put this down to my reaction on seeing the seven others leave me for dead so early into the race. My gloom soon lifted, however, when I heard a voice shouting from the crowd. 'Ian, Ian,' someone was yelling. I scanned the rows and rows of people in front of me before seeing Linford Christie standing up, his face beaming and his hands clapping. 'You're the man,' he shouted, 'You're the man.' Yeah, and that's not all. I was only 2.31 seconds behind the rest of the field!

As all this was going on the big screen began to show the whole race again, honing in on lane eight. We were all therefore subjected to the sight of No. 43, this time running in slow motion, completing the 60 metres. There must have been a good few in the crowd who failed to realise that this run was, in fact, being repeated in slow motion.

Stuart Storey's summing up on television said it all. 'A man lacking power, in fact lacking in most things as far as sprinting's concerned,' he said. 'But he's really working hard. The rest have finished way before him, but it's an experience and a half for him.'

Roger Black called me 'crazy' when asked for his thoughts by Sue Barker; and John Regis made the valid point that the promotion I sought by my end of race dip 'was not to be'.

Meanwhile, back on the trackside, Mark Lewis-Francis was the first to approach me. Smiling, he threw his arms around me and said, simply: 'Well done, and thanks for not beating me.' I told him it was a pleasure.

The post-race shenanigans were not quite over. Christine Boxer, the former middle-distance runner turned BBC track-side interviewer, now wanted a live chat. Among various questions she asked me if I was satisfied with my run. I pointed out that I had just produced my personal best for the 60 metres, and any athlete in a major meeting cannot ask for much more than that. The fact that this had also been my first ever timed 60 metres race was glossed over.

The ensuing final was won by Coby Miller, in the lightning-quick time of 6.55 seconds. I consoled myself with the fact that I had been beaten in my semi-final by the eventual winner. Leonard Myles-Mills finished second, with Deji Aliu third. Mark Lewis-Francis finished fifth, with Christian Malcolm two hundredths of a second behind, in sixth. Christian's afternoon would later improve immeasurably when he not only won the 200 metres final but also recorded the fastest time at that distance indoors in the world.

As I sat and watched all this from high up in the NIA's seating area, I concluded that in this particular sporting challenge, my limitations had been exposed even more than elsewhere. Moreover, my below-par performance had been observed by three million television viewers – as I found out later – as well as a capacity crowd at the National Indoor Arena.

To my surprise, however, I seemed to be the only person embarrassed by the experience. Athlete after athlete made a point of congratulating me afterwards. 'Now you have an idea what we have to go through,' Dwain Chambers said, shaking my hand and his head at the same time. 'I don't blame you for being distracted by the others. It's one of the hardest things to avoid in a race.'

And then my deflated ego received a sudden and unexpected burst of air. An official handed me a piece of paper with the reaction times of the second semi-final. This refers to the period of time taken between the gun sounding off and the feet leaving the blocks. Incredibly, I was fourth fastest in my race – ahead of the winner, Coby Miller, and the former European champion Jason Livingstone, among others. Moreover, I even beat Christian Malcolm's reaction time in the final. 'I'll have to work with you on my starts,' Christian said, when he saw the evidence thrust into his hand.

The words 'straws' and 'clutching' may come to mind here, but I left Birmingham that night thoroughly contented with the undeniable fact that over two or three metres I was a proven, world-class sprinter.

It is just the remaining 57 metres that need working on.

Backstage at the N.I.A. with Jason Livingstone

The 60 metres line-up

On your marks...

'...Go'

Congratulations and
commiserations with
Mark Lewis-Francis

Post-race
interview for
BBC's
'Grandstand'

Padded up and ready to bat for Yorkshire

Not out!

Looking for runs

On the offensive

The lonely walk back to the pavilion

A difficult

chance...

... goes begging

The victorious

Yorkshire team

Luciano Burti leads me on the karting circuit

With my driving instructor – a certain Jackie Stewart

Post-run rest aboard Eddie Irvine's yacht with fitness trainer Nick Harris (left) in Italy

On the grid

Irvine
snatches the

chapter six

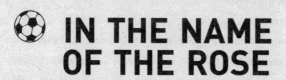

IN THE NAME OF THE ROSE

Within days of the indoor athletics season ending, the country's cricketers (other than those involved in England's Test series against Sri Lanka) were preparing for their traditional pre-season tours. This was the chance for players from many of the eighteen first-class counties to escape to sunnier climes, to play top-quality cricket in readiness for the start of the new season in April, and to build up team spirit and camaraderie before the long and arduous summer that lay ahead.

Yorkshire were about to leave for a two-week tour of South Africa when I contacted them with a suggestion that I could join their ranks and bolster their middle order. I had chosen the White Rose county above all others because of their tradition, their successful past, their array of legendary former players and the fact that at their Leeds-based Test venue, Headingley, they enjoyed better support from the cricket-crazed locals than just about any other team in the country.

Steve Oldham, Yorkshire's cricket development manager and a former player for the county, returned my call with a suggestion that I should speak to David Byas the county's long-serving captain. 'If it's okay with Dave, then it's okay with us,' he pronounced.

I followed his advice and sent a long explanatory fax to Byas at his farm in Driffield, an hour's drive from Leeds. I made much of the fact that I used to keep wicket at school, and explained my earlier sports participatory experiences. Later that week, having run my proposal past Yorkshire chief executive Chris Hassell, he made contact. 'Come and join us for a week in South Africa,' he said. 'You can train for most of the week, and then play in a one-day match we have fixed up against Boland. That okay with you?'

It most certainly was. I had just been given the go-ahead to make my debut for a county that in the past has featured such names as Hutton and Sutcliffe, Boycott and Close, Trueman and Illingworth, and even Dickie Bird, and in the present boasts England regulars Darren Gough, Michael Vaughan and Craig White. We agreed it would be a good idea to meet up at Headingley just before leaving for South Africa, in order for me to train for a day and to introduce myself to the rest of the team.

I duly arrived at the indoor cricket school, just across the road from the cricket ground, two days before the squad was set to leave for Pretoria. The indoor school seemed fairly dilapidated but managed to serve its main purpose, with a number of nets, a bowling machine and an area large enough to practise fielding and throwing.

As I had no idea what David Byas looked like, I asked one of the young lads waiting to start the day's work. 'You can't mistake him,' he told me. 'Dave's tall and old.' Sure enough, there in the dressing room was Byas, tall and – by the lad's standards but not, unfortunately, by mine – old. In fact, the old man was merely a month older than me.

'Welcome aboard,' Byas said, before introducing me to Gavin Hamilton, the former England and Scotland international player, who had just dumped his bags in the dressing room. Chris Silverwood and Richard Blakey, both former Test players as well, ambled over to introduce themselves; it transpired that they had in fact been to a launch party I had held for one of my earlier books in London. ('We were playing Surrey at The Oval and Adam Hollioake, the Surrey captain, brought us along,' Blakey explained.) Then Byas introduced me to the rest of the squad and suggested we began the day's training.

After a few laps jogging around the nets Byas remembered how I had mentioned my schoolboy wicket-keeping experiences. Throwing me some gloves he told me to stand behind him as, at great speed, he edged balls at me and at one of the three slip-fielders who had joined me for practice, Almost every opportunity that came to me was put down – I found it difficult to adjust to the dim light and the speeding ball, and, moreover, the last time I had kept wicket was some nineteen years ago.

Things picked up, however, when we began fielding practice. We first had to collect a moving yellow rubber ball and take a shy at a wicket; then Blakey allowed me to take turns with him standing behind the wicket as various batsmen fended off some of the county's spin bowlers. Simon Guy – Yorkshire's number two wicketkeeper, who intended to give Blakey a good run for his money this season – lent me his inners and his keeper's gloves, as well as his pads. 'You got a mouthguard?' he asked. It was something that had not crossed my mind before, even though I possessed one from my rugby-playing experiences with Leicester and Wigan. 'I always wear one these days,' he insisted. 'I just got fed up with constantly getting smacked in the mouth.'

Finally, once everyone else had had a go, it was my turn to bat. Gary Ramsden, a young and promising fast bowler, lent me his bat, gloves, pads, thigh pad and elbow guard: by the time I was ready to waddle down the pitch to face the bowling machine, I resembled a modern day knight-in-armour. My innings began disastrously. The bowling machine had been turned up to top speed and it duly clean bowled me with its first two balls. I consoled myself with the fact that it was at least a year since I had last wielded a cricket bat – perhaps I was just out of practice. Eventually my bat began to make contact with the ball, although the various expert onlookers still had plenty to say about my technique.

'You're crouching too much,' said Arnie Sidebottom, the former Yorkshire and England fast bowler. 'Stand up a little straighter so that your head's over the ball.' Byas chipped in, too. 'You're moving your front foot before your body, when it has to be the other way round,' he explained. 'That way you won't lose your balance.' It was a little unnerving to find a technique that had served me perfectly well at school and in local village cricket matches being taken apart, but I had to remind myself that it was not every day I would be playing for one of the top first-class counties.

Over lunch Byas and Sidebottom outlined the squad's final preparations for the trip to South Africa.

Chris Silverwood and Ryan Sidebottom – Arnie's son – would not be coming, having just returned from the England 'A' tour to the West Indies; while Gough, Vaughan, White and Matthew Hoggard were still in Sri Lanka with England. In all, sixteen players would be flying to Johannesburg and then driving on to Pretoria, where I was to join them two days later. Byas also made a point of introducing me to Anthony McGrath, the former England 'A' player and one of the country's most exciting batsmen. 'I'm the social secretary on tour,' McGrath explained. 'That means I'm in charge of the team dinners, the court cases, the fines, the lot.' He paused and gave me a knowing look. 'I've got a feeling you're going to keep me busy.' How right he was.

The afternoon was spent at the David Lloyd Centre in Leeds, where our activities would have shattered the image that many people still have of modern-day cricket. Over two hours the squad endured various sprint sessions followed by some circuit training. Ian Fisher, the spin bowler, conducted the torture. 'I've got some fitness and conditioning experience having taken some instruction courses,' he explained. Split up into groups of four or five, we had to perform a series of exercises, for example running ten metres, throwing ourselves to the floor to do ten press-ups, running a further twenty metres and then performing ten burpees, and then sprinting back again to the start. The team that came last had to face a forfeit, usually an extra ten press-ups or twenty sit-ups. For the first few sessions our team managed to escape this punishment, but as I tired and became what my team-mates liked to term 'The Weakest Link', we found ourselves invariably last.

It certainly took me by surprise. I was hoping for an easier ride after my earlier sporting exertions, but this was obviously not going to be the case at all. The circuit session proved just as hard as the first exercises. Here I was partnered with Byas, and we each had to carry out a series of twelve thirty-second exercises interspersed with a thirty-second recovery period. It added up to an intense six minutes: the exercises ranged from press-ups and burpees to lifting a weighted bar up to your armpits, raising your thighs and head off the floor from a lying position, and balancing on just your forearms and toes.

Each time the circuit was completed there followed a mad rush to the nearest water fountain. On my return the first time Gavin Hamilton burst out laughing. 'Tried to escape, Ian?' he asked, observing my red and flustered face. After the second time he continued the theme. 'How far did you get this time? The ring road?' On completion of the third circuit even Gavin appeared exhausted, although he still found enough energy to undertake a four mile run with Ian Fisher. 'You coming?' he asked. We all shook our heads and hurriedly dressed. 'It's no fun unless it's at least a half marathon,' Simon Guy countered by way of an excuse.

As I gulped down a pint of orange juice upstairs in the health club, still mopping my sweating brow, I told Byas how surprised I was by the level of fitness training we had just undergone. It was not that it was any harder than other fitness sessions I had experienced while writing this book, but the fact that it was not any easier, either, had taken me aback. 'We've come on a lot in the past five years,' explained Byas, who is now thirty-seven years old and has fifteen seasons' experience of first-team cricket with Yorkshire under his belt. 'It wasn't that long ago that fitness was almost frowned upon, and that certain unfit individuals were seen as role models because they could play the game well and have big guts. Today we're all looking for an extra edge, and the fact that fitness, diet and psychology are all now becoming elements of the game proves that our whole approach has become far more professional.'

Extra elements are particularly important to Byas. This was to be his sixth season in charge of Yorkshire and, despite the host of top players that the county had fielded during this time, no silverware had been won. 'I've never won a thing at Yorkshire,' Byas said. 'It's something I'm desperate to put right.' In fairness Yorkshire had come close on many occasions, especially the 2000 season, when they had finished runners-up in the Sunday League and third in the First Division, and this without the services of their numerous Test players for much of the summer. 'It doesn't help, but we just have to get on with it,' commented Byas. 'I can't see many counties faring as well as we have done recently with the loss of such key players as Gough, Vaughan and White. This season, though, I'm really hopeful. I think we've got good strength in depth, good spirit – and a new coach joining us in South Africa who might just add that extra five per cent we need. Maybe you can get us off to a good start this season, Ian.' Byas added with a wink. 'See you in Pretoria, and don't be late.'

I endured a predictably bad night's sleep en route to South Africa. The large, rather rotund man sitting next to me snored through most of the flight, twice nesting his head on my shoulder, and there was nowhere to stretch my legs. At least I could have a few hours' sleep in my room before joining Yorkshire at lunch, I thought, as the taxi delivered me to the team hotel just across the road from Pretoria's Centurion Park international cricket ground.

Alas, this was not to be. As I was checking in Byas emerged at reception. 'Ah, good timing, Ian,' he said. 'We're leaving in fifteen minutes for the ground. See you here, then.' So much for my plans. By the time I had reached my room, dumped my holdall and suitcase, changed into some training gear and returned to reception, the team had already left for Centurion Park. The hotel driver took me across moments later. When I showed my face in the dressing room, the first words of welcome came from McGrath, the social secretary. 'That's a fine, then, Ian,' he said, with a beaming smile.

'What?' I said. 'What for?'

'Lateness,' McGrath replied, handing me a piece of paper headed, 'Tour Fines 2001: South Africa'. Underneath the title were detailed the following list of crimes and punishments:

Lateness: 10 rand per minute.
Left items: 10 rand per item.
Wrong kit: 20 rand per item.
Item search: 20 rand per item.
Dressing room farts: 10 rand.
Toothpicks: 10 rand.

It went on to state: 'Any questions concerning fines should be saved for the first fine meeting. Any questions about fines to the committee will result in a 10 rand fine.'

All this threw up a multitude of questions, but already the rest of the players were making their way out on to the pitch to begin their warm-up with a five-minute jog. 'Don't forget your toothpick,' said James Middlebrook, the young spin bowler, as we began the run. 'And your cheese sandwich,' added Paul Hutchison, the fast left-arm bowler.

I wondered if they had all taken leave of their senses but felt unable to answer back. Despite my confidence in my general fitness, a combination of fatigue and the fact that I had been plunged straight into training at an altitude of 6,000 feet made even this simple exertion taxing. It was not long before my face was wet with sweat, and my stomach knotted with stitches.

Wayne Morton the former England physiotherapist, had joined the squad for a week. Morton had worked with Yorkshire for seventeen years but had recently set up his own private practice. The team would be without a fitness/conditioning coach and physio until the arrival of its new appointment, Matt Carrico, later in the week, and so Morton had agreed to step into the breach.

Yorkshire were playing their first game of the tour this day, a fifty-over match against Northerns. Once we had all stretched, under Wayne Morton's instructions, there followed fielding practice with, first, slip-catching, then high ball takes and finally running, picking up and throwing. Those not playing in the game – myself, bowler Tom Baker, spinner and social committee treasurer Richard Dawson, batsman Vic Craven and Simon Guy, together with Morton and Sidebottom – made our way over to the nets for an hour's bowling and batting practice. Meanwhile Northerns built up an impressive 306-3 in their fifty overs on what was a pitch favourable to the batting side with a fast and vast outfield.

'What do you do, then?' Arnie asked, referring to my bowling style, as I prepared to deliver my first ball in the nets.

'Nothing,' I replied. 'I just send them down at the batsman, at a slow to medium pace, with absolutely no deviation, bounce, swing or spin at all.' Which is precisely what I did, providing any opponent with welcome relief from the various fast bowlers and spinners. I was a little more in my element when it was my turn to bat, however, and although hardly impressing any of the observers, I managed to improve my own confidence with a few meaty drives. Each time the ball flew in the air the bowler claimed a catch. Each time I insisted that the ball had found a gap in the field.

During lunch some of my earlier confusion was cleared up. It turned out that we all had to be in possession of a toothpick at all times except for during a cricket match. Members of the committee – McGrath, Dawson and vice-chairman Gavin Hamilton – could ask us to present it at any time, and failure to do so would result in a ten rand fine. And what about the cheese sandwich?

McGrath – or 'Mags', as everyone called him – explained. 'Tomorrow night we have our first team meeting and court session,' he said. 'All the players have to produce the following: one cheese sandwich, one stamp, one joker taken from a pack of cards, and a packet of beef "wors" sausage. The punishment for failing in this task will be severe. And you've been fined already, haven't you?'

The threat of fines was already being taken seriously. Players were making a big point of leaving the confines of the dressing room before ostentatiously passing wind, to much amusement. Accusations and counter-accusations were being uttered from all directions, and there was still the matter of who would be the recipient of a hideous red multi-patterned shirt, at the end of the day. 'It's awarded to whoever makes an idiot of himself,' McGrath added, when he caught sight of my perplexed expression. 'And after each time it's worn, something else equally stupid is added to it. You wouldn't want to be the one wearing it at the end of the tour.'

Byas called for a team conference in the changing room. 'I can see a few heads down in here, but there's no reason for that,' he said. 'We can win this game. Our batters are better than theirs, and if they can score 306 then so can we. Let's be positive, use the open spaces and look for the singles as well.' His words were to be proved right, although the afternoon started poorly. Matthew Wood, the affable opening batsman, had his hand broken by a ball that suddenly lifted off a length and smashed into the unprotected part of his glove. He would return later that day with his arm in plaster and his tour effectively over. It was not merely a literal blow for the young man. He would be out of action for the next six weeks, which meant that the crucial pre-season period and the start of the one-day competitions and county championships would pass him by, at a time when competition for places was rife. If Wood was disappointed, however, he hid it well and, until he returned home three days later, he remained in good spirits while fulfilling his new-found role as team gofer.

McGrath, meanwhile, was in imperious form, mixing his shots with nudges, textbook strokes and a few powerful drives. He had spent the winter in Australia, seemingly intent on enjoying a big season back home after promising well a few seasons ago. Indeed, he and Marcus Trescothick had both seemed to be on a par when they had toured with the England 'A' team, and I had the distinct feeling that Trescothick's sudden emergence as a Test player with England must have given McGrath a timely reminder that he, too, possessed similar talent that had yet to be fully realised. It was time to prove this. His 150 not out against Northerns that afternoon, as well as the captain's bludgeoning 75, ensured that Yorkshire reached the required total with more than an over to spare. It was, by anyone's standards, an impressive victory, and the best way to begin the tour. 'It proves that you can win a cricket match from almost any position,' Byas said later, clearly pleased with the day's workout. 'I bet if I had asked everyone half-way through the day whether they believed they could win the game most would have said no. For that reason it's been a marvellous lesson. I'm glad the opposition scored as many runs as they did. It set us a challenge, and we overcame it.'

While the match was going on the non-players had been enduring an afternoon of pain. During a half-hour run on the roads surrounding Centurion Park, I soon found myself dropping back through the heat and the altitude. Following this, Morton had us performing what he termed 'BA shuttles'. 'It means bad attitude shuttles,' he explained. 'It finds out who really wants it. Mind you, it could also stand for blowing out of your arse.'

BA shuttles comprised a series of six twenty-metre runs, to be completed in thirty seconds and then repeated after a recovery period. The first recovery period was thirty seconds; the second, twenty seconds; and the third a mere ten seconds. By the time we had finished our fourth series of shuttle runs most of us were flat on our backs – only to be told that the whole process would now be repeated. The exercise was hard, but it made perfect sense. The Yorkshire management want their players fit enough to be running twos and threes well into their second and third hour at the crease – as McGrath ably demonstrated that afternoon. These shuttles amounted to exactly the same as running from one end of the wicket to the other.

It must have taken well over an hour for me to recover fully from all this. So much for a relaxing week! There was just enough time to see McGrath knock off the winning runs before we were all summoned out on to the pitch for what turned out to be a tradition with the team.

'Football,' Hamilton declared. 'We always have the oldies versus the youngsters. You'll be with us, the oldies, but that's good.'

'Why?' I asked.

'Because we never lose. Oh, and by the way, I always score the goals. My stock phrase is that I get paid £80,000 a year to put the ball into the back of the net. It really winds the others up.'

True to his word, Hamilton scored all four goals as the oldies beat the youngsters 4–2. Despite the exacting day already endured, the game was played at a tempo so fast and competitive it was as though winning this meant more than beating Northerns. Play was punctuated with accusations of cheating and pleas to referee Matthew Wood, and Richard Blakey irritated everyone with his trademark ploy: a long hoof into touch from a foot away, which merely reduced the time the youngsters had to claw their way back into the match. The match ended in acrimony when Wood awarded the youngsters a consolation goal that clearly should not have been theirs. Gary 'Mouse' Fellows (his colleagues believe Gary shares certain facial similarities with a mouse) launched himself into a spectacular diving header that went well wide, but Wood's explanation later was that it deserved a goal. 'I'll allow it for effort and enthusiasm,' he decreed, to much consternation from the oldies.

Back in the dressing room, Simon Widdup, the opening batsman, was awarded with the disgusting shirt – a decision which was met with a round of applause. During the game that day Widdup had attempted to field the ball on the run in the cover area just as his large wide-brimmed hat flopped over his head and fully covered his face. And so he would be forced to wear the 'prize' shirt that night in the hotel, and anywhere else he chose to go. Failure to do so was not worth contemplating.

Before dinner there was some important shopping to do. A nearby general store had clearly been visited already because the man behind the counter had packs of playing cards next to packets of beef sausage in the delicatessen area. 'I've been asked not to sell any of this to anyone from the Yorkshire cricket team,' he announced. I asked him who told him this. 'Someone wearing a Yorkshire shirt,' he replied.

So things were getting dirty already. I bought the cards, the sausage and a stamp at the shop, realising that a cheese sandwich could come from room service. I had just acquired a cocktail stick from the bar when Gavin Hamilton approached me. 'Do you have your toothpick on you?' he asked, in his role as social committee vice-chairman. I told him I did. 'May I see it?' he insisted. I showed him the stick, complaining that he should trust me. 'Thank you,' he replied. 'I will be asking you frequently during the week.'

Dinner was taken at a local Italian restaurant with most of the team. Richard Blakey amused us with his stories of his punk days in the 1970s, and of the time when he arrived at a black tie dinner dressed as a Viking, having been purposely misinformed by his club colleagues. Simon Widdup, resplendent in his Miami Vice shirt, declined to venture out of the hotel.

Tuesday morning meant an early start – too early for Widdup, who compounded his shirt-wearing punishment the night before by reporting for duty a couple of minutes late. 'That's another fine,' he was gleefully told by the committee. Yorkshire would be playing Northerns again at Centurion Park, although the opposition was to include more Academy players this time. We embarked on our customary warm-up of a ten-minute jog followed by a stretching session and then catching and fielding practice overseen by Wayne Morton. Unlike the previous day, when I had trained in my Leicester Tigers white rugby shorts and a sports t-shirt, some Yorkshire training kit was now provided for me: a blue pair of shorts, and two tops, one blue and one white, with 'Yorkshire Tea', the county's sponsors, written all over the chest. It transpired that the night before each of the week's morning training sessions we would be told which shirt to wear. Failure to wear the correct shirt would warrant a fine.

Byas lost the toss again, and returned to the pavilion cursing. 'I always call heads,' he explained as he told everyone that Yorkshire would be fielding first. 'But I seem to be on a bad run at the moment.'

I made a rather obvious suggestion. 'Ever thought about calling tails instead?' I asked. The captain shook his head, as if I had suggested an act of treachery. 'Nope, I'm sticking with heads.'

While Northerns struggled to 128 all out the non-players – this time McGrath, Widdup, Fisher, Ramsden and myself – had another nets session, taking turns bowling and batting with each other. Arnie Sidebottom joined us and started to ping his fast deliveries down the track at us. Normally one would not take too much notice of a late-order batsman and fast bowler giving you advice about your batting technique, but Arnie was different. 'I came to Yorkshire as an opening batsman,' he explained. 'Only later did I turn into an opening bowler instead.'

He also admitted that the last time he had been to Centurion Park was when he was part of the England rebel tour to a then isolated South Africa back in the late 1970s when the country's abhorrent apartheid system was still very much in place. The rebel team also included the likes of Geoff Boycott and Graham Gooch. 'We had no idea how much trouble it would cause,' he said, shaking his head as he recollected the protesters, the barbed wire and the police. 'It was good to get home again after that experience.'

The previous day we had strolled back to the dressing room after the net session to watch some cricket and prepare for the afternoon's fitness exertions, but this time we were sent off for a twenty-five-minute run. That may not seem much, but at 6,000 feet it tested our reserves to the full. One-half of the non-players chose the road again, but McGrath,

Widdup and I plumped for twelve times round a rugby pitch instead. As if this were not enough, Morton and Fisher then subjected me to some extra close-in fielding practice, throwing the ball from their standing positions some 20 feet apart, and expecting me to race across to take what was often a diving catch. Twenty of these in succession proved to be physically demanding, to say the least.

Once recovered from these morning activities I sat with Gavin Hamilton during lunch. Hamilton came to everyone's notice during the 1999 cricket World Cup when, playing for Scotland, he shone with both bat and ball. In fact, so impressive was the all-rounder's performance that England snapped him up. But then it went all wrong. 'One Test appearance,' he recalled. 'In Johannesburg, at the Wanderers Club.'

'How did it go?' I asked.

'It was a bloody disaster,' Hamilton replied. 'I scored two ducks, and took no wickets. Then that was that. I haven't been called up again. I'm desperate to get another chance, though. I'm desperate to prove that I am good enough to play Test cricket, and to succeed at that level. I don't like to talk about it much, but it eats away at me.' It was an interesting and rare drop of the defences by a man who was usually the life and soul of the tour party, telling jokes and living out his role as social committee vice-chairman to the full.

Yorkshire rattled off the required amount with the loss of only two wickets after lunch, with Fellows scoring a good-looking half century, and Hamilton, Dawson and Michael Lumb, the son of former Yorkshire batsman Richard Lumb, making useful contributions. This was not the good news it seemed. With play over by half-past three, Wayne Morton's face suddenly brightened. 'Some extra time on our hands,' he observed. 'That means time for some more fitness, then,' he added, to general groans from the squad. Several of the players asked Fellows why he had not taken a great deal longer in knocking off the runs. There followed a further forty minutes of shuttle running and sprints, leaving all of us exhausted. Yet the obligatory game of football still followed, with the oldies winning this time by a margin of 4–0. The day's work had left me so tired that I played in goal and managed, somehow, to keep a clean sheet. This prompted Hamilton – who failed to score but insisted that his presence alone had created space for others to find the net – to christen me Jim Leighton, after the former Scotland and Manchester United goalkeeper.

'Is that because I played well, then, Gav?' I asked.

'No,' he replied. 'It's because you look like him.' He would call me Jim for much of the remaining week.

Before returning to the hotel David Byas gave another team talk, applauding Yorkshire for their efforts and congratulating them on another convincing win. Simon Guy was awarded the dreaded shirt for a comment that cannot be repeated in these pages, suffice to say that his assumption concerning a man and a woman in the crowd was embarrassingly wide of the mark.

We were all supposed to report to a conference room in the hotel at 7.30 sharp. This would be the first team meeting of the week, and also the 'court session' that I had been warned about. Outside the closed doors the squad assembled, all carrying their jokers and stamps, cheese sandwiches and beef wors. There seemed to be an air of nervousness. The door swung open and Hamilton invited everyone to enter. There, sitting at the head of a table, were McGrath and Dawson, presently joined by Hamilton. The rest of us sat around a long table opposite them.

Right away I was summoned. McGrath explained that it was customary for a newcomer to the squad to down a pint of lager in front of everyone else. This task completed, I sat down only to be told that I had the most fines, due to my tardiness on the first morning and because I had left some equipment lying on the ground. In total, I owed the committee fifty rand.

After this the whole squad, one by one, had to deliver their requisite items to the top table. It was fast becoming obvious that I was unwittingly providing much of the entertainment that evening. I had ordered a cheese sandwich from room service an hour earlier and had spent forty-five minutes looking at it before giving in and eating half of it. Gavin Hamilton spotted my crime immediately. 'Ian has produced only half a cheese sandwich,' he pronounced with obvious glee. Another pint of lager was handed to me and drunk. They accepted, slightly begrudgingly, my stamp, joker and beef sausage, and then declared that the whole packet of beef wors had to be eaten before the end of the meeting.

As this local delicacy was universally considered revolting, most of us found ways to dispose of it without having to consume any of it. Gary Ramsden was the appointed 'bartender' that night, which meant he had to make sure we all had fresh cans of lager by our sides. Whenever he passed by with a bin bag we threw bits of sausage, or empty cans crammed full of wors, into the sack. At least it was something I got right in a night otherwise dominated by my mistakes.

The joker, as the committee explained, could be used once during the week when fined. On producing the card the fine would be annulled. The cheese sandwich, meanwhile, was provided as a snack for the players during the court session. As most of the sandwiches had been sweating and curling up for much of the previous day, they followed the beef wors into any escape route possible.

McGrath had asked us to initial the back of the stamps. He pulled out five, including mine, and ordered the owners to come forward, drop to our knees and down another glass of lager, in a movement he described as a 'Mexican wave'. Then came the cards game, in which a pack of cards was placed on top of a glass, and each of us was asked, in turn, to blow off a card without knocking off the whole pack. It was obvious that everyone else was well-practised at this because by the time it came to my turn, Morton, Blakey and Byas had successfully managed to blow off just one or two cards, usually from a crouched, kneeling or lying down position. Predictably, when I took my place on the floor, the whole pack fell off. Equally predictably, my punishment – in the form of another glass of beer – was handed over, and had to be drunk in one movement.

Just when my evening was lurching towards disaster McGrath initiated the court proceedings. The charge was that someone had stolen his Scrabble rule book. Calling on Richard Blakey to be an impartial judge, he called up his three chief suspects: Fellows, Fisher and Hamilton. All denied the charge, but when Wood, Lumb and Craven were interviewed as witnesses, the finger of suspicion pointed firmly at Hamilton, whose protests of innocence would have been more convincing if he had managed to keep a straight face. The end result was a hefty fine for Hamilton, plus smaller fines levelled at both Fisher and Fellows, who were charged as accomplices. All three insisted that they had been stitched up and accused McGrath – allegedly seen dumping the said rule book in a wastepaper bin at Heathrow Airport – to have instigated the crime himself. The argument, by now not entirely jocular, raged on as we all retired to the bar. The Pretoria Three, aware of previous injustices in the British judicial system, demanded an appeal and a retrial.

The reason for the timing of all this merriment was that the following day would be one without any fitness or cricket. This was the day when Yorkshire would be upping camp and moving south to Cape Town – which meant an early coach journey to Johannesburg, and bleary eyes all round. At the airport Gavin Hamilton was still asking if certain individuals, me included, were carrying their toothpicks. Matthew Wood, who was still with us and would not be going home until the following day, was growing increasingly helpless with his arm in plaster. I cut up his omelette into small squares for him, but drew the line when he needed to go and relieve himself in the airport toilets.

Cape Town was noticeably warmer and, at sea level, noticeably easier on the lungs, too. It was the second time I had been to the jewel on the Cape, but I was not alone in my excitement as we flew past Table Mountain and landed. 'Home,' Hamilton exclaimed, having played six winters of cricket here. Many of his team-mates had also experienced club and provincial cricket down here in Western Province. Most seemed to know the best bars, clubs and beaches, and while some opted for a couple of hours at the municipal swimming pool across the road from the hotel in Newlands, Blakey drove me, Craven, Dawson, Ramsden and Middlebrook in a hired Kombi down to Clifton Beach.

While the younger lads went for strolls along the beach to observe the 'scenery' – and with the sun beating down on a beach packed with beautiful young women, their dropped jaws and obvious stares were about as discreet as the way we had hidden our beef wors the night before – Blakey and I lay on the beach and chatted.

Yorkshire's first choice wicketkeeper/batsman had also played for England, twice in Test matches in India under Graham Gooch's captaincy, and also three times in one-day internationals. Like Hamilton, he was not giving up his chance of perhaps returning to the international fold. 'All it takes is a good start to the season, a couple of tons perhaps early on, and you get noticed again,' he reasoned, as he slapped suncream on to his muscular body. 'We're all aware at the start of the season of how a good start might lead to things.'

Life as a cricketer had its understandable ups and downs. That particular moment illustrated the ups. 'I'm actually getting paid for doing this!' he said, with a grin. 'I'm seeing the world, enjoying myself, and playing a sport I love. And, as you saw from last night's team meeting, growing up is put on hold when you play cricket.' The downs cannot be ignored, however. 'It's very hard to keep a happy marriage in this game,' admitted the divorced Blakey. 'The demands of the game, the travelling and the time spent away from home makes it very tough on a family. And many fall into the trap of suddenly discovering one day, when their career is over, that they have nothing to fall back on. To some, this can be a depressing time that they never recover from. That's why I'm already involved in other work, such as marketing and speaking, as well as writing a column in my local newspaper.'

He and Byas were by now the longest-serving current players in the squad. Blakey had even played with Boycott, a man whose high reputation as a batsman was checked by his perceived selfishness. Blakey, though, will not hear a bad word said about the man. 'He was always willing to help me out when I arrived at the county as a youngster,' he insisted. 'You only had to ask and he'd be giving you advice. As you can imagine, coming from him, it was worth listening to.' He added: 'Despite what people might think, he also prided himself on his fitness and general state of health. That's one of the main reasons why he was able to build long innings.' Blakey, in this sense, was similar. Despite being thirty-four years of age he was probably the fittest player in the squad, and whenever he had the chance he undertook extra training – sprinting, jogging and performing press-ups and burpees while the rest of us sat watching the cricket with our tired legs up.

We had to dash back from the beach in time to meet Yorkshire's new coach, Wayne Clark, who was flying in to Cape Town that evening. Our plans for a seafood dinner at Camps Bay had been aborted when a local rammed her car into the back of our parked Kombi. With the sea and beach to our left, and Table Mountain to our right, we reasoned that there were worse places to be involved in a pile-up than here. 'Like the M1 on a wet, Wednesday afternoon just outside Leeds,' considered Blakey, who took charge of all the insurance details.

Clark, formerly player with and then coach of Western Australia, would be meeting his new team for the first time that night, and it was important that a reception committee would be there to greet him. It would not be easy for an Australian to get to know a sea of strange faces, let alone to please the county's committee men back home in Leeds who expected an instant return to the glory days of the past, but Byas, for one, was extremely optimistic. 'I think he's going to be good news for us,' he reported, having driven Clark from the airport to the hotel. The social committee was impressed, too, when they asked him without any notice to present a toothpick and found he had one in his possession. 'I often carry one with me,' Clark explained.

It was here that McGrath handed out invitations to the next team

meeting, which was to take place on Friday night after a Yorkshire team –
including me this time – had played Boland. 'The committee would like to
invite you to "Cape Fear",' the invitation announced. 'Dress, plain white
collar or t-shirt. Reply to chairman's room by Friday, 9 a.m. Letters must
include 50 rand and the words "specifically", "exceedingly", "you know
you love it", and "s'bad lad".'

'What on earth does "s'bad lad" mean?' I asked.

'It's a Yorkshireism for "not so bad, lad",' Paul Hutchison explained.

Right! We were also instructed to produce four more items for the
meeting: a TV remote control, a can of Aussie beer, a ping-pong ball and
a packet of soup. A natural combination, if ever there was one.

Wayne Clark's first day in charge saw us reporting for an early start
at 8.30. A short journey in three Kombis, including the battered one
from the Clifton Beach prang the day before, took us to the Newlands
cricket ground, where Western Province were playing Border in a four-day
provincial cup final. The day was already searingly hot, and on arrival
we discovered that we were not permitted on to the fresh grass of the
Newlands stadium to warm up, instead having to use a rather shabby
field across the road.

Having just arrived from Australia Clark was understandably in the
throes of jet lag, but he nevertheless gamely participated in every aspect
of practice. Some members of the team were disappointed when they
discovered that he had been briefed about my role with Yorkshire. They
were rather hoping he would believe their story that I was the county's
major new signing for the forthcoming season. They were looking forward
to seeing Clark's jaw drop when he saw me play.

My grand entrance was somewhat delayed because Arnie Sidebottom
wanted me to help out around the fringes rather than bowl in the
nets. 'It is Wayne's first day,' he reasoned, making this sound like
a perfectly acceptable explanation. Instead together with the injured
Matthew Wood I had to make do with fetching water for the hot and
sweating team. I eventually helped out the two wicketkeepers, Richard

Blakey and Simon Guy, by purposefully missing the ball when batting to give them chances behind the stumps to make difficult stops. One or two suggested I would find this exercise easier than the others because it was my natural game.

By the time I was summoned to the nets everyone else had batted. I thought only Sidebottom would be bowling against me, but a ready queue of eager and revitalised bowlers lined up, including Widdup, Guy, Byas – and Hamilton, who started pounding down fast bouncers. 'You've got to hook them,' he insisted, as each ball whistled past my nose. When I managed to pull one of the captain's slower bouncers most of the team reckoned it would have gone for a six but Byas, in keeping with every bowler in the nets, saw it differently. 'I had a man out there on the boundary, and the ball would have fallen right into his lap,' he argued. Hamilton steamed in even quicker, especially after I had managed to smack the ball straight past him. In the end I would say it was an honourable draw. I failed to connect with a meaty hook, and he failed to get me out – or hit me, for that matter.

After some extra fielding practice with Sidebottom – who sent balls skywards for us to catch, and then low along the ground for us to collect one-handed and throw back to him – Byas announced the team for the next day's game against Boland. 'Blakey, Widdup, McGrath, Stafford, Byas, Lumb, Hamilton, Fisher, Dawson, Hutchison and Middlebrook', he declared. 'And it's in that order. That means that you're batting at number four,' he said, looking at me. 'I'd like to wish Ian all the best for his debut for Yorkshire tomorrow.' A round of applause followed. Arnie Sidebottom smiled and then rolled his eyes. 'God help us,' he said.

Sidebottom had already entertained us that morning with his stories from his playing days. Although his various reminiscences of Yorkshire players such as Brian Close – his personal hero – Boycott, Graham Stevenson, Freddie Trueman and others were interesting, what really caught my attention were his various tales concerning his other life as a professional footballer with Manchester United.

Indeed, Sidebottom is the last man in England to have played both professional cricket and football at the highest level, and appeared in one of the two sports for his country. Not long after he left United for Huddersfield Town, Yorkshire made it clear that it was proving impossible for Arnie to play both sports as the two seasons increasingly overlapped each other. He was given a stark choice: cricket, or football. Sidebottom chose cricket, having had a fat contract dangled in front of his nose in the days when wages in football were nothing like they are today, and has never looked back. Yet he still remembers his days at Old Trafford with particular fondness.

'My debut was Bobby Charlton's last match,' the former centre-back recalled. 'It was at a packed Old Trafford and I was obviously very nervous because Charlton's swansong made it very high profile. My first touch of the ball was a nightmare. I went to clear it upfield and sliced it straight into touch instead. We lost 0–1, and it was only Sheffield United. It wasn't how Charlton or I would have wanted it.'

It transpired that Sidebottom had played with, and against, the best. 'I remember having to mark Johann Cruyff once,' he said, shaking his head and laughing at himself. 'He ran rings round me throughout the match. Another time I came on as a substitute against Benfica. The only good thing about that was the fact that Eusebio had just left the field injured. That saved me from making a complete embarrassment of myself.'

Yet Sidebottom's all-time hero was George Best. 'I would honestly put him above Pelé and Maradona,' he said. 'George could do anything he wanted with the ball. I remember when we played Chelsea and Ron "Chopper" Harris tried repeatedly to kick George to pieces. It got to the stage when George had had enough. He summoned Harris over with his finger, dribbled the ball between the defender's legs and went past him, only to stop, run back and nutmeg Harris again. The crowd went crazy and Chopper went berserk. The other thing about Bestie is that he was fantastic with the kids and the autograph hunters.' Arnie could probably have gone on all day, and it was fascinating to listen to him, but now it was time to leave Newlands and take the afternoon off in preparation for the next day's game against Boland.

I had arranged to spend some time with the captain. Byas was keen for me to see Newlands during a match. 'It's the best cricket ground in South Africa,' he insisted, 'and probably the world.' First, over milkshakes in a Cape Town bar, we talked cricket. Byas, like Hamilton and Blakey, had had his share of disappointment when it came to the England team.

'I was called up into the final thirteen for a Test match at Trent Bridge in 1995 because both Mike Atherton and Graeme Hick had back problems,' he recalled. 'In the end I wasn't required because both of them recovered. I thought, and indeed I was told, that this would at least guarantee me a place on the winter tour, but that didn't come my way either. But I've never given up hope. In fact, the day I give up aspirations of playing for England will be the day I give up cricket.'

He asked me for my thoughts about the Yorkshire squad. I told him I had been impressed with both their team spirit and their ability to draw the line between enjoying themselves and producing a professional performance when it mattered on the pitch. Byas recalled previous adventures on tour.

'We were in Zimbabwe and Botswana on one of our pre-season tours a few years back, and we decided to spend a day trekking through the jungle as part of a fitness and teamwork exercise,' he recounted. 'In the end we were as good as lost, and our moods weren't exactly improved by the sight of numerous paw prints that came quite clearly from a big cat, plus various snake imprints in the ground. Another time, on mountain bikes, we were chased – and I really mean chased – by around a hundred baboons. We all laugh about it now, but at the time we were pretty scared.'

Looking up at Table Mountain – which dominates the Cape Town skyline from every point in the city – the captain also recollected the time when the squad ran all the way to the summit, caught the cable car down, and then cycled back up to the top again. 'None of us will ever forget that experience, I can promise you.'

Success at Yorkshire clearly meant a great deal to Byas. 'There are two aspects to the club that I still think need to be improved,' he said. 'One is our mental approach to the game. I'm hoping Wayne Clark will help here. I think we can only improve as players if we are mentally prepared for the game, because cricket depends a great deal on the confidence of the player. Secondly, I'd like to see some of the younger players involving themselves in activities outside cricket when they have some time on their hands, especially in the winter. Some of them find it difficult to appreciate how lucky they are. Don't get me wrong. They're all fine cricketers, and deserve their chance in the professional game, but it's not what I call work. Not real work. Maybe some of them should try it. It would make them appreciate what they do a little more, and also make them determined to make the most of their talent.'

As we wandered over to Newlands this reminded me of the afternoon I had spent in Tuscany with the Everton player, John Collins, who had made similar comments. Byas, it transpired, had always possessed a work ethic – in part, no doubt, due to having been brought up on a farm, which he now runs with a partner.

'Even now, when asked, I describe myself as a farmer who plays cricket,' the captain explained as we settled down on the grassy bank inside Newlands, where we sunned ourselves while watching Western Province hand out a thorough beating to Border. This helped explain why Byas was still not only one of the strongest of the Yorkshire team but also was more than capable of keeping up with players some fifteen years younger than him. 'I don't like to ask anyone to do anything I can't,' he admitted.

Back home in England foot and mouth disease was ravaging the country. I wasn't sure whether I should remind Byas of this, but he seemed more than happy to talk about it. Happily, the epidemic had not yet reached the eastern coast of Yorkshire, where his farm was, but Byas believed that it was probably only a matter of time.

'We've got a hell of a lot of livestock on our farm,' he revealed.

'There's no doubt about it. If foot and mouth reaches our farm, we're talking about a lifetime of work destroyed. Compensation from the government will mean that it won't kill us off completely, but it will still, nevertheless, be a devastating blow.'

He shook his head and stared down at the grass. 'It's incredible, when you think about it, what the farming industry has had to deal with over the past few years,' he continued. 'We've had swine fever, BSE, the slow death of the whole agricultural industry, and now foot and mouth. Farmers are killing themselves over this.'

Coincidentally his mobile telephone rang and he spoke for a couple of minutes. 'I thought that might be the bad news from home,' he said, as he turned his telephone off. 'Luckily, it wasn't.'

As we lay on that grassy bank at Newlands, gazing up at Table Mountain and tanning ourselves in the South African summer while it rained back home in England, things took on a certain perspective. Here was a man waiting to discover if a lifetime's work had just been obliterated. Yet he remained perfectly relaxed about it. 'If it happens it happens,' he said, shrugging his shoulders. 'It's all part of a farmer's plight. You have to be philosophical about these things. And you have to be fatalistic, too. Besides, I still have my cricket.'

There was just enough time to catch the shops before closing time. This was important because there were four items that needed to be produced for the Friday night team gathering. The remote control was easy. We could just borrow one from our rooms. The packet of soup had already been sorted out. But the ping-pong ball and the can of Aussie beer needed to be arranged. Fortunately a sports shop in Newlands was able to provide the ping-pong ball, but we had no luck with the Australian beer. Back in the hotel one of the reception staff said he would be visiting the waterfront area that night and would bring some back for me. This was good to hear, especially as everyone else in the squad was complaining that they could not find any Australian beer. I wrote my official RSVP to McGrath – using the hotel office to type out my letter, and inserting the four required phrases into the missive – and slipped it under his door before retiring for an early night. Tomorrow, after all, would be my big day – the day when I would make my debut, and almost certainly my final appearance, for Yorkshire.

Friday morning meant a particularly early start. We would be playing Boland in Hermanus, a resort town a good hour-and-a-half's drive from Cape Town. We left in a convoy of Kombis. I found myself in the lead vehicle, which was driven by the captain and also accommodated coaches Clark and Sidebottom, as well as McGrath. It proved to be an interesting drive through the stunning Sir Lowry's Pass, which was engulfed in early morning fog. At one point we had to slow right down to avoid hitting a large group of baboons who had decided to park their pink backsides on the road. 'Brings back memories,' Byas shouted out from the driver's wheel, as Sidebottom and McGrath nodded their heads.

Eventually we arrived at a cricket ground in Hermanus, which was still hampered by fog. Newlands this most certainly was not. Indeed the ground more resembled the kind of cricket venue you find in most small towns in England. Still, this was Yorkshire versus Boland, a game both sides wanted to win, and a game in which my big chance had come. The modest ground was of little concern.

Our usual warm-up of a jog, a stretch and various fielding exercises also included a quick game of touch rugby between the oldies and the youngsters. Once again the older team prevailed, winning by three tries to two, having been 2–1 down at one stage. The predictable banter between the two followed, with the likes of Hamilton and Morton asking the youngsters if there was any game at all that they felt they could win. The oldies milked the occasion to the maximum once more, using phrases such as 'experience', 'guile' and 'maturity' to explain their unbeaten streak.

To everyone's surprise Byas actually called correctly when the two captains marched out into the middle of the wicket and tossed a coin.

For the first time on the tour Yorkshire would bat first in what would be another fifty-over game. This meant that I would need to pad up immediately. After all, two quick wickets could fall and I could soon find myself in. My personal preference was to enter the fray when the scoreboard read something like 140–2 after thirty-five overs. There was always the chance, however, that it could be 14–2 after ten overs instead.

Most of the team members inspected the pitch and wicket and came to the conclusion that it would be difficult to notch up a big total. The pitch was slow, which meant that the ball would not come on to the batsman, so there would be little pace to utilise. Those batting would have to work for their runs. The outfield, too, was not that quick. Byas came to the conclusion that he would be happy with any score exceeding 200.

Gary Ramsden, who was not playing that day, kindly lent me his equipment. This amounted to two batting pads, two thigh pads, a helmet, a pair of batting gloves and, crucially, his bat. Thankfully, while on my ping-pong shopping expedition the day before, I had finally purchased a cricket box. After five days of touring, I could tell that the others were dreading my asking them if I could borrow their box.

Then it was simply a question of waiting. Blakey and Widdup opened the innings for Yorkshire. Progress was steady, if a little slow. Widdup was the first to go, on twenty-six, after he and Blakey had made a sound start for the county. McGrath strolled purposefully out into the middle, but even he was failing to hit too many forceful strokes to begin with. A number of confident appeals for LBWs, run-outs and even a catch came and went. Each time my heart missed a beat as I half rose from my seat to make the walk out into the middle of the pitch. James Middlebrook threw a few balls for me to practise some strokes while we waited for my time to come.

After thirty overs, and with the score at ninety, Blakey's wicket finally fell. He had made a slow but important nineteen runs, ensuring that Yorkshire had plenty of batting in reserve. Unfortunately, that reserve began with me. Trying to remain calm, and attempting to exude coolness, I stood up, placed the helmet on my head, slipped on my gloves and marched out to take my stand at the crease. In the time-honoured fashion of departing and incoming batsmen, not a word, not even a glance, was exchanged between Blakey and myself. No batsman, no matter how well he may have fared, likes to be out, and it is an unwritten rule in cricket – at least at this level – that the dismissed batsmen is left to his own devices before a conversation is initiated. Bats are regularly thrown down in disgust and anger inside, and sometimes outside, the dressing room on such occasions. Besides, I was too busy trying to keep down my heart rate as I approached the wicket.

Nobody in the Boland team knew who or what I was, of course, and the same went for the umpires. Goodness knows what they would make of me and my technique – or lack of it. And goodness knows what they would make of a Yorkshire team playing me at number four in the batting order. Maybe they would see it as a ray of hope – that someone as unorthodox and as inelegant as myself was deemed good enough to be selected as one of the key batsmen in one of England's top county teams. I'm not sure they know to this day who that number four batsman really was.

No matter. McGrath strolled over for a few comforting words. 'Take your time, Ian,' he reassured. 'We have plenty of overs to spare. Play yourself in, look for a few singles, and just play your natural game.'

I had certain goals to achieve, goals shared by probably every batsman in the world – from Sachin Tendulkar and Steve Waugh, to Ian Stafford. Goal number one: avoid, at all costs, a golden duck. This, thankfully, was achieved, when the fast bowler sent a useful delivery just short of a good length flashing past my off stump. I'd like to say that I let it pass. I certainly attempted to give that impression. The truth is I played and missed.

Goal number two was to get off the mark. A couple of years earlier I had failed to do this when, playing for New South Wales against Australia, I was dismissed for a fourth ball duck. This had been preying on my mind all day and now, as the bowler sprinted towards me, the horrifying recollection had lodged itself in the forefront of my mind.

It felt particularly good, therefore, just to strike the ball with the middle of my bat. The ball zipped along the ground and straight to a fielder for no run, but at least I had produced a worthy shot – something I had failed to do, with three misses and an edge to second slip, two years ago. With the last ball of the over I managed to knock a low, full toss down to long leg, and sprint to the other end. Since raising my bat in celebration of having avoided a duck would have been met with dismay by the small crowd of spectators, not to mention the Boland fielders, I managed to keep my emotions in check. However, a small ironic cheer could be heard coming from the watching Yorkshire squad. I realised that I had kept the strike away from the in-form McGrath, who found himself standing at the other end of the wicket watching all this with a mixture of bemusement and incredulity.

A couple of balls later an intended cut was turned into a thick inside edge down to fine leg from a spin bowler who was managing to turn the ball. McGrath promptly smacked the next ball for four, and in so doing made it obvious how our partnership would flourish. I would be the pusher and nudger, he would be the man who bludgeoned the ball. It was imperative, therefore, for me to ensure that he enjoyed most of the strike.

In the next over, luck fell my way. Always susceptible to a ball a fraction short of a length on my off-stump, I fished at an out-swinging ball and edged it. Despite the little amount of time a batsman has in such situations, he always manages to respond to the fateful sound of the nick by turning round and watching the wicketkeeper or slip dive for the catch. In this instance there was only a keeper, and although he did well to stoop low to his right, the ball plopped out of his glove to the ground. It was a difficult chance, but it was definitely a chance, nevertheless. I twiddled my bat around a number of times, just as Alec Stewart likes to do, and attempted to exude an unconcerned air. Deep down, I realised that I could, and possibly should, have been taking the long and lonely walk back to the pavilion.

Slowly time and runs ticked by. Another edge presented me with a single; a forward push out to cover added a quick run. A connection with a short ball on leg stump nearly resulted in a boundary. Indeed, so convinced was I that my healthy pull would evade the fielder loitering by the ropes, that I jogged for one run, only to be foiled by a magnificent stop and throw. In reality, we should have scored a couple of runs then. While training in t-shirt and shorts I was not exactly the fittest nor the fastest in the Yorkshire squad; and now, bogged down with pads and bats, gloves and a helmet, my going was slow indeed.

McGrath, meanwhile, continued in the same vein as he had during the first game of the tour, back in Pretoria against Northerns. He reached and passed his fifty as the overs came and went. I began to get in the wars. First, attempting a quick single, I was hit in the small of the back by the ball when a fielder tried to throw down my stumps. Then, in the next over, it occurred to me as I ambled down the wicket that if the cover fieldsman who had just picked up the ball were to knock down my stumps with a direct hit, I would be in serious trouble. In desperation – seeing, in the corner of my eye, the ball rocketing towards where I was headed – I threw myself forward in an untidy dive, somehow managing to produce a somersault in the process, smashing my bat against my helmet, and severely grazing my arm.

'You all right?' asked the umpire, as I shot to my feet and tried to give off the impression that nothing had happened. I noticed that the umpire was struggling to keep a straight face, while laughter could be heard back at the pavilion. Somehow, I could not imagine England's Michael Vaughan, who may well find himself at number four for Yorkshire at some point during the season, performing the same acrobatics.

My third goal was to reach double figures, and this was duly achieved with a late cut that actually came off. Now we were motoring. I was beginning to set my sights on a new goal – a cool half century, followed by a ton – when McGrath strolled down the wicket for a quick, mid-over chat. 'It's time to go for our shots,' he suggested. 'Just play as if you were in the nets.'

He was right. There were plenty of good batsmen waiting in the pavilion, and I could not be seen to be holding them up nor slowing down the score. A sweep of the spin bowler brought me a further two runs, and in-between two singles that came from my pushes out on to the on-side, McGrath smashed a six and a four over the bowler's head. 'That's great,' McGrath said as we held yet another mid-wicket discussion. 'Fourteen runs off the over. If we can keep this up we'll do very well.' Maybe, I thought, as I made my way back to the crease. But I had scored two of those fourteen runs. It did not feel like an equal partnership here.

Now there were just eight overs remaining. I realised that I had to go for broke. Boland recalled their opening bowler, the man who had already dismissed Blakey. I had already decided what shot I was going to play as he steamed in to unleash the ball. With a bit of luck the ball would be sent straight back over his head before crashing into the white concrete sight-screen behind him. That, at least, was the theory. The cruel reality was somewhat different. I missed the ball completely and heard the noise that every batsman dreads. Taking the quickest of glances back at the splayed wickets, I began to walk back to the pavilion. To my surprise the rest of the Yorkshire team emerged to clap me in, their applause augmented by the small contingent of Yorkshire supporters who had come out on tour to South Africa to enjoy a cricket holiday. Somewhat sheepishly I raised my bat, realising I was probably the first and last Yorkshire player to do so with a score of fourteen next to his name. Yet, for me, fourteen runs represented a triumph. I was desperate to make a contribution to the good cause, and I felt I had.

The fourteen sounds a little more convincing when seen in context. I had been at the crease for over an hour, and shared a partnership of eighty-eight with McGrath. He had contributed sixty-four to this, with ten extras, which underlines the obvious fact that he was the dominant batsman in the partnership, but at least it enabled Yorkshire to have a thrash in the last eight overs with plenty of batsmen to spare. This they proceeded to do, with Byas scoring a quick fourteen before being dismissed by the same man who bagged my wicket; McGrath reaching his second successive century of the tour before holing out to cover point; and Lumb and Hamilton knocking up useful scores in the teens as well with a late assault on the Boland bowling. After fifty overs Yorkshire had scored 235 runs for the loss of five wickets. The captain was a contented man. 'That's thirty-five runs more than I thought we'd get,' he said.

I felt now was as good a time as any to ask the new coach for a contract. Wayne Clark laughed. 'Erm, let me get back to you with that one, Ian,' he answered. 'But you did all right.' Later on, over lunch, the Australian was even adding weight to my contribution. 'Never mind the fourteen runs, look at your partnership with McGrath,' he argued. 'Maybe you two should become a regular item.' His encouragement was probably spurred on by the secret promise I had made to him and the captain that if my man back at the Newlands hotel delivered more than one can of Australian beer, they would be the first recipients.

After my failure in Australia back in 1999, I felt a happy man. It was only fourteen, and a rather lucky fourteen at that, but at least I had played some part in the match, when quite easily that might not have been the case. Such is the way of the batsman. I could have scored two runs that day, and been at the crease for ten minutes, if the wicketkeeper had kept hold of that edge. As a batsman, one missed chance and you are out; but if you survive those chances, nobody talks about anything but your final total. The outcome is mostly down to your talent, but some of it is clearly in the lap of the gods.

Matt Carrico had finally arrived while I had been at the crease. Carrico, an American who lives in Leeds, had formerly been a BUPA and PGA European golf tour physiotherapist before he was headhunted by Wayne Morton. An affable man, to whom the team took an instant liking, he was slightly hampered by just one thing: he knew nothing, really nothing, about cricket. Over lunch I explained one or two cricketing terms, such as 'bouncer', 'googly' and 'Chinaman'. Matt certainly knew his stuff when it came to physiotherapy, but his cricket education was set to be a steep learning curve.

When it was our turn to field I felt surprisingly tired by my exertions. Blakey had suggested to Byas that he and I could share wicketkeeping duties, with maybe me taking over duty behind the stumps for the last twenty overs. The captain, sporting his favoured wide-brimmed fielding hat, decided this was not such a good idea. 'There has to be a semblance of seriousness about this,' he argued, which was as good a put-down as any I'd received over the year I had spent playing with Britain's top sportsmen and teams.

Every so often I would swing my arms rather ostentatiously in the close proximity of Byas in the hope that he might call upon me to bowl. As Boland's wickets began to tumble, and it became obvious that they would not come close to reaching our total, McGrath would make a point of asking me which end I would be bowling from, always within earshot of the captain.

Hamilton, too, joined in the fun. Once, when just about everyone else in the side had shouted out words of support as he trudged back to his mark ready to bowl another fast delivery, he turned to me and said: 'Any chance of encouragement, Ian?'

'Come on Gav,' I replied, as he began his run-up. A couple of seconds later the batsman was making his way back to the pavilion after a smartly taken catch by Middlebrook at slip.

'That was brilliant,' Hamilton said to me, as we exchanged high fives. 'Can you do that for every ball?'

Most of the time Byas fielded me at either mid-on or square leg, but for a few overs he placed me just a few feet away from the batsman. This is the most dangerous position in fielding. Connect with a pull or a hook from the meat of the bat, and you can be in serious trouble. It did not occur to me to ask for a helmet, although later in the afternoon I noticed others wore them in the same position. Only once did the ball fly in my general direction and, despite a flying leap to my left side, I was not even close to catching it. The event was met by a series of 'Oohs' and 'Aahs' from the rest of the Yorkshire side. 'Sharp chance that, Ian,' added Blakey from behind the stumps.

The longer the game went on, the stiffer I felt. My innings had clearly taken a lot out of me, and my running and especially my throwing was beginning to become embarrassing. Thankfully, it made little difference. Dawson and Fisher's spin bowling, together with Hamilton's early wickets, did the damage, and Boland were skittled out a hundred runs short of our total. Yorkshire had just secured their third win out of three on tour.

In the dressing room afterwards Byas delivered his now custom-ary speech, congratulating everyone for another winning performance. McGrath, too, made his customary announcement. It was time for the hideous shirt to be passed on. This time would be worse because not only had a further element been added to the outfit, but also the recipient would have to wear it out in Cape Town that night for the team meal, which was bound to descend quickly into a major drinking session.

There are times in life when you just know what is on the horizon. This was one such occasion. 'The committee have voted unanimously on this,' McGrath announced. 'For diving full length, producing a somersault, cutting his arm, hitting himself on his helmet with his bat and then, worst of all, jumping to his feet quicker than any of us have ever seen anyone do so before, and pretend that nothing had happened and nobody had seen a thing, the award is presented to Ian Stafford.'

Simon Guy handed me the shirt, together with a batman mask. Everyone applauded, as though I had just received a major award. I looked at the shirt and the mask, a black plastic monstrosity with ears. This would be my attire for the evening. Needless to say, I could hardly wait.

A smirking Simon Widdup, an earlier shirt-wearer, described the moment that had clinched it. 'I was sitting on the boundary with a couple of the others,' he said. 'As soon as you somersaulted and then tried to make out it hadn't happened, we looked at each other and said: "shirt".'

When I emerged in the hotel lobby that evening I discovered that not only was I the last to arrive but also that I was two minutes late. 'That's another fine,' announced McGrath once everyone had stopped laughing at the sight of the figure in the ridiculous shirt and batman mask who appeared out of the elevator.

A long table awaited us in the nearby bar. Laid out in front of each place was a bottle of Castle lager, a glass of Guinness, and a large vodka and Red Bull. Drinks had to be handled with the left hand only, and any conversation directed at a member of the committee had to be conducted with the ping-pong ball in the mouth. I never discovered why we needed the packet of soup or the TV remote control.

Before the evening got underway in earnest some members of the Warwickshire team suddenly appeared in the same bar. They had just arrived in South Africa to begin their tour, and exchanged hellos with many of the Yorkshire team. Although stiff opponents for much of the summer, the players were all members of the cricket 'circus' that tours Britain's towns and cities during the summer months. Over the years, most get to know each other well.

Wayne Clark and Matt Carrico were subjected to the same introductory drink that I had been forced to down before the court session three nights earlier. Then the three of us, starting with me, were ordered to sing a song of our choice for forty-five seconds, without faltering, whilst standing on a chair in the full view of not only the Yorkshire squad but also the rest of the restaurant. I chose 'American Pie'; Wayne sang some unrecognisable Australian country folk song; and poor Matt, who had only arrived in the country that day after an overnight flight from England, ended the excruciatingly embarrassing sequence with that old favourite, 'You've Lost That Lovin' Feeling'. McGrath then read out his favourite letters in reply to his invitation for the night's fun. The fact that I had become the first person in the history of Yorkshire cricket to type, as opposed to scrawl, a reply meant that I received a rebate for my earlier fine for lateness.

Wayne Morton, an old hand at such events after his many years with both Yorkshire and England, took charge of the proceedings as various toasts were made, designed primarily to catch out David Byas. As the younger lads drank more, so they grew braver. 'I'll have a drink with anyone who's a farmer,' announced one, causing the captain to point his threatening finger at him before taking his drink. 'I'll have a drink with anyone who wore wellington boots this winter,' said another. Again, Byas had to stand up, and down the contents of his glass. 'I'll drink with anyone who drives a Vauxhall,' said a third. Byas was already half-way to his feet before the toast had even been completed. Three nights earlier at the court session, as my error-strewn evening led to ever more glasses of beer, he had informed me that when you have been around as long as he has you don't get caught out in such sessions. Now, to the delight of the rest of the squad, the captain was receiving his long overdue comeuppance.

And so the evening lurched onwards, and downwards, with speeches and fines, drinks and laughter. The night before turned into the morning after, the day I would be returning home. Sore heads were replaced by a mid-afternoon fitness session of surprising intensity and a rousing speech from Wayne Clark, who had thoroughly enjoyed the night's antics. 'Nothing like good team spirit,' he declared, smirking broadly. 'And I'm impressed with the way you have approached the tour so far,' he added, clearly delighted with the first three wins. 'Never forget, we're a team first and foremost, not a collection of individuals. Concentrate on the basics and success will come.'

I had just managed to buy the next addition to the red shirt – a diver's balaclava – before it was time to hand it, together with the shirt and mask, over to McGrath. Some poor soul would be wearing the lot following the end of the three-day game against Western Province Academy that was to start the next day.

Shaking each and every member of the Yorkshire squad by the hand I thanked them for their support, and bade them farewell. 'Remember,' I told them, as the car arrived to take me to the airport, 'if you do need me to bat for you this season, just give us a call.'

Everyone smiled and waved, but strangely nobody said a word.

chapter seven

 **THE FINAL LAP**

'You are a complete pain in the arse.' It was not the first time I had been greeted with such an enthusiastic welcome, and no doubt will not be the last, but it was symptomatic of not only the mood but also the manner in which Eddie Irvine and I had sparred and jousted over the past few months. This, believe it or not, was almost a compliment from the Ulsterman, Formula One driver and unashamed playboy of the paddock, even if it was uttered moments before he was about to face me, head to head, in a two-car race at Silverstone.

The race was to be the culmination of six months spent, off and on, in the company of the Jaguar Formula One racing team. During this time the Jaguar team had seen some extraordinary comings and goings, while I endured my various stints playing rugby league for Wigan, running in world-class sprints and making my cricket debut for Yorkshire CCC.

The very notion that I would not excel as a racing driver was too ridiculous, of course, to contemplate. I am a man, after all. And, as I have been told many a time by racing school instructors and Formula One drivers, for most of the male population this is apparently the only ingredient necessary. If further proof of my abilities were needed I can add the fact that I once overtook Michael Schumacher on a Silverstone bend.

It was after testing one early summer evening, and Schumacher, the world champion then as he is now, was making his way home using a small part of the circuit to find the site exit. To my delight I drew up behind his Ferrari sports car and, failing to quell an irresistible, puerile urge, I pulled out, slammed my foot down on my acceleration pedal, and shot past him. As the two cars drew momentarily level we exchanged glances, mine triumphant and his, squinting in the low sunlight, somewhat scathing. 'There goes another prat who can now boast to his friends that he overtook Michael Schumacher,' the German most probably concluded.

Armed with such an impressive curriculum vitae I felt it was only right that I should skip the many years of driving through the ranks and the hundreds of thousands of pounds required in this sport and approach Jaguar with the proposition that I should become one of their Formula One drivers.

Why Jaguar? Well, apart from Ferrari, who else in motor sport can boast such a prestigious and long-standing reputation? The famous green livery was not yet one year into its Formula One career, but it had already made its mark – if not in terms of Grand Prix wins, at least by adding its hallowed name to the seventeen races that made up the Formula One season. With the likes of Jackie Stewart still involved, and subsequently Bobby Rahal and Niki Lauda also coming on board, the outfit was riddled with achievement and motor racing history.

And then there was Eddie Irvine. Difficult, arrogant, absurd at times, and rude. Very rude. Yet he was someone who fascinated me. There must be more to the only driver in today's group of racing automatons who resembles a throwback to the playboys of the 1970s and early 1980s, a man who brazenly promotes his lifestyle of yachts and planes, cars, homes and, above all, women. He had, after all, finished second in the drivers' championship behind Mika Hakkinen only the year before, when racing for Ferrari; and his long track record in Formula One, with first Jordan, then Ferrari and now Jaguar, suggested that beneath the party-going exterior there was a very accomplished racing driver. But what of the man himself? The next few months were to answer that question.

My connection with Jaguar was eased through by my previous acquaintances with the marketing manager, Simon Crane, whom I had known in his former guise as the chief executive of Loftus Road plc; and Cameron Kelleher, the media and public relations manager, who had worked with me at *The Times* newspaper back in the late 1980s.

Simon and Cameron agreed that I could join up with Jaguar, with the ultimate aim of challenging Irvine to a race in a single-seater motor racing car. First, however, it would be opportune to gain some driving experience. Johnny Herbert was the number two driver for Jaguar at the time, a man whose racing career, like that of most Formula One drivers, had started in karting. And so it was to Bill Sisley, the owner of the Buckmore Park karting circuit near Chatham in Kent, that I was first to turn. If Buckmore Park had been good enough for Sisley's friend Herbert to start out at, then it most certainly would be good enough for me.

Over the course of half a dozen or so lessons Bill, together with a number of other instructors, introduced me to the basics of motor racing. These comprised racing lines (to produce the shortest and therefore the quickest route, and the smoothest ride, and to make it harder to be overtaken), acceleration (on the straights and emerging from the bends), braking (as late and as smooth as possible), heeling and toeing (the art of braking while keeping the other foot on the throttle), overtaking – and the experience of spinning off and crashing, which was a frightening event at first as the kart span hopelessly out of control and careered into a wall of tyres. However, once it became clear that the vehicle would remain upright throughout all this and that, time after time, you emerged unscathed, so a fearless urge to push harder became dominant.

I entered one of Buckmore Park's race nights, a chance for amateur racing drivers who spend their weekends around the country karting, speed hill climbing or touring, to pit their racing skills against each other. Under the circuit's floodlights, as the evening dew made the track increasingly slippery, I recorded a reasonable place of twentieth out of forty-three. Nothing to make Eddie Irvine quake in his luxury yacht, of course, but it was a start.

Jaguar felt it would be appropriate if I were to witness their operation at the sharp end of their business. In other words, experience a Grand Prix from within the camp of a Formula One team. They invited me out to Monza, for the Italian Grand Prix of 2000, and the home of Ferrari. Saturday, the day of qualifying, was spent enjoying the largesse of Formula One. Lunch, at the £500,000 motor home which formed part of the £1.5 million facilities available to VIP guests and sponsors, was taken alongside the likes of the German and AC Milan football star Oliver Bierhoff, Italian football superstar Alessandro Del Piero and, somewhat bizarrely, television personality Carol Vorderman.

Irvine and Herbert qualified in fourteenth and eighteenth positions respectively. It had been that kind of year for Jaguar, who had just gone back into Formula One. More, much more, had been expected of the team – but people had allowed the image of Jaguar to overshadow the stark fact that no team achieves much in terms of points in their first year. In fact, the four points that Irvine had achieved earlier in the season would be it for the year.

During the course of the afternoon I met a number of key Formula One faces. Bernie Ecclestone, Mr Formula One himself, was strutting around the paddock surveying his empire, as were team owners Ron Dennis, Flavio Briatore and Eddie Jordan. The drivers, too, made brief appearances in between testing and debriefs, always followed by a posse of photographers and girls. I stopped for a brief chat with Jenson Button, who spent some of the time talking about his impending move from Williams to Benetton, but was often distracted by the gaggle of long-legged models who paraded up and down the paddock as if they were on a catwalk. Which, in a way, they were.

Luciano Burti, Jaguar's test driver, was introduced to me. He would be taking over from Herbert as the number two driver the following season, with Herbert looking for a drive in the Cart championship in the

United States. Burti, a polite and friendly young man who was desperate to prove himself in Formula One, promised to help me in my bid to beat Irvine. 'You can do it,' he told me, with only a slight hint of a smirk on his face. Herbert, who drove me back to our hotel, put it differently. 'If you try and beat Eddie in a race, he'll beat you up,' the diminutive Englishman promised. His mood was not at its best as he contemplated starting the Italian Grand Prix from eighteenth on the grid. 'All I need is a seventeen-car shunt and I've got a chance,' he mused.

Race day itself proved to demand far more than simply driving a car in a Grand Prix. No sport in the world has such a symbiotic relationship with sponsors as does Formula One, and it is on such days that the sponsors get their money's worth. And so Irvine and Herbert's timetable on the day of the Italian Grand Prix read like this:

0800–0900: Pit walkabout.

0930–1000: F1 warm-up on the circuit.

1110–1115: Pit walkabout.

1115–1135: F1 drivers' parade.

1140: Driver appearances at hospitality venues. Lunch.

1400: Italian Grand Prix.

The 'Italian Grand Prix' part of all this turned out to be the shortest commitment of the lot. Both Irvine and Herbert were out before the end of a chaotic first lap dominated by accidents. Irvine went first, after Mika Salo collided with him; Herbert followed, when Pedro de la Rosa shunted into the back of his car. Despite the multiple pile-ups, and the freak, tragic death of a marshall hit by a flying wheel, the race continued and, to the joy of the Ferrari-supporting Tifosi, Schumacher won in a race that would go some way to confirming his return to being the world champion. Others, however, felt that the race should have been stopped, especially when news of the fatality became the talk of the pits, paddock and stands.

'We've had better days,' Gary Anderson, Jaguar's technical director, said afterwards, which was something of an understatement. 'There's little satisfaction to be taken from a race in which both cars are out after the first two turns.' Herbert was philosophical. 'I would have liked to finish my European Formula One career on a high but that's life,' he said, with a shrug of his shoulders. And Irvine? Well, Eddie was in a rush to nip back on his motorbike to his Milan apartment. There was, after all, a party to go to that night. 'When you are braking from that sort of speed into a chicane then three into two won't go,' he said, by way of explaining how he ended up out of the race after a matter of seconds. 'It's just one of those things.'

Simon Crane was not quite as ready to accept the harsh realities of Grand Prix racing. 'Last year, before Stewart Ford Racing sold out to Jaguar, Phil Collins came along as one of our guests,' he told me, with a weary expression, 'and we recorded a first and a fourth. When you come we can't even last twenty seconds.' It was good to know it was all my fault.

The season was over by the time I linked up with Jaguar again. Schumacher had duly won his third world title, his first for Ferrari; Herbert had departed looking for a drive in the United States; and, after just a few weeks' break, Irvine and now Burti found themselves in Barcelona in the second week of December, where they were testing in readiness for the new season – set to begin three months later with the Malaysian Grand Prix.

It was here that I joined them with a view to getting to know Burti and, in particular, Irvine, and undergo some training with Jaguar's conditioning expert, Nick Harris. 'A Formula One driver requires the stamina of a long-distance runner, the strength of a wrestler, the reaction of a tennis player and the agility of a ballet dancer,' Harris had told me in Monza, while dubiously eyeing up my own physical features. Harris was to work with me in Barcelona in an attempt to transform me into someone who was at least bodily capable of racing the likes of Irvine.

Harris was an interesting character. A sports science graduate, his

main interest was in the physiological aspects of training and conditioning. Having worked with football and rugby players in his time, as well
as powerboat drivers, he could talk at length on any subject relevant to
his position. 'Because of the gravitational forces experienced in Formula
One it's crucial that stability comes from soft tissues,' he explained, as
he rubbed down a prostrate Burti in the Jaguar motor home. 'That's
why we go through a progressive stretching exercise that replicates
the type of contraction drivers go through. I have to mobilise the
soft tissues and the vertebrae in readiness for stress. A stable head
position is necessary for a driver because jerking movements leave you
disorientated.'

As Harris explained the process I observed Burti, who resembled a
walking advertising billboard. Splattered all over his Jaguar green race
suit were logos from HSBC, HP, Rolex, One 2 One, DHL Worldwide
Express, Becks, Michelin, Texaco, Lear and Worldcom, to name just a
few. Irvine, meanwhile, was catnapping during breaks in testing. In the
past few days he had been a guest on Channel 4's 'TFI Friday', alongside
such luminaries as John McEnroe and Kylie Minogue. He had arrived in
Barcelona the night before, courtesy of his own Lear jet. (I had arrived
in Barcelona the night before too, courtesy of easyJet.)

The pit lane that morning was a frantic hive of activity. Next door
to the Jaguar garage the BMW–Williams team were hard at work with
Ralf Schumacher and new boy, Pablo Juan Montoya. The Colombian,
a star in American Indycar racing, would create most of the furtive
glances stemming from elsewhere. Benetton and Prost were further along
the lane.

By this time, the first of a series of changes in personnel at Jaguar
had taken place. Out had gone Gary Anderson, and in had come the
team's new technical director, Steve Nichols. He was eager to see just
how good Jaguar's two cars – a R1B and a standard 2000-spec R1 – would
run on the Michelin tyres the team had turned to. Over the airwaves
we listened to Irvine's opinions as he raced around the Spanish Grand

Prix venue. 'It's grippy, digging in a bit on the bumps,' reported Jaguar's number one driver. 'In the high-speed corners it's pushing like a pig.'

Nick Harris had already insisted that I swallow a vitamin B tablet that morning. 'Creates energy from food and helps to produce healthy blood cells,' he said. This was followed by a fruit shake and a pasta-based lunch, as eaten by Irvine and Burti. It was in the afternoon that Irvine first began to show some interest in my existence. Once he had been told of my previous sporting adventures, the competitive animal inside him seemed to rear its head.

Inside the motor home sat a Concept 2000, a state of the art rowing machine. Irvine challenged me to have a crack at 2,500 metres. 'What time can you do it in?' he asked. Although I have spent many an hour on a rowing machine, I had never timed myself in a flat out, 2,500 session. 'I don't know,' I replied. 'Ten minutes?'

Irvine snorted. 'My granny could beat that,' he said, uttering one of his favoured sayings. 'Bet you can't better my best time of 9 minutes, 29 seconds.' He sauntered out of the motor home. 'I'll be back shortly to see how you're doing.'

The challenge was on. Harris set up the machine, informed me that I needed to average around 1 minute 51 seconds for each 500 metres, and started the watch. Fortunately, the following week I was to report for training duty with the Wigan Warriors rugby league team before playing in the big Boxing Day derby game against St Helens, and so although I may not have been the finest physical specimen, I had at least built up some all-round strength.

By the time Irvine had returned to the motor home, fully expecting to find me in the midst of abject failure, I was half-way to completing the 2,500 metres and ahead of schedule. Aware that I was on course to beating his mark, he resorted first to psychological ploys, and then downright abuse.

He began by sitting to my side, observing me from just a few inches away. Swigging from a bottle of water, as torrents of sweat poured down my face, he began commenting how good the water tasted, before handing the bottle to Harris across my path as I slid back and forth on the rowing machine. When he discovered this had little effect, he turned to name-calling. 'You're fat,' he said. 'You're old.' Emma Owen, the hapless public relations officer from Jaguar who had been handed the dubious pleasure of looking after Eddie and me, looked astounded by these goings-on. The time read 8 minutes and I was now some distance ahead of his 8-minute mark.

Irvine continued his ploy. 'You're a faggot, a poof.' By now I was beginning to groan and make loud breathing noises as I drew near to my goal. 'Is that the noise you make when you're shagging?' he asked. Moments later I reached 2,500 metres in a time of 9 minutes, 9 seconds. I had beaten Irvine by 20 seconds. The Formula One driver shook my hand and changed his demeanour completely.

'Okay, I'll give you that one,' he said. 'That's 1–0 to you. You may be fat and old but you've got decent will-power. But don't think you've won anything. You've just taken the lead, that's all.'

The lead in what, exactly? 'Well, there's our race, for a start,' Irvine replied. 'And I gather you want to come out to spend a day with me some place. We'll have to do something there. Maybe the yacht's a good place? How about a swimming race?'

I asked him why he had suggested this. 'I used to be an Irish international swimmer when I was a teenager,' he admitted. 'So I'll definitely beat you in that. Or we could do a mini triathlon?'

We agreed that the battle would continue, in some form, somewhere else. While Irvine returned to yet more testing out on the circuit Harris set me back to work on the Concept 2000, this time performing four three-minute bursts at ninety per cent, with ninety-second intervals to recover. 'It's exactly what I get Eddie to do,' he informed me, as I panted like a thirsty dog afterwards.

As we drove back to the hotel, Irvine appeared in high spirits and decided that we would be interested in hearing how he bedded a couple of former Miss Irelands plus a Miss Germany. As you do. It was clear, though, as he made his way to his room, that the rowing machine challenge earlier in the day was still on his mind.

'You know something?' he said, as he unlocked his hotel room door. 'You may have recorded a faster time than me, but I definitely have a much quicker recovery period than you.' Well, at least that had been sorted out.

Nick Harris had devised a particularly intense fitness session for me the following morning. Near the entrance to the circuit a couple of steep hills swept down towards the track. It was here that Harris took me to perform ten 200-metre sprints. Each sprint would be preceded by an exercise. Before the first run, for example, I had to produce twenty press-ups. Before the second, twenty star jumps. Before the third, twenty burpees. Before the fourth, twenty sit-ups. And so on. My recovery period in-between each sprint would be ninety seconds, which was just about the time it took me to stagger back to my starting position. It was a relatively short session, but extremely demanding, and doubly useful. This was relevant not only to motor racing but also to rugby league – the following week in Wigan, I was to find the shuttle work to be a little less demanding than it might have been.

Over lunch Irvine seemed surprisingly keen to talk. Despite recording only four points in the season just past, in some contrast to the runner-up spot he had bagged the year before, he insisted that he had never been happier. 'Finishing second in the world championship with Ferrari means very little to me,' he insisted. 'I don't look back on it as any real achievement, nor with any discernible pride. Given the choice between doing it with Ferrari or with Jaguar then I can tell you that I would much rather it was with Jaguar.'

It seemed an odd admission from a man who was so close to getting his hands on Formula One's holy grail. 'But Ferrari wasn't my team,' Irvine explained. 'It was Michael Schumacher's. He was the guy who was meant to win the world championship for them, not me. Ferrari had everything at their disposal – the money, the knowledge, the best guys. I just sat in the car and drove it. My input wasn't asked for. That's why I can't look back on my runner-up year with much pride at all.'

What of 2000, then, a year in which Jaguar fell way short of expectation, and Irvine found himself back among the also-rans? 'Funnily enough, it's probably been my most enjoyable season ever in Formula One,' he replied, blinking in the bright glare of the Spanish winter sun. 'Sure, in terms of results it was pretty disastrous, but I reckon I'm driving better than ever. For example, the best Grand Prix I've ever driven in my career was not one of the races I've won, but in Budapest last season, when I don't think I made a single mistake – yet I didn't even win a point.'

So what is so special about driving for a team doing no better than lurking in the middle of the grid? 'I'll tell you what it is,' Irvine said, jabbing his pasta with a fork. 'People think I came here for the money. Nothing could be further from the truth. I feel that Jaguar is partly my baby. It's something I'm trying to help build. I have a great deal of input here, and that's how I like it. How good will it be if Jaguar can compete with the top guys in a few years' time? It's a mountain to climb, but it will be a fantastic achievement and one I want to be a part of.'

I began to see Irvine in a very different light as we demolished Harris's high-protein lunch. For a man who has made his millions, won his many Grands Prix, who has been close to the top of Formula One for nearly a decade and, quite ostentatiously, enjoys all the trimmings his role as a Grand Prix racing driver can offer, his appetite for the sport remains healthy. At thirty-five years of age he understands that time is running out, but maintains that he is far from finished. 'Formula One racing is not about age, it's about hunger,' he said. 'Just look at Nigel Mansell. He was still desperate for it up into his forties. Don't forget, I was a late starter.'

There was one other factor too, one that belied his playboy image. He had finished second once before in the world championship, driving a Ferrari with Michael Schumacher as his dominant team-mate. Now he wanted to achieve at the very least second again, and this time on his terms.

'I was lucky that Schumacher had an accident that gave me the chance to go for the title,' he admitted. 'But, as soon as he returned later in the season, I realised I wasn't going to become world champion. If I can challenge for the world title again then I'll prove to everyone, especially myself, that it wasn't just a one-off.'

As he rose from his seat, grabbed his helmet and made his way to the motor home door all set for another session on the Barcelona circuit, I asked one, final question. What, in his opinion, was the best moment in Formula One racing, the reason, above all else, that he does this?

Irvine's reply was instant. 'When you know you've just completed a bloody good race. Sometimes it doesn't hit you until you're sitting on the plane flying home afterwards. If it's been an easy win then you'll suddenly clench your fist and say, "Yes!" If it's been a close chase, though, and you win by, say, two-tenths of a second, then when you cross that line it's relief that you've beaten the bastard behind you. Up until then anything could happen, and it has. It's like having a gun held to your head and the trigger is never quite pulled. As soon as you know you've won there's an explosion of emotion that cannot be replicated. That's a pretty special moment, too.'

Irvine was leaving for home that night, courtesy of his private jet which had waited for him at nearby Gerona Airport. Burti would have one more day's testing. The Brazilian was attempting to complete over one hundred laps in Barcelona in preparation for his first full season in Formula One. Jaguar's test driver the previous season, he had been given the chance to drive in the Austrian Grand Prix alongside Herbert after Irvine pulled out at the last moment with a stomach bug. Burti had no time to acclimatise to the conditions, let alone the track, but completed the Grand Prix in eleventh position.

It would be the beginning of a crucial three days. 'I was delighted to have shown what I could do,' he explained, as we sat in the motor home. 'I had been waiting some time for my chance. But the following week Jaguar were seeing how Dario Franchitti [the Indycar driver] would fare in testing. They had him down as their next driver for Formula One. The fact that I did better than expected in the Austrian Grand Prix merely persuaded Jaguar to put Dario up against me. I don't think they really saw it as a head to head, rather more just the chance for Dario to be given a little competition.'

The 'little competition' then went out and recorded significantly quicker times than Franchitti. The Indycar driver was told he was not, after all, required, and flew back to the United States. Burti, against all expectations, had just won himself a lucrative seat in the Jaguar Formula One car for the 2001 season. 'I've never doubted my ability,' said the man who was drawn into Formula One after watching Ayrton Senna race in the Brazilian Grand Prix in their home city of São Paulo. 'And I'm not intending to spend my Formula One career at the back of the grid, either. I'm here to win. If I don't, I won't hang about. I'll find a car, whether in Formula One or not, that will help me become a champion.' Ambitious words from an ambitious young man, although Burti's friendly persona and courteous manner belied his burning drive, and contrasted somewhat with Jaguar's number one driver.

Christmas came and went, as did my Boxing Day match with the Wigan Warriors. In the second week of January I was invited to the official unveiling of Jaguar's new car at their Whitley engineering centre on the outskirts of Coventry. It was a glitzy affair, although notably low key compared to the year before, in which the American telecommunications giant AT&T had been announced as Jaguar's latest big-name sponsor. Irvine, Burti and development driver Tomas Scheckter removed some tarpaulin to reveal the new car – all shiny and green – as a hundred camera bulbs flashed from the massed rank of motor racing and car industry photographers.

A further and significant addition had been made to the personnel at Jaguar Racing. Bobby Rahal, the forty-eight-year-old former Cart and Indy 500 champion had been appointed as the new team principal and chief executive officer, and it was he who made the main, and highly polished, presentation. A kart race had been set up for the following day at Silverstone between Burti and myself, all as part of my preparation for the big race with Irvine. 'All set for tomorrow?' Burti asked, as he passed by. 'I fancy I'll be recording my first win of the season.' I told him not to be so presumptuous. 'I finished twentieth out of forty-three at Buckmore Park four months ago,' I said. 'I reckon I'm even better now.' Burti seemed less than concerned by this bravado.

Tomas Scheckter ambled over to say hello, too. The son of the South African former world champion Jody Scheckter, Tomas was eager to be involved in anything to do with Jaguar in his personal quest for a Formula One drive, even if it meant racing against me. When it became clear, twenty-four hours later, that Burti's testing was taking longer than expected, Tomas required no persuading to step in and face me at the Silverstone kart track.

He took the competition seriously, too. As we twisted and turned, braked and then sped away around the tight kart circuit Scheckter proceeded to bump me from behind when he needed to overtake me, and from the side as we jostled for the best position rounding a bend. Like a child in a playground he was clearly enjoying himself as he shook his fist at me after one particular heavy collision. After half an hour, and some sixty-odd laps, the organisers asked us to stop and gave us our lap times. Scheckter's best was 20.35 seconds; mine was some two seconds slower, at 22.41 seconds.

Tomas looked pleased with himself. I pointed out that the circuit had been cold and damp, that I hadn't karted for over four months, that he clearly had a faster kart than me and that I was significantly heavier than him. His eyes widened and a big, toothy smile appeared. 'That's good,' he said. 'That's very good. You're making lots of excuses. You're starting to sound like a Formula One driver now.'

At twenty years old Tomas was not even born when his father became world champion, although the connotations of the surname have stuck with him ever since. 'It's helped and hindered me,' he said. 'Because I'm a Scheckter people expect me to win every time, but it's not my dad racing in the car, it's me.'

It transpired that father Jody was anything but supportive at first when his son announced he wanted to enter motor racing. 'After my mum gave me a kart my dad tried to make me stop. I'd go to kart races and everyone else would have their fathers there shouting out their support, but my father said it was too dangerous and didn't want me racing at all. After a few years he could see that I was serious, though, and when he saw me win my first race at sixteen he told me he would support me for one year in Europe. If I wasn't any good I would go to university and do something else. I said fair enough, and won my second race.'

And now? 'And now I'm testing for Jaguar, which is both good and bad.' Why? 'It's good because two years ago I would have given anything just to touch a Formula One car. Testing for Jaguar provides me with the opportunity to impress a Formula One team. I'm a lot nearer to becoming a racing driver at the highest level. But it's bad, too, because I'm a racing driver and I'm not racing. That's why I've enjoyed karting against you today. It gave me some competition.'

I wondered how he was treated by Irvine. 'Eddie treats me as a junior, but that's part of his personality. He makes me laugh and he's achieved a lot in motor racing, whereas I'm just a little squirt who sits in his motor home and gets in the way. But my time will come.'

Like any other racing driver, Scheckter had great belief in himself. He was impatient to be given his chance, but knew, as he surveyed the scene at Jaguar, that with luck his time would indeed come, just as it had for Burti and, well before him, Irvine. As for me, I drove home just pleased with the fact that Tomas had referred to me as 'competition'.

Seven days later I was back at the Silverstone kart track. Luciano Burti, to my surprise, was disappointed not to have faced my so-called challenge the week before and still fancied the race. Jaguar arranged another kart session at the Silverstone track just for Burti and me. Scheckter had played his part, too, in all this. Apparently on returning to the motor home he had reported that I was a very talented driver, and had pushed him all the way. Not only that, but Tomas had told an astonished Burti that, although he had recorded a slightly faster time, there was less than half a second between the two of us when all the lap times were added together.

The conditions were noticeably worse this time. The temperature was so cold that there was still the odd patch of ice on the circuit, which led to a number of spins from my kart and half a dozen crashes into the wall. After twenty-five laps it was clear to Burti that Scheckter had exaggerated my karting prowess. Like the South African test driver, Luciano's best time was just over two seconds faster than mine, although we were both some five seconds slower than the previous week due to the unfavourable conditions. 'So, that's 1–1,' Burti announced, as he shook my hand. I hadn't even known we were in a competition, but the Brazilian had heard of my rowing race with Irvine and revealed that my time for 2,500 metres was nineteen seconds faster than his. He may have come across as a different animal to Irvine, but the same competitiveness lurked. In fact, it reminded me of a conversation I had with Jacques Villeneuve a couple of years earlier, just after he had become world champion. I asked him what he would do if I beat him in a game of Space Invaders. He replied: 'I'd go away, find a Space Invaders machine, practise until I was convinced I was better than you, challenge you to a rematch and beat you.'

Back at the Jaguar garage Irvine was dressed up in a suit, with a young and attractive model draped on each arm. I was attired in a waterproof sports anorak provided by the Wigan Warriors, and a black bobble hat that befitted the weather. 'Bloody hell,' Eddie announced, when he saw me enter the scene. 'It's Ali G!'

We asked each other what we were doing. Irvine was in the process of filming a commercial for Becks beer, one of Jaguar Racing's chief sponsors. I told him about my session with Burti on the kart track.

'You'd probably beat me if we had a kart race,' he conceded. 'I'm useless at karting. Never been any good at it. They're too small for me, and not fast enough to my liking. Now, I hear we'll be racing in Formula Fords. Even they're not fast enough, but they'll do. You'll be found out then, that's for sure.'

Burti had appeared and caught the last few exchanges between Irvine and me. 'You know what you ought to do,' he said, taking me to one side. 'You should spend a few days at a racing drivers' school. The difference between you and me may not seem that much in terms of time, but that two-second gap is a massive one to make up. That's where driving school will help. You want to give Eddie a race, don't you?' Luciano was right. In my lifetime I may have driven hundreds of thousands of miles in a road car, and I had now covered many laps in a kart at both Buckmore Park and Silverstone. I may even be a man. Yet if I seriously wanted to provide some kind of competition to Eddie Irvine, a couple of days' tuition from a recognised racing drivers' school would not go amiss.

I contacted Ken Bowes at the Silverstone Drive School and told him of my ultimate goal to race Irvine in April. He agreed with my suggestion that a few lessons might improve my chances, and set up a couple of days with his instructors. Before all this was to happen, however, I needed to meet two significant people.

Bobby Rahal may not mean a great deal to non-aficionados of motor racing, especially those in Britain, but in the US Rahal is as well known as anyone in the sport. His highly successful career in cart and Indycar racing is in some contrast to a Grand Prix career of two races with the now defunct Wolf Formula One team, alongside team-mate Jody Scheckter. You might have expected a man who had arrived at Jaguar Racing intent on shaking the place up after the previous year's disappointments to be less than enamoured with the prospect of his drivers hanging out with a wannabe Formula One star, and even less enthusiastic with the notion that his number one driver would be challenging me to a head-to-head, winner-takes-all race at Silverstone. Yet he admitted to being intrigued.

'Didn't you fight Roy Jones Jr, the world light-heavyweight boxing champion, the other year?' he asked, when he invited me to his neat office at Jaguar headquarters in Milton Keynes. 'Then you must be brave, talented or mad. You need a little bit of all three ingredients to be a good racing driver.'

I decided not to tell him that although I may possess a little of his first category, and a great deal of his last one, the middle ingredient was where my chief problem lay. Besides, I was more interested in what persuaded him to give up his successful and lucrative career in motor-sport administration in the States to take over the reins at Jaguar Racing.

'I called a friend of mine in California and asked him for some advice,' he answered. 'I had a racing team in the States, owned eight automobile dealerships and, if I had wanted to, could have sat out the rest of my life on a beach. My friend told me he had just seen a ninety-five-year-old woman interviewed on television. When asked if she had any regrets she replied that she wished she had climbed more mountains. She was speaking figuratively, of course, but that answer provided me with mine.' He continued: 'Hell, there may be lots of reasons why I chose to take up the job: I'd lived here in Britain before and made many friends; it's a great experience for my family; I wasn't ready to sit on a beach; I'd never achieved what I wanted to in my short career as a Formula One driver. But when it all boiled down, this was my greatest challenge. How many times in life are you given the chance to direct a Formula One team? I looked upon this as my final mountain. This is my Everest. If I'd said no I would have regretted it for the rest of my life.'

Rahal conceded that there are significant differences between Indycar racing and Formula One. 'In Indycar the race is the show. In Formula One the show is the show.' Yet it was his deeply embedded love of motor sport, and in particular Formula One, that enticed him.

'I never got *Hot Rod* magazine as a kid. I read *Road and Track*. That informed me about Formula One. You wanna know who my hero was? It wasn't A.J. Foyt. It was Jimmy Clark. I can tell you exactly what I was doing when JFK was shot. I can tell you exactly where I was when Bobby Kennedy was shot. I can tell you exactly what was happening when Martin Luther King was shot. And I can most certainly tell you exactly where I was when I read about Jim Clark's death.' He nodded his head and stared down at the floor in a moment's contemplation. 'It's up there,' he added. 'At least it is for me.'

Rahal impressed me. Not only is he a professional performer, but he is passionate as well. And he didn't pull any punches, either. Asked what state he found Jaguar Racing in when he took over he replied: 'The patient was on life support. There was a crisis in leadership and in morale. There had been an abdication of responsibility and I was appalled to witness it because I'd never seen that in racing before.'

And now? 'Well, now we have a heartbeat again. We're breathing on our own again. We've got a lot of good people here, but at the end of last year they didn't feel they were worth a dime. Now we have people intent on achieving their personal goals, and by so doing they will take the company with them. Our intention from now on is to under-promise, and over-deliver.'

The second character I needed to meet was Jackie Stewart. Three times Formula One world champion in the late 1960s and early 1970s, he had sold his Stewart Formula One team to the Ford motor company which, in turn, had set up the new team with Jaguar, but the Scot remained on board in a directorial capacity. Against his better judgement he had agreed to first drive me around the Silverstone Grand Prix circuit, and then shift over to the passenger seat and experience my racing skills at first hand. I was excited by the prospect, but also nervous. After all, having a driving lesson from Jackie Stewart was like busking in front of Luciano Pavarotti.

We met outside the British Racing Drivers' Club beside the Silverstone circuit. I was a little concerned that Stewart might remember me from our last meeting. I had interviewed him for a national newspaper, and although we got along fine, and the subsequent feature had worked out well, the manner of our departure was a little unfortunate. We had met at the plush Howard Hotel in London, where Jackie was staying. After numerous expensive cups of coffee and plates of biscuits Jackie suddenly remembered he had a function with the Prime Minister, at 10 Downing Street, to attend. I bade him farewell, and it was only when I was driving up to my house an hour later that I realised that I had walked out of the lounge area without paying. The next morning Jackie's personal assistant told me how Stewart had been collared by a doorman for the bill. What made matters worse was that he was not carrying enough change on him, and had to send his driver out into the streets to find a cash machine.

Fortunately Stewart could not remember me – and I was hardly going to remind him of the incident. Besides, as he placed his tartan-patterned helmet on to his head, he seemed eager to get inside the Jaguar XKR sports car provided especially for the lesson and burn up the Silverstone circuit.

I'd like to say that it was an enjoyable experience, and in some ways it was. After all, to be able to sit and then drive alongside one of the greatest and most charismatic figures in motor sport – indeed all sport – while a crowd of onlookers watched us circumnavigate the track at high speed during a lunchtime break in F1 testing, was a great privilege indeed. The only problem was that Jackie was a little nervous and demanding when I was at the wheel.

'Brake,' he would first say, quietly. 'Brake,' he would then state, a little more firmly. 'BRAKE!' he would finally shout. 'Now, accelerate, accelerate.' My confident veneer was crumbling under the pressure of showing Jackie what I could do. 'You're not listening to me, are you?'

Stewart would bellow as I missed the correct racing line around Club corner. Perhaps the worst moment was when he grabbed my wheel. We were travelling at a speed of 135 mph and, as my two hands were also gripping the wheel at the time, it proved to be a hairy moment. Jackie clearly felt it was necessary to lean across and wrestle the wheel with me. I, possibly oblivious to the danger I was placing the two of us in, was perfectly content and felt that two further hands, plus one body leaning across me as we travelled at high speed, was in neither of our interests.

'We were a whisker away from going off then,' Jackie reported, once I had regained sole control of the wheel. 'And I tell you what. If we'd gone in to the wall we would have known about it. You wouldn't have felt too well tomorrow, that's for sure.' Both of us could not get out of the car quickly enough when the lesson was over, although by the time we had retired to the smart BRDC lounge our heart rates had died down.

So, Jackie, what did we learn today? 'You're not bad, but you're not that good either, and neither would I expect you to be with your lack of experience,' he answered. 'I'm sorry if I had to shout at you a few times, but you weren't listening to me and you weren't doing what you were told – and that's because you were consumed with the function of driving.'

And what, exactly, does that mean? 'It means that only the great drivers can man-manage themselves during a race. Almost always, the problem with drivers – and I mean more experienced ones than you, even – is that they have poor preparation when it comes to taking corners at speed. Inexperienced drivers are aggressive with the steering wheel because they haven't timed their approach to the corner correctly, and the result is car instability. If you've prepared properly then you have time. If you haven't, then you become very busy. You must understand that you need to be gentle and sensitive with a racing car. It's like being driven by a good chauffeur. I don't want to feel the brakes, the gear changes nor the throttle. The truly great racing drivers were always smooth with their movements.'

Digressing slightly I asked whom, in his opinion, were the true greats. 'Fangio, for sure,' Stewart replied in an instant. 'Jim Clark. Prost, Lauda, Senna, and even though he never became world champion, Stirling Moss.' And Schumacher? 'Yes, he's the man of this era. I'd class him with the others.' Was his own omission pure modesty? 'Well,' he said, with an apologetic shrug. 'I'd like to think I might be included in that list, but that's for others to say.'

Stewart wanted to get back to my report. 'There are two ways to insult a man,' he stated. 'One is to say that he is a bad lover. The other is to say that he is a bad driver. Now, I don't know whether you're a bad lover or not, but a bad driver is one who doesn't learn from his mistakes and listen to good advice. So, my advice to you is to identify when to make the turns, and prepare some way in advance before you reach a corner so that when the time comes you have already worked everything out and you will be looking ahead to the next challenge.'

Did he think I stood any chance of giving Irvine a competitive race? Stewart pulled a face. 'I think you might struggle,' he said. 'If you beat him, then maybe you've been an undiscovered talent lost to motor racing. Somehow, I can't see it happening.'

Somehow, neither could I, although the two days I had booked in at the Silverstone Drive School might improve my chances. There, on my first morning, I found myself alongside eleven other wannabe drivers. Some of them wanted to add single-seater cars to their list of racing vehicles such as touring cars and trucks, but most had dreams of becoming, ultimately, a Formula One racing driver. All had karted in their time, and some had financial backing. This course – four days for them, and two for me because of my forthcoming cricket commitment with Yorkshire in South Africa – would reveal whether they possessed any real talent.

'You see some men arrive here full of hopes and dreams, and leave shattered by the experience,' John Pratt, the chief instructor told me as my mission was explained to him. 'The reality is that to become a Formula One driver you must be that one man in a million. Let's face it, we all want to do it, but look how many achieve it. Yet still we can dream that maybe we are that one man.'

Over the course of the next two days I became accustomed to Silverstone's Stowe circuit – where Irvine and I would be staging our race – first driving a saloon car, then a Formula First single-seater racing car, and finally a Van Diemen works Formula Ford, three cars down the scale from an F1 car. Interspersed with the driving came a series of lectures, designed to increase our awareness of the art of racing. Phrases such as exit speeds and apex points filled my head as the importance of following the correct racing lines, cornering, and preparation for what lay ahead on the circuit was drummed into us. As Pratt promised, the two days taught me to look ahead some four times as far as I would normally do as a driver on an ordinary road.

Once in the single-seater cars this bore fruit as we all completed lap after lap on the 0.8 mile circuit. Of course the theory was easier than the practice. My main area of fault was an inconsistency when it came to cornering. On the Stowe circuit there were two particularly challenging corners that followed fast straights, requiring a late and hard brake followed by a sharp turn. I knew instantly when I got it right because of the smoothness of my passage and the speed with which I was able to exit from the corner, but often I would find myself braking too early or too late, or simply approaching the corner too fast. In the latter case this would result in a high-speed spin, something that would create blind panic at first until I realised that I was reasonably safe.

Other factors were also incorporated into the two days, such as skidding sessions in a saloon car, and learning to recognise the various flags displayed during races – from blue (Let the car behind pass), to yellow (Caution! Slow down, no overtaking, be prepared to stop) and, of course, the black and white chequered flag (End of session, slow down and come into the pits).

The most fun, the fastest laps and the real sense of becoming a motor racing driver came when presented with the chance to drive the

Van Diemen Formula Ford. Over three sessions, each consisting of three fifteen-minute periods, the dozen students (split into two groups of six) underwent lapping in the Van Diemen's, with each session followed by a debriefing from the instructors. Initially we were told to keep our revs down to 4,500, but after the first session had been completed safely and competently we were encouraged to increase to 5,000. Sleet was falling as we sped around the Stowe circuit, and our hands were numb with the cold at the end of the day, but by then I had lapped the circuit over a hundred times.

Indeed, if I had been a contestant on 'Mastermind' that night my specialist subject would have been the Stowe Circuit at Silverstone. A lap would begin towards the end of the straight connecting the south and north corners. The north corner, arguably the trickiest on the circuit, would require a hard brake and a gear change down to second before a quick exit out and into the second-fastest part of the circuit, the straight between north and west.

It was as you approached the end of this straight that preparation for what lay ahead really came to the fore. As soon as you had braked, changed gear down to second and exited from the apex of the corner, you had to face two consecutive turns. This meant keeping to the outside before hitting the first apex and then the second. Get any part of this exercise wrong and you could be sure to find yourself battling to keep the car on the tarmac. A small, straight part of the circuit followed before a less demanding corner turned you back into the main straight and towards the finish line. I was told that the course record in a Formula Ford is just over thirty-six seconds. I was recording nearer forty-six. Still, as I thanked Pratt and his team at the Silverstone Drive School I felt strangely confident of at least not showing myself up too much against the 1999 Formula One world championship runner-up. Despite all my previous sporting experiences, I still appeared more than capable of self-delusion.

By now the 2001 world championship was well under way. Australia,

Malaysia and Brazil had been and gone with Michael Schumacher setting off at a furious pace in defence of his world title. David Coulthard was in hottest pursuit, although BMW–Williams were looking good with Montoya and Ralf Schumacher beginning to flex their muscles. Jaguar, meanwhile, had scored no points in three Grands Prix, although with a number of finishes around tenth place, at least a little consistency had been discovered. Points would be needed, and sooner rather than later, but for the time being everyone remained confident. Niki Lauda, the three-times Formula One world champion, had come on board, too. The Austrian had been appointed to the Ford-run Premier Automotive Group as head of their Premier Performance Division. This meant that he would be coordinating the Ford-owned Jaguar Racing team and Cosworth Racing. With men like Lauda and Rahal overseeing the whole operation, an improvement in results would be expected.

On the deck of the *Anaconda*, life remained serene. Winter had truly turned into spring, at least in Santa Margherita, where Irvine's luxury yacht was moored. Half an hour's drive from Genoa, and just around the headland from the picturesque harbour village of Portofino, this is one of the loveliest enclaves along the north-west Italian coast, and a favoured spot for Irvine to rest and relax in.

It was going to be an interesting exercise to spend time with the man away from the Formula One scene. Up until this point I had only been in his company at either a Grand Prix or at testing at Silverstone or Barcelona. Now, on his invitation, I found myself standing on the quay staring at his expensive boat. It was ten o'clock in the morning, and no sign of life was in evidence. The crew, it was explained to me later, were on leave for a couple of days.

I telephoned Nick Harris on his mobile, not quite knowing whether he was even in Santa Margherita. In fact, despite the invitation to visit him on his yacht, I wasn't entirely confident that Irvine would be there either. A sleepy-sounding Harris answered his phone. 'I'm on the boat. Where are you?' he asked.

'Standing right outside,' I told him and, within moments, Harris had appeared and beckoned me aboard. 'Eddie's asleep,' he said, before gesticulating to have a look around. The *Anaconda* is impressive, with its five bedrooms, bathrooms and a sauna, plus Irvine's obligatory jet ski. On the deck stood a Concept 2000 rowing machine, the very same one that had tested my strength back in Barcelona. 'Eddie and I had a workout last night on the deck,' he explained.

We sat down by his table, surveyed the busy quayside and made the most of the warmth of the Italian spring sunshine. The peace would be shattered within minutes. 'Bloody hell, haven't we got rid of you yet?' It was, of course, Eddie. 'People should be sacked for allowing you into the Jaguar team,' he continued. 'In fact, why the bloody hell do so many people agree to let you join them. They must be all mad!'

He returned a few seconds later with three glasses of orange juice, shook my hand and said: 'Welcome aboard.' His American girlfriend, Catherine, was still asleep, although her yappy little dog, Hayley, had emerged and seemed intent on licking my legs all over. 'We've got great security here,' Eddie observed, as he stuck his face outward and upwards towards the morning sun. 'Make a false move and you'll be licked to death.'

As we sat there in the sunshine and gazed quietly out to the sea and, beyond, the bustling streets of Santa Margherita, the only noises that punctuated the serenity were the slapping of the sea water against the hull of the yacht, and the distant sounds of mopeds. 'You see why I like living on a boat?' Irvine said, finally. 'I can live anywhere I like on the *Anaconda*. Today it's Santa Margherita. Before the Spanish Grand Prix we'll shoot across to Barcelona. I'll stop at Antibes on the way back. Or maybe Monte Carlo. It's much better than buying a house in all these places.'

Irvine appeared far more relaxed than at any other time we had met.

Despite his customary abusive greeting, his manner was as warm as the Mediterranean sun that day. He seemed what he largely is: content with his lot. Indeed, he was even interested to hear of my previous experiences, and of my future plans. I mentioned a possible date with an international singer. 'Can you sing, then?' he asked. I told him I used to be a singing and guitar-playing busker as a student, which prompted him to fetch his guitar. Thrusting the instrument into my hands he sat back with his arms folded across his chest, looked at me and said: 'Go on, then. Show us what you can do.'

Slightly uncomfortably I began to strum a few chords before singing Del Amitri's 'Nothing Ever Happens' to Irvine and Harris, who had sat down alongside his employer to double my audience. Eddie had been learning the guitar on and off for the past couple of years, but his travelling commitments had made it difficult to progress. 'I hate taking anything more than I have to when I travel,' he explained. 'That's why the guitar stays here. But I'm annoyed that I'm not a better guitarist, and I really intend to improve.'

Rather like the aftermath of the rowing machine challenge, Irvine was generous in his praise. 'Oh, you're much better at strumming than me. And I can't finger pick at all.' He dashed into his room and re-emerged with an old, lined exercise book. On the cover someone had scrawled: 'Eddie's Furst Snog Book.' Inside he had written out half a dozen songs, complete with chords.

'Play us this one,' he ordered, pointing to Johnny Cash's 'I Can See Clearly Now'. I followed this with the old buskers' favourite, 'Streets of London'. Eddie was keen to learn the Ralph McTell classic, writing down the words and chords in his exercise book. When I started to play 'Leaving on a Jet Plane' he revealed that the song had always been his favourite as a small boy. This followed 'Streets of London' into his book.

Curious onlookers stared towards the *Anaconda* as Irvine and I passed the guitar back and forth to swap songs. His strumming was rather too methodical, and he seemed uneasy about the prospect of singing, but he was prepared to play me some of the songs he had learnt. Led Zeppelin's 'Stairway to Heaven', Oasis's 'Wonderwall' and U2's 'One' followed, with him singing 'One' when I asked him to remind me how it went. His singing voice revealed a far stronger Irish accent than his natural conversational tone.

A good three-quarters of an hour of this impromptu jamming session passed before Nick Harris reminded us that we were all due to undergo an exercise session. Irvine, after all, would be competing in the San Marino Grand Prix five days later in Imola, before then facing an even stiffer challenge: me, at Silverstone.

The session turned out to be an 11-kilometre run, the distance between Santa Margherita and Portofino, and back. It was a fair distance, and rather warm too, but there are few more scenic routes to take for a run than the coastal road between the two settlements. As we jogged alongside the turquoise sea Irvine spent much of the time waxing lyrically about the beauty of this part of the Italian Mediterranean coast. I commented on his rather unusual style of running – a strange jog stemming from his hips, which made him resemble AA Milne's Tigger.

'Short legs,' he explained, as we headed towards Portofino. Then he revised his initial explanation. 'Actually, it's because of all the practice I get in using the area of my pelvis.'

This line of thinking continued when we arrived in the picturesque village of Portofino, with its blue, green and pink pastel-coloured houses and bars. A young Italian woman asked if she could photograph Irvine. 'Why are you here?' she asked.

Eddie, nearly fluent in Italian after his time spent driving for Ferrari, answered: 'To see you'. It was pretty toe-curling stuff, but Irvine was enjoying his morning trek out. Later, when a local shouted 'Ciao, Eddie', Irvine had a ready explanation for me. 'I pay him £100 a day to do that just so that I can impress people like you,' he said.

After a drink of water and a quick exploration of Portofino, we were on our way back. Irvine favoured running up hills, and each time we approached one he accelerated, taking Harris with him, and leaving me floundering behind. It took much of my effort to catch them up again, only to be left behind once more when Irvine attacked the next hill. I soon began to realise that Eddie was enjoying doing this to me. In fact, this was his chance to avenge his defeat on the rowing machine. By the time we had returned to Santa Margherita and the *Anaconda*, some forty-five minutes after leaving for Portofino, Irvine and Harris had opened up a thirty-second lead over me. 'You're told these people are fit,' Eddie said to Nick, ensuring that I could hear his comments. 'Then you discover the truth when you go running out on the road.' I didn't tell him at the time, but I was secretly pleased to have run 11 kilometres and to have finished what I saw as a mere thirty seconds behind a fit Formula One driver.

Back on the boat, after a cool-down stretch, a shower and a change of clothes the three of us strolled along the quayside before finding a smart restaurant for lunch. As we sat surveying the Mediterranean again I remarked that Irvine had come a long way from the modest Northern Irish town of Newtownards.

It provoked an excited response. 'I couldn't even dream of living like this because I had no idea this lifestyle existed,' he explained. 'I mean, for anyone. It's ridiculous, frankly, that I'm able to do this. The thought of me becoming a Formula One driver was laughable. It was impossible, really. I had no money. I had no kart. I only started racing for the fun of it, and even when I realised I was quite good at it my ambition was just to get paid for doing it. I couldn't see beyond touring cars, and the way I saw it, if I could end up earning £100,000 a year, then I'd be the richest man on earth. To have said to myself that I'd end up living like this is like me saying now that I'm buying a house on the moon.'

Has he worked out how it has all happened for him, then? 'Oh yes,' he replied, as the waiter produced some tomato and mozzarella. 'I know exactly how it happened. I was there in the right place, I used my head when I needed to make a lot of right decisions, was prepared to invest some of the money I subsequently earned when I had to, and did the job when asked to. How much of that is down to luck? All I can say is that I see guys who don't make it to the top in motor sport, and I can understand why.'

What, then, of the lifestyle? Irvine is no apologist when it comes to his hedonistic outlook. 'Look, when I'm at the circuit I'm very professional. When I'm in a car I work hard. But when I'm away, then I play hard. The way I see it, you only live once and I've been given a fantastic opportunity to have the best life in the world. I'm not going to turn it down, am I?'

His eyes wandered all over his yacht before then shaking his head in bemusement. 'It's unreal,' he said. 'It's fucking unreal. I'm not just talking about the money. I've got the most brilliant friends in the world. I have such a laugh. My life is just one big party.'

You would expect the kid from a small Northern Irish town to have changed his outlook in life once the money, the fame and the women began to fall on to his lap. He refutes this. 'I'm having a real blast, but it's not because of the money or the lifestyle. It's because I'm being me. I have friends a great deal richer than me who don't have half the fun I do. I was having a blast when I was living in digs in London. I had a blast when I raced Formula 3000 in Japan. Nothing has changed in that sense, except that my wealth allows me to do bigger and better things.'

What, then, are the best aspects of his 'unreal' lifestyle? Irvine takes a long swig from a bottle of water, wipes his mouth and launches into a short soliloquy. 'When you pick up a beautiful girl then it's amazing,' he answered. 'I still get a huge thrill out of it, and to me that's complete joy.' I told him he sounded like a teenager looking forward to a weekend party in a village hall. 'Nothing wrong in that,' he replied.

'When I'm on the boat then it's pure tranquillity. It serves as an antidote to the other elements of my life, the racing and the partying. Mind you, I've had some amazing parties on the boat, too. And when I'm racing in a Grand Prix, then it's sheer adrenalin. Contrary to popular belief, the racing's very much the most important part of my life. I think about it an awful lot, much more than people assume. I can't seem to ever switch off, and I think it's because driving a Formula One car still provides the biggest thrill in my life.'

On the subject of racing I reminded him that, once he had dealt with the San Marino Grand Prix, he faced the threat of me in a Formula Ford the following week. This provoked some predictable banter. 'You'll find it a humiliating experience,' he promised. 'It's not going to be a race because you won't even see me.'

I countered: 'I will when I overtake you.'

Irvine wasn't finished. 'You'll do well to come second,' he said. 'In fact, I'll probably find it so boring I'll bring a book along or something to occupy myself while I'm driving.'

I told him he had just motivated me to give him a good beating. 'We'll see,' he said. 'We'll see.'

Thursday, 19 April 2001. My final day with Jaguar, indeed my final day living out my fantasies with the best of British sport. Playing for Everton at Goodison Park suddenly seemed like a long time ago. Much had happened since those sunny training sessions in Tuscany with Walter Smith's men and now, despite the other dangers faced in both codes of rugby and in the wrestling ring, together with my other painful and sometimes humiliating experiences, I arrived at Silverstone in a nervous state of mind. Could I give Eddie any kind of competitive race? In trying to do so, could it all end up in a mangled mess of racing car somewhere off the track? But my major concern was more basic: would Irvine even turn up? The thing I had learnt about Eddie more than anything else was that, for all our friendly conversations, runs, rowing machine races and guitar jamming sessions, you never knew from one day to the next how he would react to a given situation. It made him interesting, but it also made him infuriating to work with.

The Silverstone Drive School awaited my arrival. The Stowe circuit had been set aside purely for my use, and later Eddie's. Everyone agreed that I needed a good hour's practice in my Van Diemen Formula Ford before Irvine arrived, just to reacquaint myself with the vehicle in the hope of minimising my defeat.

Nav Sidhu, who had taken over from Cameron Kelleher as Jaguar's head of media relations, arrived at the Drive School with a Jaguar racing suit, the kind worn by Irvine and Burti at a Grand Prix. 'Got to look the part,' Nav said, as I squeezed my frame into the suit. I had already purchased a pair of dinky black racing boots, and a pair of gloves. The school provided me with a helmet.

The day had already turned hectic. After a whirlwind series of negotiations Jaguar had promoted the Spanish Formula One driver Pedro de la Rosa from test driver to their number two, behind Irvine. He would be making his Formula One debut for Jaguar at the Spanish Grand Prix ten days later. Tomas Scheckter would remain the development driver. Burti, meanwhile, had switched over to the Prost Formula One team, and would also be starting his first Grand Prix for his new team in Barcelona. As this was a day for testing – hence Irvine's availability at Silverstone – all Burti had to do was to pick up his bags and walk a few metres along the paddock, the distance separating the Jaguar and Prost garages. I saw him later in the day and he seemed unperturbed by the sudden disruption in his life. For him, a new chapter in his Formula One life had started, much sooner than he or anyone had expected. Everyone seemed happy with the arrangement. It was Jaguar that had poached de la Rosa from Prost as their test driver in the first place, and for a while the threat of writs dominated the conversation within the Jaguar Racing camp. With Burti joining Prost, however, peace returned to the paddock.

On the other side of the Silverstone Circuit, meanwhile, the peace was about to be shattered. John Pratt, the driving school's chief instructor, had arrived to oversee my lesson. 'It's a bit of a crash course,' he said. 'And I don't mean that in a literal sense.' Before I was even allowed to sit in the Van Diemen, however, there came the now familiar act of signing a waiver form. I've lost count of how many waivers I have had to sign over the past three years, but by now I had grown immune to the deathly tone of phrases adopted in the form.

'I agree to save harmless and keep indemnified Silverstone Drive, the British Racing Drivers' Club, Silverstone Circuits Ltd and their sponsors and their respective officials, servants, representatives and agents, the drivers of vehicles and any other person or organisation using Silverstone Drive facilities in respect of all claims, costs, expenses and demands in respect of death of, or injury to, or loss of or damage to me or my property arising in pursuance of my undergoing instruction and use of Silverstone Drive facilities,' it read. In other words, just as in previous experiences, if I happen to cop it, it's my fault, and nobody else's. I signed my name at the bottom of the form.

The correct name for the red racing car waiting for me in the Silverstone garage is a Van Diemen RF97 Formula Ford. For any petrol heads reading this, it has an 1800 cc, sixteen valve, four cylinder Zetec engine, with double overhead camshafts. Running on unleaded petrol, the Van Diemen boasts 195 horse power, and a maximum rev counter of 7,055. Supplied by the Silverstone Drive School for the British Racing Drivers' Club single-seater championships, the Van Diemen runs on Dunlop control race tyres, and possesses a Hewland LD four-speed race gear box. Weighing just 520 kilos, due to its fibreglass bodywork, it has a standard, three-pedal layout, and an 'H' pattern conventional gear box, except for the fact that the gear lever is to your right and operated by your right hand.

Wedging yourself into a Van Diemen is like cramming your foot into a shoe using a shoehorn. You sit in a semi-reclined position, and have only limited visibility to the front and the rear. The wing mirrors are so tiny that you need bionic vision to make full use of them. I complained to John Pratt that for such an expensive vehicle it was disappointing to find there was no stereo system. 'Ah, but the air conditioning's brilliant,' he replied.

Once you have squeezed yourself into one of these machines a five-point racing harness straps you in so firmly that you feel like an additional part of the car. Space is at a premium. The very narrow racing boots, for example, are so designed because there is so little room in the Van Diemen's foot well to manoeuvre the pedals. And with the Nonex racing suit, made out of fire-resistant cotton, you are reminded of the dangers. 'Everyone breathes a sigh of relief at the end of a day's racing,' admitted one of the instructors.

Over the next hour I got to grips with the Formula Ford, first by merely driving around the Stowe circuit, and then by testing my racing skills with some late braking, accelerations from the exit points, and fast dashes down the straights. Pratt took me out in a saloon car to remind me of the correct angles to take, and then conducted a debriefing session after observing me career around the circuit. In particular, I was advised to stick to second and third gear, increasing the revs and my speed in the process. 'You've got a better chance if you can drive at ninety-five per cent, ensuring that you don't make any mistakes,' Pratt added.

Irvine arrived just as it began to sleet. I was still out on the circuit, but managed to see my opponent out of the corner of my eye as he watched me for a few moments.

Stupidly, I tried even harder in a naive attempt to impress, which resulted in my spinning off at speed as I attempted to tackle the west curve. As if my performance in a Formula Ford was really going to impress one of the world's top Formula One drivers.

Predictably, Irvine was singularly unimpressed when I drove back into the pits and shook his hand. 'I've just been watching you practise,' he remarked, as he lowered his frame into the cockpit of a Van Diemen. 'You're even worse at motor racing than you are at running.'

This comment caused a ripple of laughter from the watching crew of Jaguar figures and Silverstone Drive officials and mechanics who had assembled to watch the ensuing drama. 'It's time to stop the talking, Eddie,' I said, in a false show of bravado. 'It's time to start the walking.'

Irvine burst out of the pit for a few laps of the Stowe circuit. It had been a good number of years since he had raced in a Formula Ford, and I was hoping this might help me claw back some of the huge gulf between us as racing drivers. Watching him tear up the straights, I concluded that Irvine found no difficulty reacquainting himself with the car.

Five minutes later he returned, positioned his car on the grid, and looked across at me. Someone gave him the official waiver form to sign, alongside my name. It did not matter whether it was Eddie Irvine or Ian Stafford, the waiver needed signatures. As I had arrived at the circuit first I was given the choice of car. I plumped for car number one; Irvine took number two. For some reason this helped to decrease my nerves. The hour's practice in the Van Diemen meant that at least I felt confident of lapping the circuit quickly. I would be finding out in a matter of moments whether this would be quickly enough.

John Pratt stood in-between us holding a flag. It had been agreed that I would go out first, with Irvine following half a lap later. This was to avoid any danger of a first corner collision, and to give both of us an extra goal in the race: Irvine had to catch me, and I had to prevent him from doing so. 'Don't you force me off the track,' Eddie warned, his expression growing serious for an instant. 'How good will it be if I miss the Spanish Grand Prix because I've had an accident racing you?'

Quite. The prospect of Niki Lauda being informed that Jaguar's number one Grand Prix driver had been taken out of the equation by a wannabe racer in a Formula Ford did not bear thinking about. Fortunately, neither of us had much time to mull over the consequences. Pratt raised the flag high above his head and started to wave it in a series of frantic motions.

I slammed my foot down on to the gas pedal and shot away. Half a lap later Irvine followed suit. As I burst down the back straight, I could see him speeding down the opposite pit straight across the small and tight circuit. The car was noisy and jerky, the wind sneaked in under my helmet to make my eyes water and cloud up my view, and the tarmac, just a few inches below my backside, hurtled past to create a feeling of great danger. Using all my powers of concentration I handled the first lap as well as I had hoped, and believed that the Ulsterman had made little ground on me. Determined to maintain my advantage, however, I made a crucial error as I turned for the north corner on lap two. Despite all the advice I had received from the Silverstone Drive School and from Jackie Stewart, I approached the corner too quickly. It is a common error created by the fact that your car is required to slow from around 95 mph to 28 mph in a couple of seconds, but one that was costly. My desperate attempts to negotiate it resulted in a high-speed spin.

Punching my dashboard in frustration I managed to turn the car around and headed back on to the circuit just as Irvine shot by. After one-and-a-half laps he had caught me up. Then, quite unexpectedly, came my moment of glory. At least this is how it appeared at the time. Within a lap I had caught Irvine, and I was now pressing him hard from behind. It seemed to me that my opponent was not yet used to his car, and when he nearly went off himself at the north corner my confidence grew. It was as we approached the west corner, reducing speeds from just under 100 mph to 60 mph, that I made my move. Irvine had remained on the outside of the track, allowing me the space to overtake him on the inside as we both cornered. It was a difficult manoeuvre because within a split second of edging back in front of him I was forced to deal with the next two, consecutive turns, known as 'The Esses'. By the time I had managed these, slowing to 31 mph and then turning back into the main pit straight at 56 mph, I held a one-second lead.

It was difficult to control myself as we completed the fourth lap. I had just overtaken Eddie Irvine, the 1999 runner-up in the Formula One drivers' world championship. He had not crashed, or retired, or made any mistake whatsoever. Instead he had been outwitted by my superior driving skills. I had shown him who was the boss of the Stowe circuit. I was the man.

This line of thinking might have continued for the rest of the race if it had not been shattered by first the noise, and then the sight of a red Van Diemen bursting past so quickly on pit straight that I barely had time to see it. From seemingly nowhere, Irvine had left me looking pedestrian.

This shook me up. After all, I was driving my fastest. Indeed, my counter showed I was pushing the car up to 7,000 revs, just a fraction short of its maximum capability. Apart from the second lap spin-off I had not made any major mistakes, and was driving more smoothly and faster than ever before. Yet Irvine, seemingly at will, made me look as if I was driving a milk float.

By the time I had caught him up again, and even overtaken him for the second time, my earlier joy and confidence had diminished to a grim realisation that after his initial rustiness Irvine was so good – and so much better than me – that he was toying with his opponent. It was still fulfilling to overtake him for a second time, and for a while I managed to block him out as he tried to readdress superiority. This resulted in Irvine piling on the pressure from behind – and a hundred nervous glances into my wing mirror. By ten laps, however, it was clear that Irvine, far from being bored as he had predicted in Italy, was enjoying making me look a poor second. It wasn't even that the man was travelling at greater speeds than me. It was the fact that he was smoother, and that he entered the slow corners more quickly than me, and the fast corners more slowly, enabling a better exit.

I began to gamble, pushing the car faster than I was comfortable with, and braking suicidally late into the corners in an attempt to show Irvine I was not finished. The quicker I went, the faster Irvine shot past. At one point I looked across at him for a split second and was convinced I saw a grin on his face as he passed me for the fifth time. He had created a dogfight between us as we careered towards the fifteenth lap, but it was a dogfight he was always in control of.

James Thomas, from Jaguar Racing, was the man held with the responsibility of waving the chequered flag to denote the end of the race. Irvine shot past first, with me just behind as the flag fluttered in the strong wind. Grinding to a halt in the pits we were met by a round of applause from the onlookers. 'It was a good race,' Pratt informed me as I hauled my body out of the Van Diemen's cockpit. 'Apart from the early spin you didn't really put a foot wrong. It just goes to show how good drivers like Eddie are.'

And it just goes to show how naive I had been in hoping to provide a serious challenge to Irvine. He leapt out of his Van Diemen like a spring lamb, ready to take on an afternoon's testing in the Jaguar Formula One car. I, in contrast, felt exhausted by the physical and mental exertions of racing Irvine. It had only been fifteen laps, but the pressure and anxiety had taken its toll.

We were presented with the race statistics. Eddie's fastest lap was timed at 37.7 seconds, which was close to the all-time lap record. Mine was measured at 40.3 seconds. Well, what's 2.6 seconds between friends? Our fastest times were recorded at 98 mph as we sped down the back straight from the north to the west corners.

Irvine shook my hand and smiled. 'I enjoyed the race,' he said. 'It was good fun. And by my reckoning, that makes it 2–1.' He had still not forgotten our rowing-machine challenge and our road run in Italy. Now he was happy.

I spent the rest of the afternoon in the paddock with the Jaguar crew, still sporting the Grand Prix driver's race suit. The effect was both astonishing and amusing. Each time I took a walk, motor racing photographers snapped away with their cameras. I saw people make surreptitious comments as I passed them by. And I even received a number of eyelash-fluttering smiles from female groupies. The driver's suit, clearly, made an impression, even if the man inside failed to do so. At one stage I found myself embroiled in a conversation with one of Jaguar's VIP guests. 'Is it as cold when you're driving in the car as it is just walking about today?' he asked, referring to the biting April sleet and wind. For a moment I thought about being honest. Then I changed my mind. 'Oh no,' I replied, conjuring up all my powers of delusion. 'Once you're in those babies it's hot.'

As the daylight began to disappear so Irvine emerged from his day's testing, ready to drive to Oxford and take his personal plane back to Milan. Seeing me, he ambled over for a final joust. 'You want to know what I think?' he asked.

'Go on, then,' I said, preparing for the worst.

'When it comes to running and racing I'd leave it to the big boys if I were you,' he announced. 'But I'll tell you what. You're better at rowing than me. And you're definitely a better guitarist, too.' It was as good a compliment as I could hope to receive from Formula One's most colourful racing driver.

It was time to return my racing suit, time to stop playing at being a racing driver, and time to drive home. The day had confirmed what I had suspected and feared all along. That however good I may believe I am, the best leave me standing.

And as I drove through a blizzard and back down south I realised that a comment Irvine had made to me on his yacht rang true. 'You're not really very good at anything, are you?' he had said. 'Except that you are very good at not being very good.'

There are a large number of sportsmen dotted around the country, from Liverpool to Leicester, Wigan to Leeds and to Birmingham, who know exactly what Irvine meant. I had just spent the last eighteen months proving his point.

epilogue

Life at the Jaguar Formula One racing team remained busy and troublesome after I left their ranks, perhaps more so than ever before. As if a poor start to the season, the arrival of Niki Lauda and Pedro de la Rosa, plus various comings and goings among the technical staff, not to mention the departure of Luciano Burti, were not enough, Jaguar recorded no finishes, and therefore no points at the following Grand Prix at Barcelona. Eddie Irvine was faring reasonably well until the car packed in. De la Rosa, in his first Grand Prix for Jaguar in front of his home crowd, lasted only seven laps until he was involved in a collision.

Unhappily, both for Jaguar and for myself, development driver Tomas Scheckter left the company under a dark cloud following a court case that inevitably became public. I hope the young man bounces back in motor sport, if only because I liked him, and was appreciative of the kart race we battled out at Silverstone. In this instance, being the son of a famous father has worked against him. The surname made Tomas instant news.

Eddie, in the meantime, was the subject of various speculative pieces in the press suggesting that Jaguar Racing were growing tired of what they saw as a carefree attitude to his job as team leader. He rejected such claims, naturally, arguing that few drivers tested more than him. From my point of view, whatever Irvine's perceived failings may be – and for some bizarre reason, I rather like him – there is only so much you can do with a car that seems slower than many of its rivals. By the time the Monaco Grand Prix arrived, however, things were beginning to look up. Irvine recorded a third place in the race behind Schumacher, a first podium position for Jaguar, and four valuable points. De la Rosa then scored a point in Canada, and a further two at Monza, which left the sport wondering why Jaguar's number two driver was outscoring Irvine. Meanwhile, Bobby Rahal returned to America, officially to concentrate on his motor business. This departure was met with little surprise. Formula One had been predicting for some time that Lauda and Rahal would not work together. The season ended, however, on a high, with Eddie, once again, answering his critics with a fourth place at the US Grand Prix in Indianapolis. He finished with six points to his name in the F1 drivers' championship, de la Rosa boasted three, and Jaguar completed the season in eighth position. It was hardly spectacular, but with a new, £15 million wind tunnel now in use, and with de la Rosa and Irvine both scoring points towards the end of the season under Lauda's sole leadership, optimism for a better future can be found within Jaguar. As for Eddie Irvine, he has refuted claims that he would be retiring from Formula One at the end of this current season, when his three-year contract with Jaguar ends. After all, as he would say himself, he's still having too much of a blast.

It's been up and down at Everton football club, too, where this book, and my journey of self-discovery, began. According to manager Walter Smith, some fifty-eight players had either joined or left the club since my questionable contribution to the blue cause. Many of these moves had been high-profile, too.

In came the likes of Paul Gascoigne and Duncan Ferguson, but out went top stars such as John Collins (to Fulham), Don Hutchison (to Sunderland, then West Ham), Nicky Barmby (to Liverpool), Francis Jeffers (to Arsenal), Michael Ball (to Glasgow Rangers) and Craig Short (to Blackburn). Terry Phelan also left for Fulham, and promptly fell into dispute with Mohamed Al Fayed's outfit. Mitch Ward returned to Yorkshire, with Barnsley; Richard Dunne moved on to Manchester City and, after a long association with Everton Football Club, Dave Watson hung up his boots to become manager of Tranmere Rovers.

Yet a good number of the team – my team – are still there, plying their trade at Goodison Park. Although Richard Gough has just retired, Kevin Campbell is still knocking in the goals; Paul Gerrard remains between the sticks; and Dave Unsworth, David Weir, Scot Gemmill and Alex Cleland continue to bolster the forwards, mid-field and defence.

None of them could argue that it has been a glowingly successful time since my departure. Smith's hopes of returning Everton to at least the Premiership top ten have foundered among the board turmoil that saw owner Peter Johnson leave and impresario Bill Kenwright take over. Everton finished sixteenth in the Premiership in 2000–01, and were reasonably placed in eleventh this season at the time of writing. Still the money is tight, the fans far from enamoured, and the team is some way from producing a realistic challenge for honours.

Smith and I still converse on a regular basis and, despite the pressure he finds himself under from the media and the fans, the Scot has not lost his sense of humour. 'One more bad result and I'm recalling you,' he tells me regularly. 'I've told the lads at training that if they perform as badly again I'm going to sign Ian Stafford.' Life could have gone smoother at Goodison Park over the past few months. Yet it has not quite reached the stage where this author is awarded a second trial.

Pat Roach can be found still in Birmingham, dodging and weaving, and ducking and diving between his various interests. He still wrestles, although he has kept his appearances down to half a dozen in the past year due to other commitments. These commitments include a film called *Crustacean* and, perhaps more significantly, he has recorded a new series of 'Auf Wiedersehen Pet', some fifteen years after the group of German-based builders were last seen on British screens. When we spoke last he apologised for fighting in a tag team with someone else. 'I know it's two-timing,' he said. 'But you can't fight with a legend such as The Red Shadow every week, can you?'

John Freemantle continues to promote his all-in wrestling nights across the south coast and, for some strange reason, in Crewe, too. The Professional Wrestling Federation is going strong – even stronger, according to Freemantle, than when I made my red-caped appearance in tandem with Roach. Dick the Bruiser and Pretty Boy Stuart remain two of the ugliest stars on the PWF circuit. Freemantle continues to enquire whether The Red Shadow will return. 'Just think of the publicity,' he enthuses. 'The only unbeaten professional wrestler in the country. The legend is re-born. The Red Shadow returns.' I have told Freemantle there would have to be a good reason, a really, really good reason, for The Red Shadow to make a comeback. The PWF's promoter has promised that he will provide that reason in good time. So, grapple fans, we will just have to wait and see. Perhaps the story of The Red Shadow is not quite over yet, after all.

Unlike John Freemantle, the Leicester Tigers appear to have no need for my services at all. They have just completed what has been, even by their lofty standards, a truly remarkable season. After a steady start in the Premiership they found themselves behind Saracens in the table, but it was during the autumn internationals, when many of Leicester's bigger names were required for Test match duty, that the Tigers came to the fore. Revealing both their team spirit and their strength in depth, both second-to-none in English rugby, Leicester forged ahead and were never caught again. By March they had wrapped up their third successive championship.

Although the Tigers fell against the odds to Harlequins in the semi-final of the domestic cup competition, the Tetley's Bitter Cup, they more than made amends by winning the Heineken Cup and becoming European champions, beating Stade Français in their own backyard in Paris in the process. Even for the likes of Martin Johnson and Neil Back, this was the pinnacle of their club rugby careers. Just to round off the season, they also became the Zurich Champions by winning the inaugural play-off cup after beating Bath in the Twickenham final.

One season, three trophies, and even Dean Richards was smiling at the end.

John Wells was appointed as the England coach for the summer tour of Canada and the USA in Andy Robinson's absence on leave with the Lions in Australia. Austin Healey, Back and Johnson went with the Lions to Australia too, Johnson becoming the first man in the history of the sport to captain the Lions on two successive tours. For Johnson, the England captain during an unbeaten Six Nations run that was cut short by Ireland's withdrawal due to the foot and mouth epidemic, the captain of the European champions, and then, finally, the man asked to lead the Lions against the world champions, it was quite a year. Of course, the Lions went on to lose the series 2–1, and Healey returned chastened after some ill-advised newspaper comments. Johnson then missed the Grand Slam decider in Dublin through injury, a game England lost. Back, in the meantime during Johnson's enforced absence, was appointed the new England captain for the autumn series of England internationals. At club level, both in England and in Europe, Leicester continued their winning ways well into the 2001–02 season.

The funny thing is that, for all their triumphs, most of the boys still feel that they have one more goal to achieve. Almost every time they see me they enquire whether this might be the day that I will attempt to take the back seat on the team bus. Each time I decline, promising that it will happen, some time in the future. This has provoked unwarranted accusations of cowardice. It is not the physical assault I fear. After all, nothing could be as bad as that Wednesday afternoon defence session in Omagh. It is more the humiliation of being left, stark naked, and with no belongings, on the side of a motorway one Saturday night as the Tigers' coach heads for home. Would they do this to me, a man who wore the stripes with pride and who so nearly scored against Ulster? There's every chance.

Over in Wigan the running joke for a while was that they could only beat St Helens when I was in the team. In the Challenge

Cup at Knowsley Road, St Helens, and then in the Super League at the JJB, Wigan lost and then drew. By then Saints, clearly undisturbed by their Boxing Day defeat, had beaten the Brisbane Broncos in a memorable match to become world club champions, before then completing a remarkable treble by winning the Challenge Cup, too.

In the Super League, however, Wigan had much the better of it, although initially things were not looking good. Three successive away defeats early into the season saw Wigan part company with their affable coach, Frank Endacott. Wigan were third at the time, not exactly a disastrous position but not really good enough for a team with the Warriors' expectation. In came Australian Stuart Raper, from Castleford, and results began to pick up. The Warriors ended the season second behind the Bradford Bulls only on points difference, but having destroyed St Helens in the final eliminator, Wigan were themselves thrashed by the Bulls in the Grand Final at Old Trafford. For the second year running they ended the season with a defeat in the play-off final, and no trophy. There is no doubt about it, however, they promise to be quite a force this season, with or without me.

A couple of weeks after my sprint at the National Indoor Arena Christian Malcolm and Mark Lewis-Francis were selected for the GB team for the World Indoor championships in Lisbon. Although Malcolm was disappointing in failing to make the 60 metres final (and I never got round to working on his starts with him), he took silver in the 200 metres, and was only edged out of becoming world champion by a matter of a few hundredths of a second. Lewis-Francis, meanwhile, surprised everyone by winning a bronze medal in the 60 metres final.

In the summer Mark had an astonishing time of it, first winning the Europa Cup for Great Britain in Bremen, then achieving his major goal by becoming European junior champion. At the World Championships in Edmonton he broke ten seconds for the first time, although the time was disqualified because it was deemed wind-assisted, and then failed to make the 100 metres final, just losing out in the semi-final. Christian, meanwhile, had a bizarre World Championships. He surprised everyone by making the 100 metres final, finishing seventh, but these extra races took their toll when it came to the 200 metres. On form he could and possibly should have become world champion. Instead, he could only finish fifth.

My other training partners travelled to warm destinations in the spring, swapping the cold fog of Haringey and Bath for the pleasures of California and South Africa, before returning for the start of the 2001 athletics season. The World Championships should have been the chance for Dwain Chambers to have atoned himself after what he saw as his Olympic failure the year before. Unfortunately, a motorcycle crash and subsequent injuries in April 2001 hampered his training, and although Dwain made the 100 metres final in Edmonton, he could only trail in fifth behind the winner, Maurice Greene. At least he had the pleasure of beating the silver medallist, Tim Montgomery, in becoming the Goodwill Games champion in Australia later, but he would have readily swapped this title for a world medal. Jason Gardner's season was ruined by nagging injuries, Colin Jackson did not even enter the World Championships, preferring to enjoy the circuit at a relaxed and carefree stage of his career, and poor old Tony Jarrett faced the horror of false starting twice in the World Championships 110 metres hurdles semi-final, and instant disqualification.

Whether athletics fans will ever be treated to the sight of my good self squashed into an all-in-one again in a live meeting is doubtful, although the BBC do have the tape and could quite easily show a repeat of the frightening spectacle. Say, perhaps, on Halloween.

Yorkshire, in the meantime, continued with their tour of South Africa, drawing against Western Province Academy, although claiming a moral victory as a result of their dominance, before losing to Western Province in a one-day game at the magnificent Newlands. In their final match on tour, however, they beat Lancashire comprehensively, another English county visiting South Africa, in a day–night game at Newlands. The final social night out was as chaotic and raucous as the two I had experienced, and poor Michael Lumb became the unfortunate recipient of the monstrosity of a shirt I was forced to wear before him. Unhappily for Lumb, the evening meant wearing the diver's balaclava, too.

Back in England, Yorkshire went on to enjoy a sensational summer in 2001, topped by becoming county champions for the first time since 1968. They led from virtually the start of the season, and were never caught, despite losing their usual array of stars to Test match duty, and Anthony McGrath and Richard Lumb for a major part of the season through injury. Although the Tykes fared worse in the one-day competitions – quarter-final defeat in the Benson & Hedges, an early exit in the Cheltenham & Gloucester, and a narrow avoidance of relegation from the Norwich Union Sunday League – nothing could detract from their county championship triumph.

For captain David Byas it was a massive personal triumph. His name will remain indelibly in the annals of Yorkshire cricket history as a result, and the fact that confirmation of Yorkshire's title should come in a win over Glamorgan at Scarborough, Byas's spiritual home, and a game in which the captain scored a century, just about made it the perfect ending to a long, long story.

Certainly that was the way Byas saw it. Within days he had announced his retirement from the game, and promptly returned full-time to farming. When I last spoke to him on his mobile phone he was sitting in his tractor ploughing a field. 'Nothing could have topped that win in Scarborough,' he explained. 'It really was the very best way to bow out.'

Of course, with Byas now gone, it does leave the door open at Yorkshire for a promising number four batsman, the kind of player who takes on the anchor role in the innings, to nudge the singles and occupy the crease for a long period of time while allowing his partner to score freely. It is up to Yorkshire to work out who this man might be, of course, but by my reckoning the answer is staring them in the face.

It might be difficult to squeeze Yorkshire in, of course. Whether I would find the time, in-between my summer appearances for Wigan, my winter games for the Leicester Tigers, my super sub performances for Everton, and my dozen races in the Formula Ford championships seems doubtful to me. Then, of course, we have the long-awaited return of 'The Red Shadow' to consider as well.

You think I'm joking, don't you? Well, probably. You see, the problem with self-deluded people is that they are unable to accept the grim truth even when it has been proven beyond any argument. Had I been an unmitigated disaster during my sporting experiences then perhaps even I would have accepted the inevitable. In fact, I really have when it comes to short sprints, at least at world-class level. I was exposed cruelly at the National Indoor Arena, not only in front of a packed crowd but also to a live television audience of three million people.

The other sports, though, have not convinced me. Through a combination of luck and being surrounded by others who disguised my failings, I just about managed to get away with most challenges presented to me. The straw that I continue to cling to sounds like a tired old record. Wigan, Yorkshire and Everton never lose when I play for them, I argue. The Leicester Tigers, 31–12 down when I joined the fray, did not concede a further point, and almost saw me score a try as well. I overtook Eddie Irvine, for goodness' sake, and with a little more practice could soon be gracing Monte Carlo, Monza and Imola. And in 'The Red Shadow', the man who imitated Muhammed Ali's 'Rope-a-dope' tactics in taking all that Dick the Bruiser and Pretty Boy Stuart could dish out before then seeing them off, we have Britain's only unbeaten practising professional wrestler.

It could have worked out even better, too. I should have ignored passing to Danny Cadamarteri at Goodison Park and, instead, turned on the proverbial sixpence before letting fly from the corner of the penalty area with a shot that flew into the roof of the net. With the Ulster try line beckoning I should have looked up and handed off my tackler before diving over for a memorable score. At the JJB Stadium it could so easily have been me intercepting that St Helens pass, and not David Hodgson. With a 20-metre run in to the try line, and with absolutely no Saints player in sight, even I could have finished the job. And if only I had not spun off during the second lap at Silverstone, too. Then Eddie would have known he had been in a real race. Next time, with a few more laps under my belt, he may not be so fortunate.

Even in the one sport in which I consider my performance to be a success I still think about what might have been. Although I am happy with my input for Yorkshire – and, let's face it, how many professional batsmen consider scoring fourteen runs as a success – I am still in disbelief that the one ball I should choose to hit over the top was straight, fast and pitched up. If only I had played a defensive push, instead, and then gone on to punish the bowler for the rest of the over. Most probably, I would still be there now, homing in on my double century.

You see what I mean? It is a sorry tale of an imagination allowed to run rife, even after the fantasy has become an uneasy bedfellow with reality. So the training and fitness goes on, the 'you've got my telephone number' remarks continue to be repeated to sporting coaches across the country, and the misguided belief that I could have been a contender – despite the obvious conclusion of this book – remains unaffected.

One day, perhaps, I may grow up. On this evidence, however, it seems some way off.

acknowledgements

The sporting adventures chronicled in this book were made possible by the support and understanding of a great many people. Many come from within some of the best teams involved in British sport today; others are charismatic sporting individuals; and others are involved in sport from the outside, as administrators, coaches or promoters. Why they agreed to help me out – probably against their better judgement – only they can truly answer, but without them my own sporting dreams would have remained figments of my imagination. It is to the following that I convey my wholehearted gratitude:

Football: To all the players, both current and in the recent past; to back-room staff and to the management team at Everton FC, I give you my thanks for your willingness to welcome into your ranks a Sunday morning parks journeyman. In particular I am in debt to Walter Smith, the manager, for the gamble he was prepared to take on my behalf. I hope, for his benefit, he never signs a worse player than me. And I hope, for everyone's benefit at Everton, that the giant will soon awake from his slumber.

Wrestling: To the Bomber, for his time, patience and partnership. We made it, didn't we, but it was only because of your deliciously maverick streak. Without Pat Roach the legend of The Red Shadow would never have been born. It is to the big man that I give my thanks, but I am also appreciative of the support that promoter John Freemantle lent me, and the charity afforded my way by Messrs Dick the Bruiser and Pretty Boy Stuart.

Rugby union: Everyone at the Leicester Tigers deserves a special mention for their camaraderie and good spirit – despite having to endure an imposter within their ranks. Like Smith at Everton, Dean Richards, the Tigers' director of rugby, took on the challenge of signing me up for a week – as if his job were not complicated enough – and kept to his promises. To all the players, from the internationals to the juniors, and to all the back-room boys and management team, thanks for the memories, the bruises and the fractures. I wouldn't have wanted it any other way.

Rugby league: It was Phil Clarke, and his brother Andy, who began to make this impossible dream a reality; it was chairman Maurice Lindsay who agreed to try me out; and it was Billy McGinty who was left with the dubious honour of turning me into a rugby league player for the mighty Wigan Warriors. Thanks especially to Billy for his good humour, enthusiasm and positive attitude in the face of such adversity; to all the playing and back-room staff at Wigan for their support and teamwork; and to Denis Betts, my chaperone.

Athletics: Without Alan Pascoe this unlikely adventure would never have happened. It was his vision that made a ridiculous proposal reality. Thanks, also, to BBC Sport, to Norwich Union, to Reebok for all the appropriate gear, to British Athletics and to everyone at Fast Track (especially Andy Kay, Jon Ridgeon, Ian Hodge) for helping me to the finish line. Respect to coaches Mike McFarlane and Malcolm Arnold, thanks too to Linford Christie, John Regis and Colin Jackson. It was a genuine honour to train alongside Dwain Chambers, Tony Jarrett and the boys and girls from Haringey, Jason Gardner, Christian Malcolm and Mark Lewis-Francis.

Cricket: My debut for Yorkshire rested on the shoulders of one man. The fault here lies with David Byas, captain of Yorkshire, for it was he who invited me to South Africa to tour with the boys. This, without a doubt, will be the worst decision he has made in what I suspect will be a successful year. My eternal thanks to all the players and staff at Yorkshire

CCC for all the on-field opportunities, and all the off-field fun. As they say in the Headingley dressing room: S'bad lad!

Motor racing: To fast Eddie, I thank you, for the fun and games in the motor home, the day on the boat, and the day at the races. You whipped me, but your rowing could be better. And as for your guitar playing! I do appreciate your time and willingness to muck in, and I hope some of it was fun for you, too. My gratitude to Luciano Burti – good luck at Prost – Tomas Scheckter, Johnny Herbert, Jackie Stewart, Bobby Rahal, Nick Harris, Nav Sidhu, everyone at Silverstone Drive, and Bill Sisley at Buckmore Park. My special thanks to Jaguar Racing for allowing me into the inner sanctum, especially to the now-departed Simon Crane, Cameron Kelleher and, last but by no means least, the long-suffering, incredibly patient and tolerant Emma Owen. We got there in the end!

In general yet more thanks to Sarah Connors, Amanda Lee and everyone at the Back on Track sports injuries and physiotherapy clinic in Catford for not only maintaining this beaten up old banger, but also having to listen to such utter rubbish for so long.

Holmes Place in Bromley provided the best possible facilities for me to whip myself into some kind of shape before facing the challenges in the book. No matter what specific exercise was required, Holmes Place was able to provide everything I needed. Special thanks to Dave Foreacre and manager John Lavan.

Esquire magazine allowed me to find a prestigious home for many of my participatory adventures – including some of a non-sporting variety – and has retained a great support for my desire to be, seemingly, anyone but myself. To Peter Howarth, Joanne Glasbey, Amy Raphael and the team, I thank you.

It has been terrific to work with my publishers, Headline, on this project. From the moment they first expressed their faith in me and my adventures it has been a warming experience as I lurched from one beating to the next. Thanks to Ian Marshall for commissioning the book, to Celia Kent for managing the editorial process, and everyone else at Headline involved in the project.

Likewise, Gordon Banks at the NSPCC (no, not that Gordon Banks) has offered his unstinting support from the moment we first met to discuss tying up this book with the charity. It's difficult to think of a more deserving cause than the NSPCC – something, as a father, that is close to my heart – and I hope you remember this when reading this book. By buying *In Your Dreams* you have already helped.

I was always going to mention Roger Houghton in these acknowledgements, but not quite in this manner. My former literary agent – and friend – retired last Christmas. Sadly, he is no longer with us, but it was he who first went with me when I started my exploration of this participatory world, and it was he who would rock with laughter when I recounted my stories to him. Knowing Roger, he's probably doing the same thing right now.

The last mention is the most important of all. Without the support from Karen, Charlotte and Harry, this book would never have materialised. Once again it meant being away from home, or spending too long preoccupied with my thoughts, concerns and training commitments, and not enough time with my family. The children have grown used to their Dad believing he's Walter Mitty. My wife, Karen, understands the score a little more. She knows the potential dangers I have faced. She is fully aware of the self-inflicted damage. And she understands that I am not getting any younger, either. Yet she also has the good grace to let me live in my dream world, to live and relive my fantasies, and to allow the child inside the man to rear its head every so often. She cannot always understand why I would want to subject myself to elements of what you have read, but she does understand that it is what I want to do. I couldn't ask for any more than that. From anyone.

injury list

Football: Tear in right hamstring
       Hangover from big night out

Wrestling: Whiplash to the neck
       Damaged back that led to numerous calf strains
       Badly bruised abdomen
       Cut nose

Rugby union: Fractured rib
       Broken tip of right ring finger
       Small tear in right hamstring
       Cuts to left ear, forehead, left knee and right shin
       Severe bruising on buttocks, back, shoulders and thigh
         after paint-balling
       Calf strain

Rugby league: Small tear in right calf
       Minor whiplash
       Stiff back
       Bruised left-hand side of face and swollen nose

Athletics: Minor strain in right calf
       Badly damaged ego

Cricket: Fingernail removed after catching practice
Nasty moment in nets involving cricket ball and my crotch
Two hangovers, one particularly bad, after two team sessions

Motor racing: Bruised and shaken body after karting race against Burti
Total exhaustion after rowing-machine challenge
Sore, stiff neck after racing Irvine